Dr. Lester J. Kuyper

Grace Upon Grace

Essays in Honor of
Lester J. Kuyper

edited by
JAMES I. COOK

WILLIAM B. EERDMANS PUBLISHING COMPANY
Grand Rapids, Michigan

Library of Congress Cataloging in Publication Data

Main entry under title:
Grace upon grace.

"A bibliography of the writings of Lester J. Kuyper": p. 153.
CONTENTS: Hesselink, I. J. Lester J. Kuyper: faith and fidelity.—Berkhof, H. The (Un)changeability of God.—Muilenburg, J. The Biblical view of time—Gehman, H.S. The oath in the Old Testament: its vocabulary, idiom, and syntax; its semantics and theology in the Masoretic text and the Septuagint. [etc.]
1. Bible—Theology—Addresses, essays, lectures. 2. Kuyper, Lester Jacob, 1904-. 3. Kuyper, Lester Jacob, 1904- —Bibliography. I. Cook, James I., 1925-. II. Kuyper, Lester Jacob, 1904- BS543.G7   220.6'6   75-12903

ISBN 0-8028-3463-9

CONTENTS

PREFACE

Lester J. Kuyper belongs to the company of Old Testament scholars whose lives and labors personify the close relationship between the two testaments. His devotion to the scriptures of the Old Testament is only exceeded and crowned by his love for and commitment to the Lord of the New. For that reason the title "grace upon grace" (John 1:16) was chosen for this volume published in honor of his seventieth birthday and the conclusion of his professorial work of thirty-five years at Western Theological Seminary. Father Raymond Brown has in my thinking educed the theological significance of that phrase by the translation "love in place of love," a rendering that makes plain that the covenant love experienced by the Old Testament people of God has been newly and fully given in Jesus Christ and the gospel to the New Testament people of God. Each facet of our colleague's distinguished career reveals that he is both recipient of and witness to that gift.

Some portions of the Bible are predominantly Old Testament in emphasis, some are a mixture of Old and New Testaments, and some are primarily New Testament in emphasis. That is a fair description of the varied emphases in the teaching and preaching of our honored colleague and also, fittingly, of this *Festschrift*. The essays are offered as both reflection of and appreciation for his inclusive contribution to biblical studies.

I wish to express sincere thanks to those who have contributed to this volume, to the editor of the *Harvard Theological Review* for permission to reprint the article of the late Professor James Muilenburg, to the editor of the *Journal of Ecumenical Studies* for permission to reprint the article of Professor J. Coert Rylaarsdam, to William B. Eerdmans, Jr., for his kind encouragement, to colleagues I. John Hesselink, M. Eugene Osterhaven, Richard C. Oudersluys, and Donald J. Bruggink for their counsel and advice, to librarians Mildred Schuppert and Norman J. Kansfield for their skilled assistance, and to Eleanor Hoffman and Estella Karsten for their careful work in typing and reading proof.

James I. Cook
Editor

ABBREVIATIONS

AB—Anchor Bible

ASV—American Standard Version

ATD—Das Alte Testament Deutsch

BA—Biblical Archaeologist

BH³—Biblia Hebraica, 3d ed.

BHS—Biblia Hebraica Stuttgartensia

BJ—Bible de Jérusalem

BZAW—Beihefte zur Zeitschrift für die Alttestamentliche Wissenschaft

CD—Church Dogmatics

G-K—Gesenius' *Hebrew Grammar* (ed. and enl. E. Kautzsch, 2d Eng. edition, ed. A. E. Cowley, 1910)

HAT—Handbuch zum Alten Testament

HUCA—Hebrew Union College Annual

IB—Interpreter's Bible

ICC—International Critical Commentary

IDB—Interpreter's Dictionary of the Bible

JB—Jerusalem Bible

JBL—Journal of Biblical Literature

KAT—Kommentar zum Alten Testament

LXX—Septuagint

MT—Masoretic Text

NAB—New American Bible

NCB—New Century Bible

NEB—New English Bible

NICNT—New International Commentary on the New Testament

RSV—Revised Standard Version

SJTh—Scottish Journal of Theology

TDNT—Theological Dictionary of the New Testament (ed. G. Kittel and G. Friedrich)

TsTh—Tijdschrift voor Theologie

TEV—Today's English Version

TZ—Theologische Zeitschrift

YHWH—Yahweh

ZAW—Zeitschrift für die Alttestamentliche Wissenschaft

ZB—Züricher Bibel

LESTER J. KUYPER:
Faith and Fidelity

I. JOHN HESSELINK

Several years ago at a meeting of the *Alte Marburger Tagung* in an old German monastery the theme was the Old Testament and its relation to contemporary problems. The fare during much of the day consisted of long, heavy lectures by representatives of the assembled theologians. The evenings, however, were free for fellowship and small talk. It was at one of these sessions that I overheard a young Old Testament scholar, Klaus Baltzer, twitting some of his friends who were New Testament specialists and who also happened to be slighter and smaller. "It is no accident," he began, with a twinkle in his eye, "that Old Testament scholars are big men." He proceeded to defend his thesis by pointing out that there is an active, earthy, sometimes violent character to the Old Testament that naturally attracts men who are robust, virile, and physically large.

It is true that some of the greatest Old Testament scholars of our time are large men—Eichrodt and von Rad being outstanding examples. But the exceptions are so numerous that it is clear that this rule was not intended seriously.

I

A BIG MAN

The friend, teacher, and colleague whom we honor in this *Festschrift*, however, is indeed a big man in every sense of the word. Tall and husky, with massive, craggy features, Lester Kuyper has been well endowed by his creator. Had he chosen to follow in the footsteps of his father, a farmer, he would have been admirably equipped to do battle with the often hostile elements of nature that he experienced as a boy in South Dakota. More demanding, in many ways, were the pressures of being a teacher in a difficult and sensitive field coupled with the great administrative responsibilities that were his in the latter part of his career. In all this, his strength and health have been great assets. God has blessed our friend richly in many ways, including his physique and endurance, and for this we give thanks.

But the stature of Lester Kuyper far transcends his size. He is a man who possesses a big heart as well as a big frame, a man with a broad outlook and a great vision. On occasion he became involved in acrimonious, emotional conflicts that racked the community, seminary, or church, for he was too honest and courageous to remain silent where he felt an important issue was at stake. But he fought for issues—freedom, truth, unity, and justice—as he understood them, and did not attack people. Nor did he become embroiled in petty, personal feuds. He is too big for that.

During such debates and conflicts he was occasionally misunderstood and maligned; but he rarely, if ever, retaliated in kind. As a result, most of the people who were his foes in debate continue to be his friends. However much they may have disagreed with him, they could not help but admire his honesty, openness, and largeness of spirit. He frequently represented unpopular, losing causes, but he never became bitter; and in many cases he was vindicated by history.

It would be unfortunate, however, to give the impression that Lester Kuyper's life has been marked by conflict. On the contrary, he is particularly noted as a man of great warmth and conviviality, sensitivity, and compassion. Above all, the genial giant from South Dakota represents a beautiful blend of piety and humor.

II

A FULL-ORBED LIFE

Lester Kuyper was not born in South Dakota but on a farm near Rock Valley, a small town in northwest Iowa. Here he learned virtues that have remained with him throughout his illustrious career: simplicity, frugality, patience, and humility. An unforgettable boyhood memory is the way in which his father responded to the terrible depression years. Although his father lost more each year, his faith remained firm and he did not give way to disillusionment or despair.

During his boyhood days he was nurtured in a simple, solidly biblical faith. From his parents he imbibed a love of the Lord and a profound respect for the church. Through the local churches of his youth he came to know the Scriptures, the Catechism, and something of the great Reformation tradition.

There were no striking turning points in his religious development, but, consonant with his personality and background, there was a steady growth in the Christian faith. From his eighth year he nourished a desire to become a missionary. This decision was largely due to the influence of the Reverend Hubert Kuyper, his father's cousin and a missionary to Japan. At the age of sixteen he made a public confession of his faith under the pastoral care of the Reverend S. J. Menning.

This simple but solid piety was to be enhanced by equally solid educational opportunities. His parents, realizing the promise of their son, enrolled him in the Northwestern Classical Academy in Orange City, Iowa (now Northwestern College), where he spent his high school years. It meant being away from home and a financial sacrifice for his parents, but this fine school provided dedicated Christian teachers who were imbued with classical ideals. Thus Lester Kuyper, the boy from the farm, had studied Latin for four years and Greek for two even before he entered college. It was also at the Academy that he met Helen Wiersma, who was to become his wife years later.

Lester Kuyper entered Hope College in 1922, but was obliged to interrupt his education in order to help his father during the depression years. Although the financial situation did not improve, after two years it was mutually agreed that Lester should return to college. Shortly after his return, he joined the Student Volunteer Movement. He recalls that among the speakers who inspired him at YMCA camps and Student Volunteer conventions the most notable was Dr. Walter Judd, then a missionary to China.

After a year of teaching Latin and English at Hospers High School in Iowa, Lester Kuyper entered Western Seminary in Holland, Michigan. In 1932 he married Helen Wiersma, who shared his missionary aspirations. While still in seminary they approached the Reformed Church Board of Foreign Missions about the possibility of serving overseas, but the financial situation of the Board was so grim in 1932—the year of his graduation from seminary—that it was impossible to send the Kuypers abroad. Instead they were urged to consider a pastorate for a few years until the financial position of the Board improved. The Kuypers accepted a call from the Ninth Reformed Church of Grand Rapids and there enjoyed a brief but happy ministry. After two years, they were informed by the Board that there were still no prospects for sending out new missionaries.

It was at this point that Lester Kuyper began to consider graduate study. The way was opened in 1936 when the Reformed Church of Clover Hill, New Jersey, called him to be their minister. The fact that the church was too small to be able to afford a full-time pastor provided an ideal opportunity for beginning graduate study at nearby Princeton Seminary. He completed his Th.M. work there under the direction of Professor Henry S. Gehman, who has remained a life-long friend. The subject of his master's thesis was "The Ras Shamra Tablets and the Bible."

The following year he began a doctoral program at Union Seminary in New York. His mentor was Professor Julius Bewer, whose gracious spirit and profound understanding of the Old Testament had a great influence on the budding Old Testament scholar. Lester Kuyper also learned from his professor that a scholarly, critical approach to the Old Testament could be combined with a warm and devout faith. Upon the completion of his doctoral thesis on "The Doctrine of Sin in the Old Testament with Special Consideration Given to the Position of Reformed Theologians of the Netherlands," he was awarded the Th.D. degree by Union Seminary in the spring of 1939.

This preparation was providentially timed. The Old Testament chair at Western Seminary was vacant. A call to this position by the Board of Trustees was promptly accepted. Two years later Lester J. Kuyper was officially installed as the Cornelius Vander Meulen Professor of Old Testament, a position he held with distinction and honor until his retirement in May 1974.

III

A STUDENT OF THE WORD

Although Lester Kuyper has served the church in many capacities, his primary and most enduring contribution has been as a professor of Old Testament for thirty-five years at Western Seminary. Others taught English Bible and introductory courses, but he taught all of the Hebrew and exegetical courses in the Old Testament field until 1963, when a third man was added to the biblical field to serve as a bridge between the Old and New Testament departments.

The fact that the Reformed Church—and Western Seminary—still requires the study of the Hebrew language, in an era when the biblical languages are generally regarded as unnecessary and irrelevant for the ministry, is a powerful testimony to the effectiveness of Professor Kuyper as a teacher. With gentle firmness and loving zeal he has cajoled and convinced hundreds of students— some of them less than eager—of the joys and benefits of learning the Hebrew language. The majority of his former students might have to admit that they have forgotten much of what they once learned, but they would concede at the same time that this inadequacy was due to their failure to utilize the tools and resources given them. Even where the technical knowledge of the Hebrew language has been lost, generations of graduates still retain a love for the Old Testament, an appreciation of its significance and relevance, and some knowledge of its proper interpretation.

Professor Kuyper's approach in the classroom was a fascinating blend of rigorous, sometimes minute scholarship with practical, pithy insights and homespun humor and application. His lectures were well prepared, but rarely was a class subjected to a non-stop lecture. Each class period was inevitably punctuated by a number of probing questions in an atmosphere of willingness to re-examine his own views. The scholarship was always evident, but it was always scholarship with a light touch.

Moreover, it was never scholarship merely for scholarship's sake. There was vast erudition, enhanced by an impressive command of languages that reached beyond Hebrew and Greek to Syriac, Arabic, Dutch, French, and German. Yet this erudition was never an end in itself but was always at the service of the student, the church, and the proclamation of the gospel. To revise Anselm's famous phrase *fides quaerens intellectum,* here we have scholarship seeking ways of serving.

At least one more thing must be said about Lester Kuyper, the scholar and teacher. Although even meticulous analyses of complicated grammatical and exegetical points were dealt with in a disarmingly light manner, and although a twinkle in the eye and moments of humor regularly graced his teaching, there was never frivolity or banality. For this man was utterly serious about his subject matter. He was quite conscious of the fact that he was treading on holy ground. He was a servant of the Lord and, more particularly, a servant of his Word. There was accordingly a profound sense of reverence for God and his revealed Word. A corollary of this attitude was a deep underlying passion that would surface again and again. He was dealing with holy things, with God's Word, and he felt this deeply. Professor Kuyper would hardly be described as a powerful orator—although he was capable of lofty flights of oratory, especially in public presentations—but discerning students could perceive behind this easygoing manner a passion for truth, a jealousy for God's honor and majesty, and a profound commitment to Jesus Christ and his church.

Because of the heavy demands of Western Seminary on its professors for teaching and availability to students, of the local churches for preaching and teaching, and of the denomination for services on its boards and commissions, little time and energy remain for strictly scholarly pursuits and academic publications. Even so, Professor Kuyper has disciplined himself throughout the years and has produced a steady stream of significant contributions to biblical scholarship.

During the first years of his career at the seminary his literary output was largely of a popular nature. Beginning in 1949, hardly a year has gone by without the appearance of an important article or essay. The vast majority of his articles and reviews have appeared in the *Reformed Review*, the scholarly journal published by the Reformed Church seminaries. At the same time he was contributing important articles to more prestigious quarterlies in the scholarly world such as *Interpretation*, the *Scottish Journal of Theology*, and *Vetus Testamentum*.

An examination of these publications reveals several recurring themes. A minor motif is the church, her nature, reform, and the quest for unity. A key essay here, which appeared in two different versions, is "The Church Reformed According to the Word of God."[1]

Much of Professor Kuyper's course work revolved about the exegesis of the book of Job, the Psalms, and the prophets. This is not reflected directly in his writings, however, except for the question of the suffering and repentance of Job, which has found written expression more than once.[2] But the interpretation of the early chapters of Genesis is an area where Professor Kuyper has worked out his position very carefully. In view of the fact that the midwestern region of the Reformed Church is still reluctant to accept even constructive biblical criticism, this also represented a rather controversial pioneering effort. His "Interpretation of Genesis Two-Three"[3] is by no means radical, but because it challenged certain traditional approaches, it was deemed dangerous, if not heretical, by some ministers. Various charges against Professor Kuyper ensued, and these were considered carefully by the executive committee of the Board of Trustees of Western Seminary in 1960. It was decided that there was nothing heretical in this approach to Genesis. This and related issues, however, continued to perturb some members of the church, and the matter was eventually dealt with by the theological commission of the denomination, which brought a recommendation to the General Synod of 1963. Again the exegetical approach and views of Professor Kuyper were vindicated. The question, in short, was whether one must interpret the first chapters of Genesis literally in order to conform to the view of the inspiration and authority of the Bible contained in the doctrinal standards of the Reformed Church. A related issue was the question of the Mosaic authorship of the Pentateuch.[4]

Judging from his publications, one might conclude that one of his favorite books in the Old Testament was Deuteronomy; and this would be a correct conclusion. Although Deuteronomy is largely concerned with the Mosaic law and the renewal of the covenant, one of its resounding refrains is the gracious election and covenant faithfulness and steadfast love (*ḥesed*) of the Lord. These are also the themes that provide the clue to a major motif in Lester Kuyper's theology. He is fully cognizant of the justice and wrath of God on the one hand, and the radicality of man's sin on the other (cf. his doctoral dissertation); but his particular interest has been the holiness, goodness, and grace of God.

A turning point in this connection, and in Professor Kuyper's theological development as a whole, came about in the research he did for his inaugural address. The subject was the righteousness of God in the Old Testament. The discovery was that the biblical portrayal of God's righteousness did not accord with the traditional dogmatic view of righteousness. In systematic theologies God's righteousness was usually presented in a strictly judicial light as the opposite pole of his mercy and grace. In the Old Testament, Professor Kuyper discovered, the righteousness of God more and more takes on salvific connotations. God saves *because* he is righteous, not despite his righteousness.

Similar discoveries were made concerning such standard doctrines as the immutability and impassibility of God. Professor Kuyper became convinced that the dogmaticians (particularly of seventeenth-century vintage) were much too influenced by the abstract concepts of the philosophers and were not sensitive enough to the dynamic nuances and tensions within Scripture. It might be said that the life-long quest of Lester Kuyper has been that of freeing theology from the shackles of a philosophical bondage—especially in regard to its concept of God.

If one were to collate the various publications of Professor Kuyper on the nature of God, especially as revealed in the Old Testament, one would have the beginnings of a beautiful, creative biblical doctrine of God.[5]

Some of this material is drawn together in Professor Kuyper's *magnum opus*, "The Scripture Unbroken," a book-length manuscript in preparation. This is virtually a theology of the Old Testament, which focuses on certain themes. One of these themes is the character of God and his dealings and relations with Israel. Another is a concern that spans his whole academic career, namely, to demonstrate and illustrate the relation and unity of the two testaments. This concern is expressed in the title, the term "unbroken" (cf. John 5:18; 7:23; 10:35) being a negative way of expressing the truth that Jesus Christ represents the fulfillment of the Old Testament scriptures. Accordingly, "the teaching of the Old Testament is applicable and regulative for all times. The validity of the Old Testament carries on beyond its own time; it cannot be broken, i.e., become null and void" ("The Scripture Unbroken," p. iii). It is this conviction which informs all of Lester Kuyper's work.

IV
A SERVANT OF THE CHURCH

To think of our honoree and friend as only an Old Testament scholar and professor would be a grave injustice, for he has also served his denomination and the church at large in varied and significant ways. It should also not be overlooked that he has served his community in a number of ways. However, most of his time and efforts have been given to the church. The most immediate and continuous benefits were derived by local churches, both the congregations to which he belonged and churches in the area. As a preacher, Bible study leader, and lecturer he has given unstintingly of himself throughout his ministry.

Nor were his services limited to his own denomination and other American churches. During the first of his sabbatical years (1958-59, 1965-66), which were spent mostly in the Netherlands, he did research and served as an exchange lecturer in the Reformed Church in the Netherlands. (Part of the first sabbatical was spent at the American School of Oriental Research in Jerusalem where he also served as an honorary lecturer). These contacts, and the friendships that resulted from them, did much to strengthen the ties between the Reformed Church in America and the Reformed Church in the Netherlands. Concrete evidence of these ties is seen in the fact that two of the contributors to this *Festschrift* are from the Netherlands.

All this notwithstanding, there is no doubt that it is on a denominational level that Professor Kuyper made his most distinctive and enduring contributions. He served six years each on the Board of Pensions, the Christian Action Commission, and the Theological Commission of the Reformed Church. His impact on these commissions was considerable; but he was to serve in an even more distinguished manner at two critical junctures in the life of his church.

In 1968 the Reformed Church rejected for the second time in less than twenty-five years the possibility of union with another member of the Presbyterian-Reformed family, this time the Presbyterian Church, U.S. The next two years were traumatic ones for the Reformed Church. Many of those who were committed to union, particularly in the eastern part of the denomination, were frustrated, bitter, and angry. The situation was so serious that committees were appointed to consider whether the Reformed Church had any future and whether the best course was simply to work for an orderly dissolution of the denomination.

It was during this most trying period in the history of the Reformed Church that the denomination called upon one of its most beloved and respected members for help and counsel. The General Synod of 1969 elected Lester Kuyper vice president, and the following year the Synod chose him for the post of president.

This was, of course, a great honor for Professor Kuyper; but it was an even greater benefit for the denomination. Few men were so well suited for this extremely difficult task, requiring the utmost sensitivity, patience, wisdom, and love. Various events and forces conspired to bring about healing and reconciliation within the Reformed Church during the next few years, but none was more important than the providential placement of Lester Kuyper at the head of his denomination when his peculiar gifts were so desperately needed.[6]

Just at the time when this crisis was being resolved, the two seminaries of the Reformed Church experienced another in the form of the resignation of their president, Dr. Herman J. Ridder, in May 1971. Once again the denomination—this time through its Board of Theological Education—called upon Lester Kuyper to serve in a critical capacity. He was originally asked to serve as interim president of Western and New Brunswick seminaries for one year; but the one year became two.

These two years were perhaps the most demanding time of his entire career. Again tensions were high because the future of the seminaries was problematic. Many felt that the only solution was the merger of the two schools. But if so, where? Relocation of either or both of the seminaries was also seriously considered. At the same time, there were also strong feelings in the eastern and western sections of the church for retaining both seminaries in their respective locations. Others were unhappy about recent developments and wanted to return to the former arrangement in which each seminary had its own administration.

Due to the uncertainty of the future, there was also considerable anxiety and tension on both campuses. It was into such a situation that Professor Kuyper was called to serve. Although only three years away from retirement, he and his wife gave themselves completely to this task. They moved back and forth between the campuses, living almost equal periods of time in Holland and New Brunswick. This required not only the sacrifice of leaving their home for long periods and setting up a household elsewhere; it also meant making new friends and adjusting to a very different situation. All of this was done with a generous and gracious spirit. What might have been a serious crisis was again averted because two gifted people were willing to give themselves unreservedly to a higher cause.

God often grants special strength and grace to those whom he calls to especially crucial and demanding tasks. This was clearly evident in the case of the Kuypers during these years when they were asked to do so much for the cause of Christ and his church. Upon the scholar-teacher with a pastoral heart there was also bestowed an increasing manifestation of the fruit of the Spirit: love, joy, peace, patience, kindness, goodness, faithfulness, gentleness, and self-control. Blessed by good health, a loving, devoted wife, and three talented, grateful children, our colleague and friend has been wonderfully used by his Lord.

We rejoice with him and his family in such a distinguished, dedicated career, which has come to a glorious climax, but which happily is not yet at an end. We give thanks for all that he has meant to us, as well as to countless friends and former students around the world. And we are grateful to God for all the good that has been accomplished through his servant, Lester J. Kuyper. *Soli Deo gloria!*

NOTES

1. Cf. *Western Seminary Bulletin*, 7, no. 4 (March 1954), 1-6; and *Interpretation*, 12 (1958), 157-173.
2. Cf. "The Repentance of Job," *Reformed Review*, 9, no. 4 (June 1956), 30-44; "The Repentance of Job: a Study of MA'AS," *Vetus Testamentum*, 9 (1959), 91-95.
3. *Reformed Review*, 13, no. 2 (December 1959), 4-14; no. 3 (March 1960), 17-29.
4. A helpful review and analysis of one aspect of this dispute is given by James I. Cook, "The Interpretation of Scripture," *Reformed Review*, 23, no. 2 (Winter 1970), 77-86.
5. See especially "The Holy One and The Holy Spirit," *Reformed Review*, 11, no. 3 (April 1958), 1-10; "The Repentance of God," *Reformed Review*, 18, no. 4 (May 1965), 3-16; and the revised version in *SJTh*, 22 (1969), 257-277; "Grace and Truth: An Old Testament Description of God, and its Use in the Johannine Gospel," *Interpretation*, 13 (January 1964), 3-19; "The Hardness of Heart According to Biblical Perspective," *SJTh*, 27 (1974), 459-474.
6. His own views and attempts at reconciliation are set forth briefly in two important articles: "Are We at an Impasse?", *Reformed Review*, 23, no. 2 (Winter 1970), 102-105, devoted to the theme, "Reconciliation Within the Church"; and his "Presidential Report to General Synod," *Church Herald*, June 18, 1971.

Grace Upon Grace

1

THE (UN)CHANGEABILITY OF GOD

HENDRIKUS BERKHOF

I

What I have seen and heard of Lester J. Kuyper's research and teaching reveals that one of his basic concerns is to permit the Old Testament to speak with its own voice and its own presuppositions to our Reformed faith. In spite of the high tribute which, for example, the Belgic Confession pays to the authority of Holy Scripture, Reformed theologians used and misused the Bible since about 1570 mainly as an arsenal of prooftexts (*dicta probantia*) for their dogmatic statements. Biblical theology was hardly more than the handmaid of dogmatics. Two centuries later, under the influence of the Enlightenment, she freed herself from this bondage. Since that time biblical and systematic studies have for the most part developed separately throughout at least one and a half centuries. This means that dogmatic theology often repeated and repeats the concepts and terminology of Protestant scholasticism without regard for the results of biblical research.

Since, let us say, the beginning of Kittel's *Theological Dictionary of the New Testament* (1933), a slow but radical change has taken place. Lester J. Kuyper, who is both a man of the church and of biblical research, has devoted much of his effort to make his church and its ministers aware of the deep difference between the blood-warm language of the Bible and the cold scholastic terminology of our dogmatic tradition. In numerous studies he has proved how different is the word of the living God in the Old Testament from the system in which our fathers domesticated it. No wonder that he was attracted particularly by those motifs and portions of the Old Testament which testify to the inscrutability of God: the motifs of justice and love; the themes of suffering and repentance; and, above all, the book of Job.

As a prominent example of Kuyper's concern to correct and enrich dogmatic theology by fresh biblical insights, I have selected his article entitled "The Suffering and the Repentance of God,"[1] in which his biblical scholarship is accompanied by a wealth of dogmatic knowledge that is as rare among biblical specialists as is the reverse among dogmatic theologians. His study penetrates as far as possible into the difficult systematic questions about the relation of the eternal God to the changing history of salvation. What is at stake is the problem of God's immutability, and in the discussion the reader encounters this typical sentence: "One may venture the surmise that the essential blessedness of God is less disturbed by a forthright acceptance of passages on changeability and repentance than by a crafty exegesis of such passages."[2]

Kuyper, however, remains within the methods and limits of his area of specialization. Looking from there to his colleagues in systematic theology, he encourages them by saying: "It seems plausible that the blessedness of God takes up within itself the variety of emotional life which would include regret, grief, and repentance."[3] Here he stops, and invites us dogmaticians to take his biblical conclusion as a starting point for our systematic thinking. I am ready to accept this invitation and to offer a response and a continuation to the insights my friend Kuyper has developed. Something like that is necessary in order to make biblical insights fruitful for preaching and teaching. At the same time the task is a difficult one, because biblical research raises questions that cannot be answered by this research alone. This is especially the case with the question of what it means for the nature of God himself to say that his blessedness takes up within itself such changes as are inherent in human history. With Kuyper, I reject both the idea that the covenant relationship is enacted outside God's heart and the view that God is either capricious or the victim of human resistance in history. How then must we see him in his changeability or unchangeability? Do the creation of our world and the course of human history create a history in God himself and thus affect his very nature?

II

During almost the whole of church history, the answer to this question was a clear, unanimous, and indignant No! Change was considered to be demeaning to God. Two motives were responsible for this attitude, the one biblical and the other philosophical. The biblical motive was God's unchanging allegiance to his covenant in spite of the disloyalty of his people. The philosophical motive was Aristotle's influential definition of Deity as the unchanging ground of all change, "the first and unmoved Mover." What the combination of these two motives meant for Christian thinking is set forth in Kuyper's article.

In recent decades this long theological tradition suddenly began to lose its appearance of being firm and self-evident, also both for a biblical and a philosophical reason. The biblical reason is given in Kuyper's study. The philosophical reason has to do with a deep alteration in our Western sense of life that has occurred since the nineteenth century. We have discovered both nature and man in their "historicality"—if that is the translation of the German *Geschichtlichkeit*.

Nature is the product of an immense process of evolution. Man also is meant to grow and change, to respond ever anew to the challenge of his surroundings. A static situation is no longer for us, as it was for our ancestors, the ideal state, but at best is the starting point of a dynamic and progressive movement. The schools of Whitehead, Heidegger, and Teilhard de Chardin are in league, though with divergent arguments, to convince us of the fact that mutability belongs to real life and that immutability belongs to evil, if not to death. To the same extent, they argue, we become estranged from a God whom we are obliged to consider as eternal immutability and even immobility. No wonder that when in this situation we read the biblical words about the repentance of God we read them with grateful surprise for fresh insight.

There is now suddenly "a cloud of witnesses" in philosophy of religion and in dogmatics attempting to combine the concept of God and the concept of change. Alfred North Whitehead makes a distinction between God's primordial nature and his derivative nature: "His derivative nature is consequent upon the creative advance of the world."[4] As such, "God is the great companion—the fellow-sufferer who understands."[5] Charles Hartshorne[6] defends the idea that God is unsurpassable except by himself. God makes himself dependent on the relations into which he enters; otherwise he would be a tyrant. He is enriched by his experiments. For Schubert M. Ogden the law of analogy requires that temporality is essential to God as well as to us. God lives in a limitless environment. Therefore, in God is a "limitless relativity and dependence."[7] Daniel D. Williams concludes from a phenomenological analysis of the concept of love: "If the categorical analysis of love explodes the notion that the conception of God must require absolute simplicity, unchangingness, and impassibility then the analogy of being may be understood so as to affirm a creative, temporal, and relational aspect in God's being."[8] The reason for that is this: "Causality without involvement is incompatible with love."[9]

Different from these more or less philosophical formulations inspired by process-philosophy are those concepts which see the changeability of God more concretely related to his revelation and salvation. The Japanese theologian Kazoh Kitamori sees the pain of God as that element which combines his wrath and his love. God suffers in the suffering of Christ: "When a father sacrifices his son in death, he must tear himself away from his fatherly nature."[10] Particularly in European theology, the concept of God's immutability was challenged on the grounds of Christology and salvation history. We think first of Karl Barth, who in his treatment of the attributes of God replaces the classical term "immutability" by "constancy" (Beständigkeit), because "the pure immobile is—death. If, then, the pure immobile is God, death is God. . . . And if death is God, then God is dead."[11] However, in him are both rest and motion. He is the living one and as such the changeable one. But in all this God maintains his constancy as the loving one in freedom. Barth goes even further in the opening pages of the next volume. In this second part of his doctrine of God, he deals mainly with eternal election.

For Barth, this action toward men belongs essentially to God's nature. From eternity the perfect and blessed God has decided to be a God of men. Therefore Jesus Christ, the historical Savior, was the creative, covenant-making Word of God, which was in the beginning with God and was himself God. That is why Barth opens this volume with the bold summation: "The doctrine of election is the sum of the Gospel. . . . It is part of the doctrine of God because originally God's election of man is a predestination not merely of man but of Himself."[12] The consequence of this is "that the determination belongs no less to Him than all that He is in and for Himself."[13] By defining God in that way, Barth abandons radically the classical distinction between God in himself (*in se*) and God in his relation toward us (*quo ad nos*).

As we shall see below, there is some ambiguity in Barth's position on this point. Whereas Barth's partner, Helmut Gollwitzer, interpreted his doctrine of God much in the line of transcendence and *aseitas*,[14] another follower of Barth, Eberhard Jüngel, gave his booklet the significant title *Gottes Sein ist im Werden*.[15] Jüngel extends Barth's insights by applying them especially to the fact that in the crucifixion of his Son, God himself passes through suffering and death. In a later publication he writes: "God's being in its oneness is more differentiated and also more temporal than we are able to conceive. . . . God himself tolerates in himself a negotiation which creates in his being room for different being."[16]

Further consequences of this insight for the doctrine of God and of the Trinity are drawn by Jürgen Moltmann in his book with the characteristic title *Der gekreuzigte Gott*.[17] For him the moment of Jesus' being forsaken by God (Mark 15:34) marks the utmost separation and at the same time the utmost unity of the Father and the Son. The crucifixion is therefore the decisive event in God's inner trinitarian life, the history of God himself into which now all human history is integrated. The trinitarian doctrine is the expression of God's suffering self-identification with his suffering and sinful world. It is therefore the expression of his changeability.

Somewhat apart from the Barthian school we take notice (as Kuyper himself did in his article) of the original study of H. M. Kuitert, entitled *De mensvor-migheid Gods*,[18] in which he defends the changeability of God as belonging to his very essence, as the expression of his steadfast covenant relationship with his people. He does not relate this insight to the suffering of Christ, but to the whole of the dramatic covenant history.

A parallel development has taken place in Roman Catholic theology. This development was partly or mainly under the influence of Teilhard de Chardin, although he himself did not devote much thought to the consequences of his ideas for the doctrine of God. For him God is the one at the beginning and at the end of the world process, in which he "realizes" himself, "perfects" himself.[19] Karl Rahner in particular has thought about the change within God due to the incarnation and the crucifixion of Christ.[20] His concise conclusion is: "God changes through the different" (*Gott ändert sich am Andern*). Not less interesting are the formulations offered by two outstanding Dutch Catholic theologians. E. Schillebeeckx writes: "The very creation and especially the incarnation suggest to us that the unchangeability of God can assume perplexingly surprising shapes, without becoming positively changeable."[21] And again: "For God is—we stammer—absolute Newness, never growing old and at the same time never changing absolute Newness."[22] And in another place: "In a way which we cannot imagine . . . our history must have a meaning not only for us but also for God."[23] And P. Schoonenberg proposes that the confession of the incarnation is undermined "if the relation expressed by it is only a reality in us and not in God."[24] And again: "God's real relations with us imply that also in God change, coming into being, and becoming must be accepted, though in a wholly divine way."[25]

Thus, within a short period of time an age-old doctrine has been challenged by many theologians. Their rather recent confession of the changeability of God has biblical, philosophical, and cultural roots. Of the biblical and cultural roots we have already spoken. We conclude this section by drawing attention to the philosophical roots. For centuries the concept of Aristotle was dominant in the doctrine of God. His authority has, consciously or unconsciously, now been replaced by that of Hegel. For Hegel, God passes through a process in which he turns to that which is contrary in order to return to himself, enriched by this cosmic detour. Men like Küng, Moltmann, Pannenberg, and Rahner do not hesitate to acknowledge his influence on their theology. In its doctrine of God, theology will always drift about between Aristotle and Hegel.

III

How true this last sentence is can be illustrated by several quotations from the authors mentioned in the section above. Although it appears that they have abandoned the concept of God's unchangeability, no one of them (with the probable exception of the non-theologian Whitehead) speaks about a becoming and developing God. All of them want to stress God's involvement in the distress of his ever changing world. All of them want to stress that what is true of God's relation to us must in some way or another also be true of God's own nature. But at the same time, all of them shrink back from making God the subject, let alone the victim of a process of change. But how can we at one and the same time abandon Aristotle and avoid Hegel? Many of the theologians mentioned above have wrestled with this question without finding a consistent solution. In some cases the inconsistencies are self-evident. Schillebeeckx continues after the sentences quoted above: "Of course, God has nothing to gain himself from our history. That would be pantheism."[26] (Nevertheless, we heard Schoonenberg draw this consequence!) D. D. Williams also corrects himself halfway, when he writes "that there is that in God which does not suffer at all. The invulnerability in God is the integrity of his being."[27] Does Williams mean by this that there is a core of being in God that withdraws from the involvement of love? Kitamori also appears to be self-contradictory when he writes: "The theology of the pain of God does not mean that pain exists in God as *substance*. The pain of God is not a 'concept of substance'—it is a 'concept of relation.'"[28] This statement leads us back to the traditional separation that we had to reject, between God-in-himself and God-toward-us. In that case, a theology of the pain of God is hardly a step beyond Philo or Calvin! Even Charles Hartshorne, who so daringly argues that God can be surpassed by himself and can be enriched by his creatures, suddenly remarks: "The difference between ordinary and divine relativity . . . is this: God is relative, but what we may call the extent of his relativity is wholly independent of circumstances, wholly non-relative."[29] If I understand this thought correctly, God decides in his sovereignty from what relations he is pleased to make himself independent. Such a remark, however, should not be made casually in that kind of book, for it puts brackets around its whole purpose and substance.

All of these real or seeming inconsistencies are a clear indication of the magnitude of the problem. It is far easier to criticize an age-old tradition than to create a new and more solid one. We sense in all these words the fear of Hegelianism, the fear that God may lose his sovereignty and become the sublime name for the world-process.

Among the thinkers we have mentioned, Barth is the most profound. Even in him, however, we notice a certain ambiguity. To my mind the outcome of his wrestling is that the changeability of God, particularly in the incarnation and humiliation of the Son, is not in his eternal nature as such, nor is it outside of this nature. The change in covenant history finds its transcendental possibility (to put it in this Kantian phraseology) in God's nature, without being itself part of that nature. God's nature is not subjected to change, but this unchanging nature implies the possibility of change, of condescendence, and of humiliation. After thinking this through, Barth ends by assuming a polarity in God's eternal trinitarian nature: The Father is the majestic, sovereign, and directing one; the Son is the dependent, obedient, and serving one; and the Spirit is the unity and harmony of these two. Because of this eternal reality in himself, God can humiliate himself in the process of time as the Son without abandoning his divinity. In fact, he can express and confirm it in this way.[30] A speculative thought? Probably; but even so it is an answer to a very real and practical question: How can God be at the same time changeable and unchangeable? We cannot deny, however, that the thoughts quoted above from *Church Dogmatics* II.2 suggested an even closer unity between God's nature and his covenant-dealing. Barth did not extend this line. He was afraid to affect God's transcendence, his *aseitas*, his being absolutely beyond the process which he created. But to the same extent, God becomes anew a more or less abstract God, even in his eternal trinitarian polarity. It seems impossible to avoid in the same measure both Aristotle and Hegel!

IV

I am now obliged, after all these criticisms, to offer—however stammeringly—my own opinion.

In chapter 1 of Ezekiel we read how the prophet was called to his service through a vision of God. First he saw four living creatures; and then four wheels beside them. Then he saw "the likeness of a firmament, shining like crystal, spread out above their heads" (v. 22). The reader is inclined to think that this firmament is the image of God himself. And indeed, throughout many centuries, inspired by Aristotle and other philosophers, we have presented God in our dogmatic treatises as a cold, radiant firmament, transcendent and immobile; or, in the opening words of the Belgic Confession, as a "unique and simple spiritual being, . . . eternal, incomprehensible, invisible, unchangeable, unending, almighty; perfectly wise, righteous, good, and a very abundant fountain of all good." The true God of the covenant, however, is very different from such a firmament, as Ezekiel's experience testifies: "And above the firmament over their heads there was the likeness of a throne, in appearance like sapphire; and seated above the likeness of a throne was a likeness as it were of a human form" (v. 26, RSV), or, as we can translate the words $d^e mut$ $k^e mar'$ $\bar{e}h'\bar{a}d\bar{a}m$: "the shape of what looked like a man" (the abstract expression "human form" is not in accordance with the original). In Ezekiel's vision, that which is most transcendent (above the firmament and above the throne) is like a man—anthropomorph! He then hears this manlike being speaking to him (v. 28). A firmament and a throne cannot speak to man nor make a history with man.

The transcendent God is the God of the covenant adventure. There is no other God behind the God who passes through a history with mankind. He is fully engaged and therefore fully defined in his encounter with us. Otherwise it is not a real encounter. It would be blasphemous to say that this history leaves God himself unaffected and unmoved. It would be equally blasphemous, however, to say that he is no more than one of the partners in this history, a partner who risks becoming an object, or even a victim, in this process. He is involved in a history that he himself created, and which therefore remains his history. It is his goal that will be attained in this history. He is eternally the Rock whose work is perfect (Deut. 32:4); but what he is eternally, he also wants to be in time as our faithful Covenant Partner on a way with us, a way full of turns, failures, and surprises. On this way he permits himself to be negated, to be victimized, to be crucified. But it is he who decided to permit this. He is fully involved in a process that he at the same time transcends. By virtue of the unchangeability of his eternal purpose, he can create and undergo such a process. In his unchangeable love, he has made himself changeable. Therefore, we may be confident that he will get the better of his rebellious creatures, and that he will get the better for them.

With this conception I believe that we are very close to Barth. We see in

God's very nature the transcendental possibility of his condescendence and involvement. The God of Israel, the Father of Jesus Christ, is the unobjectifiable unity of transcendence and condescendence, of sovereignty and participation. Unlike Barth, however, we have no inclination to relate this insight to the traditional doctrine of the Trinity. To think of one "person" or "mode of existence" in God as wholly transcendent and another one as wholly descendent, is to the detriment of what must concern us most: the complete unity of what we, from our limited viewpoint, consider to be different aspects. Moreover, we believe that Barth, by solving a problem in this way, creates another one. Is not the consequence of his concept that God, in the incarnation, is only halfway present among us, that is, present only as the second (condescendent) person?

We also differ from Barth in that we do not shrink back from a consequence he apparently does not draw: We believe that not only we, but also God, will in the end be enriched by the covenant process. Without this consequence we still would not take seriously God's partnership in salvation history. If he engages himself wholly in this adventure, that engagement must affect him as well as us.[31] The father of the prodigal son was not the same after his son returned. God is enriched by renewed sons and daughters. That is his eternal goal. That is why he is so passionately interested in human affairs. Once we know about his involvement and goal, we have no excuse for not being involved with him in his world.

NOTES TO CHAPTER ONE

1. *SJTh*, 22 (1969), 257-277.
2. *Ibid.*, pp. 273f.
3. *Ibid.*, p. 273.
4. *Process and Reality: An Essay in Cosmology* (Cambridge: Cambridge University Press, 1929), p. 488. See the whole of pp. 484-497.
5. *Ibid.*, p. 497.
6. *The Divine Reality: A Social Concept of God*, 2d ed. (New Haven: Yale University Press, 1964).
7. "The Temporality of God," in *The Reality of God and Other Essays* (New York: Harper and Row, 1966), p. 156.
8. *The Spirit and the Forms of Love* (New York: Harper and Row, 1968), p. 124.
9. *Ibid.*, p. 128.
10. *Theology of the Pain of God* (Richmond: John Knox Press, 1965), p. 115.
11. *CD*, II.1, p. 494.
12. *CD*, II.1, p. 3.
13. *Ibid.*, p. 7.
14. *Die Existenz Gottes im Bekenntnis des Glaubens* (Munich: Chr. Kaiser Verlag, 1963).
15. (Tübingen: J.C.B. Mohr, 1965), especially pp. 99f.
16. Eberhard Jüngel, "Vom Tod des lebendigen Gottes," in *Unterwegs zur Sache* (Munich: Chr. Kaiser Verlag, 1972), p. 120.
17. (Munich: Chr. Kaiser Verlag, 1972). See especially VI.5 and VI.9. An earlier, less known, but striking parallel to these thoughts is the study of the Catholic theologian Herbert Mühlen, *Die Veränderlichkeit Gottes als Horizont einer zukünftigen Christologie* (Münster: Aschendorff, 1969).
18. (Kampen: J. H. Kok, 1962). See especially pp. 235-245.
19. See the excellent study of S. M. Daecke, *Teilhard de Chardin und die evangelische Theologie* (Göttingen: Vandenhoeck & Ruprecht, 1967), especially pp. 387-397.

20. See his *Schriften zur Theologie*, 1 (Einsiedeln: Benziger Verlag, 1954), especially pp. 125-128 and 196-204. His and other Catholic as well as Protestant discussions about the changeability of God are collected by Hans Küng in an excursus (V) of his book on Hegel, *Menschwerdung Gottes* (Freiburg: Herder, 1970), especially pp. 248-655.

21. "De zin van het mens-zijn van Jesus, de Christus," *TsTh*, 2 (1962), 134.

22. *Op. cit.*, p. 132.

23. *Op. cit.*, p. 133.

24. "Christus zonder tweeheid?," *TsTh*, 6 (1966), 301.

25. *Op. cit.*, p. 306. See also his book *Hij is een God van mensen* ('s-Hertogenbosch: L. C. G. Malmberg, 1969), pp. 176-178 (note 15), where he concludes (with some hesitation) that God becomes trinitarian by the fact that he communicates himself to and is present in the man Jesus as Word, and by being in the church as Spirit. The English translation of this book bears the title *The Christ: A Study of the God-Man Relationship in the Whole of Creation and in Jesus Christ* (New York: Herder and Herder, 1971).

26. *Op. cit.*, p. 133.

27. *Op. cit.*, p. 128.

28. *Op. cit.*, p. 16.

29. *Op. cit.*, p. 82.

30. *CD*, IV.1, pp. 192-204.

31. I expressed this conviction first in *The Doctrine of the Holy Spirit* (Richmond: John Knox Press, 1964), p. 119. The trinitarian setting in which I put it at that time, I have since replaced by another concept of the Trinity. See my *Christelijk Geloof* (Nijkerk: G. F. Callenbach, 1973), §37.

2

THE BIBLICAL VIEW OF TIME*

JAMES MUILENBURG

It is by no means fortuitous that our contemporary world is deeply occupied with the problem of time. The literature that has gathered about this problem is not only abundant but also notable for the ways in which various disciplines have sought to wrestle with it. The natural scientist, the philosopher, the theologian, the historian, the sociologist, the poet, and the writer of fiction and drama have all engaged in a common encounter with the mystery of this basic givenness of our human existence. Yet, while it is true that periods like our own incite reflection on time's meaning, the problem plays a rôle in the history of human thought quite beyond that of the pressures and hazards of eras of social crisis. It is not too much to say that the whole history of human thought and reflection has been involved in one way or another with this central reality of our human existence. Civilization and culture, philosophy and religion, *Weltanschauung* and *ethos* divide at the point of their primary preoccupation with space and time. In every philosophy of history it is the concept of time that is decisive and determinative.[1] In the ancient world "the time experience is both rich and subtle. . . . Time is experienced in the periodicity and rhythm of man's own life as well as in the life of nature. Each phase of man's life—childhood, adolescence, maturity, old age—is a time of peculiar qualities."[2] From the age of Plato and Aristotle to our own, philosophers have sought to grapple with this problem. Indeed, modern thought is turning to it with an intensity of concern that makes it the dominant if not the undergirding issue in our thought and reflection.[3]

Time's hidden mystery lies deep within us all. To live is to live in time, and our consciousness and thinking are so commingled with its movement, so intimately involved in its flux and the inexorability of temporal changes, that the quest for serenity and interior tranquility never ceases to occupy us. At an early age we feel ourselves its victims. We are haunted again and again by the painful awareness that the shining moment passes, the day comes to an end, some silver cord of confidence is snapped, some dream dispelled, some faith shattered. The

*Reprinted with permission from the *Harvard Theological Review*, 54, no. 4 (October 1961), 225-252. Copyright 1961 by the President and Fellows of Harvard College. (James Muilenburg passed away May 10, 1974. Ed.)

whirligig of Time brings in its revenges. The present forever flees to the past, the future forever breaks in with relentless speed. We are forever confronted with the unexpected, the unanticipated, the new. In an instant, in the twinkling of an eye, before the completion of this sentence—if ever, indeed, this sentence is finished, something may happen which will alter its intended meaning or our very situation; indeed, the situation at each point in the speaking of our words is a different one. Nature, too, joins in the moving pageantry of time. The seasons come and go, and each leaves its mark deeply etched in our feelings and thoughts and dim presentiments. The fresh verdure of spring deepens into the full-blown luxuriance of radiant summer, and then comes October when the leaves grow ashen and sober, the leaves grow crisped and sere. The goddess of fertility dies, and the world mourns. Or the goddess becomes the victim of space and retires into the jaws of the subterranean darkness (Persephone, and the others), and it is *cold*. We need not learn this experience from the great nature myths; all of us feel it very deeply at some time or other. There is something profoundly disquieting and threatening in the temporality of existence:[4]

> *There was a time when meadow, grove, and stream,*
> *the earth and every common sight,*
> *To me did seem*
> *Apparelled in celestial light,*
> *The glory and the freshness of a dream.*
> *It is not now as it hath been of yore;—*
> *Turn whereso'er I may,*
> *By night or day,*
> *The things which I have seen I now can see no more.*

The transitoriness of life afflicts us. The grass withers, the flower fades. Surely the people is grass.[5]

> *. . . our years come to an end like a sigh.*
> *The years of our life are threescore and ten,*
> *or even by reason of strength fourscore;*
> *yet their span[6] is but toil and trouble;*
> *they are soon gone, and we fly away.*
> (Ps. 90:9b-10b)

It is not surprising that it is the poets who have entered most deeply into the perplexities that time raises for us. There is a profound reason for this which is involved in their sensitiveness to words and language and the relation of speech to the ear, and of the hearing of the ear to time. But into this matter we cannot go at present. The only writer I have read who understands this problem is St. Augustine, and to him we shall refer at a later point. But the colossal reality of time is expressed in Edith Sitwell's "The Shadow of Cain" where she senses magnificently the primeval cold in which Time is frozen after Cain's terrible fratricide; in W. H. Auden's Tillichian reflections on *kairos* and *logos* or on the heavy burden of clock time in the opening lines of "For the Time Being"; or in T. S. Eliot's *Four Quartets* where he senses the bafflement of our temporality and then flees too precipitately, as it seems to me, to a timeless world of the eternal present. And surprisingly, perhaps, it is e.e.cummings who seizes upon the mystery with perception and sensitiveness and, withal, with courage:

> *and now you are and I never now and we're*
> *a mystery which will never happen again*
> *a miracle which has never happened before—*
> *and shining this our now must turn to then*
> *our then shall be some darkness during which*
> *fingers are without hands; and I have no*
> *you; and all trees (any more than each*
> *leafless) its silent in forevering snow*
> *—but never fear (my own, my beautiful,*
> *my blossoming) for also then's until.*

We cannot hold the treasured moment even for an instant. We cannot say to it, "Verweile doch, du bist so schön."[7]

The true poets sense intuitively the mystery of words spoken in time; perhaps this is a clue to an understanding of much of what seems to us obscure and tangled and tortured in contemporary verse. But they are by the same token deeply conscious of the malaise which afflicts the soul of man and the distraughtness that disturbs contemporary civilization. They know man's inveterate propensity to spatialize the outer and inner worlds of reality. We in our modern technological society tend to measure all things in heaven and earth. We interpret values by things; we understand by statistics; we are awed by size and numbers; we plot the configurations of the soul; we lapse into stereotyped uniformities; we diagnose the ills of man and nation by graphs. Yet it is with time itself that we wage battle: time that grows incoherent, time that will not stay for scrutiny or an answer, time that is burdened with the past and slouches reelingly into an unknown future. The manifestations of our interior conflicts between space and time are witnessed in our art, in our music, in our contemporary drama.

Of the two great peoples who have exerted a major influence upon the mind and soul of Western man, Hellas and Israel, the one lived and thought primarily in the world of space, the other primarily in the world of time. The Greeks, as Matthew Arnold never wearied of saying, sought to see life steadily and to see it whole. To them the world was animate, and to it they ascribed a world soul or *nous*. In Nature they perceived a form and structure or rather a structural necessity whose perfect representation they saw in the circle. Time was thus comprehended in the cyclical round of recurring seasons, and their myths bodied them forth in dramatic celebrations. Time is subordinated to nature. This is clearly stated by Aristotle: ". . . and so time is regarded as the rotation of the sphere (cf. IV. 10, 218b: 'the revolution of the all-embracing heaven'). . . . And this is the reason of our habitual way of speaking; for we say that human affairs and those of all other things . . . seem to be in a way circular, because all these things come to pass in time and have their beginning and end as it were 'periodically.'"[8] In the words of Hans Kohn: "Their art (i.e., the Greek) was plastic, space-dominating and space-forming, as if they sought to transpose the flowing, fleeting, ever-related elements of life into rest, space, limitation, and to give the formless form. . . . The Greek turned everything into form and marble in a supreme effort to eliminate the restlessness of time from the world. He endowed the world with the instruments of scientific thought, and tamed the Dionysian overflow of events into the supreme majesty of Apollonic order."[9] John Keats has given immortal expression to this capturing of the moment of time in his "Ode to a Grecian Urn." The recently discovered Winged Victory or The Winged Victory which stands so impressively at the head of the stairs in the Louvre is said to have been taken from the prow of a Greek ship ploughing its way through the winds and blue waters of the Aegean. Here we have a superb representation of movement, of life, of surging progress in stone. We see it, too, in the battle of the centaurs from the Parthenon, the frieze from the mausoleum of Halicarnassus, and in the Alexander sarcophagus at Istanbul.

To this predominantly spatial mentality of ancient Greece the mentality of Israel posed a perfect contrast. This does not mean that Israel ignores or rejects the world of space nor does it mean that ancient Greece did not take time seriously. *Au contraire!* As Professor Heschel has put it: "To disparage space and the blessing of things of space, is to disparage the works of creation, the works which God saw and 'it was good.' The world cannot be seen exclusively *sub specie temporis.* Time and space are inter-related."[10] But space is not in control. The much misunderstood first chapter of Genesis begins with the creation of the first day.[11] God gives day and night status: "God called the light Day, and the darkness he called Night. And there was evening and there was morning, one day." Time is not dependent upon the creation of the heavenly bodies of sun and moon; they are not only created on the fourth day, but they themselves exist under the sovereignty of a God who assigns to them their special work and function. They are created for history. A comparison of the biblical references to sun, moon, and stars with those of the other Near Eastern texts discloses the radical difference between Israel and the surrounding peoples: in Israel the mystery and meaning of time is not resolved by appeal to the cosmic world of space; among the other nations the heavenly bodies are deified and *chronos* spatializes time into extension and duration.[12] In the one, time is grasped in terms of purpose, will, and decision; in the other the secrets of the stars are determined by "those who divide the heavens, who gaze at the stars, who at the new moons predict what shall befall you" (Isa. 47:13; cf. also and especially 44:24ff.).

From the beginning the religion of Israel was imageless. Nothing in heaven and earth was adequate to its representation of the holy God of the Exodus and of Sinai. The God of Israel is active, active in time and event; he cannot be transformed into space. In the ark cloistered in the Holy of Holies of the temple at Jerusalem Yahweh was doubtless believed to be truly present, but the staves beneath the ark were a perpetual witness to his mobility (cf. II Sam. 7:4-7), and finally it disappears from history without even a mention of its loss. The sanctuaries are constantly under trenchant criticism of the prophets, and Jeremiah's life is imperilled by his word that the temple must be destroyed. One of the accusations against Jesus was that he said he would destroy the temple. The sanctuaries are holy places, to be sure, but what makes them holy is that they are characteristically associated with aetiological stories that commemorate "historical" events, moments in which Yahweh had appeared to the patriarchs, or to Joshua, David, and others. Not the physical structure of space (as the nature cults would have it), but the historical event in time is remembered and treasured and passed on from generation to generation.

The forty-first chapter of Isaiah is a good illustration of the conflict between the space mentality of the nations and the time mentality of Israel. Yahweh calls the nations of the world to judgment in a solemn conclave. He raises at once the historical question involved in the conquests of Cyrus:

> Who stirred up one from the east
>> whom victory meets at every step?
> He gives up nations before him,
>> so that he tramples kings under foot;
> he makes them like dust with his sword,
>> like driven stubble with his bow.
> He pursues them and passes on safely,
>> by paths his feet have not trod.
>> (Isa. 41:23)

The nations of the world are terrified by this challenge in the realm of time and history. They flee to the world of space and resort to man's consummate attempt to make of the sovereign God of nature and of history an idol and a thing. In their fear they say to each other "Take courage!"; in their helplessness they help each other in fashioning an idol; in their weakness they make the idol strong. With Israel the situation is completely otherwise; she is addressed by her God who says "Fear not," she is given assurance of divine help, and she is promised strength, and always in the concrete context of time:

> But you, Israel, my servant,
>> Jacob, whom I have chosen,
>> the offspring of Abraham, my friend;
> You whom I took from the ends of the earth,
>> and called from its farthest corners,
> saying to you, "You are my servant,
>> I have chosen you and not cast you off";

I will strengthen you, I will help you,
I will uphold you with my victorious right hand.
(Isa. 41:8-10)

When the trial is renewed, the issue is drawn much more sharply. The nations are urged to tell of former and latter events, of what has happened and what is still to happen, "that we may know that you are gods." But they are *silent;* they have only the things that their hands have made. The problem and mystery of time cannot be spatially resolved. Time is confronted and encountered only by a transcendent Lord of time who yet reveals himself in the events of time.

But this is not meant to imply that Israel thinks speculatively concerning the meaning of time. Such speculation is absent from the Old Testament as it is absent in many other areas of theological concern. Rather it is in the actual course of her holy history that she sees the revelation of One who initiates, guides, and directs events, and interprets their meaning through his servants the prophets. In this sense Israel is the historical people, or, as Professor Tillich states it, *das geschichtliche Volk schlechthin.* Israel lives her life in a world of eventful reality to which no image or creature of space could ever do adequate justice.

Yet there were experiences in her history that provided her with the symbolism by which to express what it was that God was doing in the directing and guiding of her existence. One of the most striking of these symbols was the *way* or *road (derek).* This symbol was an expression of the onward movement of time within her life, its historical character, its ever changing vicissitudes.[13] Each stage of her journey presented her with new situations to which she was called to answer in a responsible way. The path she walked became the primary image for her ethical life. Piety was a walking with God. The road led to a destination and thus became an eschatological symbol, notably in Second Isaiah. Thus history, ethics, personal piety, providence, and eschatology were all represented by the simple figure. Heraclitus said that we never step into the same river twice. For Israel it was the way, and the motif weaves itself throughout the Old and New Testaments. Jesus makes use of it in his teaching, and the covenanters at Qumran and the early Christians were described by it.

The road was a peculiarly congenial symbol since it had figured so largely in the epochal moments of Israel's life: from Egypt to the mount of covenanting, from Sinai to the promised land, from Palestine into exile, and from Babylon to the hill of Zion. It was congenial in other respects also, for it pointed to beginning and end, to initial moments in which God revealed himself in his unmotivated grace and to consummating moments in which he fulfilled his purpose and promise. Again, this road was not a circular turning. Cyclical views were current in the nature religions of the Near East, but Israel's conception is linear, not a straight line of unilinear development, but one that moved tortuously as history itself. There was no immanent structure in history whereby the movement could be discerned by logical patterns, no form by which men might plot the course of events, no *anangkē* to which even God must submit, no law of development or progress that the wise or the *bien-instruit* could recognize. Yahweh was the Leader: he leads Abraham who walks by obedience and faith; he leads Israel by the moving pillar of cloud and pillar of fire; he leads the battalions that return to Zion. Israel does not know the way of her history; only God knows it. As the people of God, Israel moves through history under his lordship and sovereignty, his righteous leading and grace. The Deuteronomists, to be sure, see in history the working out of a logically coherent moral sovereignty, but it is God's rule, not Israel's possession of a law of inner historical development, that is central; moreover, Deuteronomic theodicy was transcended by the course of history itself and by the prophets and sages who saw more deeply into the perplexities of life in history.

An examination of one or two of the words employed in Israel's extensive vocabulary of time affords us some further insight into the way in which it was apprehended in ancient Israel. The most common word for time, *'ēt,* occurs 297 times, and is derived from the root *'nh,* "to answer" or "to meet." Thus time is occurrence; it is "that which meets you in your path through life."[14] The Old Testament has no way of distinguishing between chronological and concrete or "realistic" time.[15] The Septuagint renders the word as *kairos* in over two-thirds of all the instances of its appearance. Often the expression is used in a formal or general sense such as "in that time" or "it came to pass in that time" (*wayᵉhi bā'ēt hahū';* cf., e.g., Gen. 21:22; 38:1; Deut. 1:16, 18). The clause "it came to pass" (Heb. *wayᵉhi;* Gk. *kai egeneto*) is one of the most frequent in the Bible, which is generally omitted in the *RSV,* and represents a distinct loss since the eventfulness of biblical mentality is thereby obscured. The word *'ēt* is associated very frequently with the events and phenomena of nature or man's life in nature in the activity of farming. Thus times are described as those of rain (the former and the latter), of threshing, of pruning, of harvest, of the singing of birds, of the drying up of the wadies, of the birth of mountain goats and does.[16] Or it is characterized by the events of human life: birth, adolescence, menstruation, old age, and death. Historical periods are dated by the time of the fathers, or the days when the judges judged, or the time of David the King. Qoheleth introduces his catalog of times with the generalization, "To everything there is a season (*lakkōl zᵉmān*), and a time for every matter (*wᵉ'ēt lᵉkol ḥēfeṣ*) under heaven." His attitude toward time is hardly typical of the rest of the Old Testament, but his vivid witness to the concreteness of time is nowhere surpassed in the whole Bible:

> *a time to be born, and a time to die;*
> *a time to plant, and a time to pluck up what is planted;*
> *a time to kill, and a time to heal;*
> *a time to break down, and a time to build up;*
> *a time to weep, and a time to laugh;*
>
> · · · · ·

a time to seek, and a time to lose;
a time to keep, and a time to cast away;
a time to rend, and a time to sew;
a time to keep silence, and a time to speak;
a time to love, and a time to hate;
a time for war, and a time for peace.

(Eccl. 3:2-4a, 6-8)

To which Qoheleth adds the somewhat lugubrious reflection: "What gain has the worker from his toil?"[17] It is clear from these many passages that biblical time is *concrete time;* properly we should speak of *times* rather than time; any abstract meaning is generally remote from the writer's thought. Between man and time there is an interior, psychic relationship. The Israelite is not *primarily* concerned with duration or extent of time. He is not primarily interested in measuring its distances or in determining the extent of its duration. "For the Israelite time is not merely a form or frame. Time is charged with substance, or, rather, it is identical with substance; time is the development of the very events."[18] The character of time depends upon that which happens in it, and to these concrete happenings he stood in a living relation. Let us put it in another way: time is believed somehow to be alive. Yahweh says to Abraham in promising him the long-expected child that he will return "when the season lives or revives" (*kā'ēt ḥayyâ*), and Job implores Yahweh that the night in which he was born may not rejoice among the days of the year but be barren and cursed (Job 3:6-7). In a word, "there are as many times as there are souls. Everything has its time."[19] Jeremiah chides Israel that

Even the stork in the heavens
    knows her times;
and the turtledove, swallow, and crane
    keep the time of their coming;
but my people know not
    the ordinance of the LORD.

(Jer. 8:7)

This concreteness of Israel's thinking is emphasized by the other words in the terminology of time: day, month, and year. Every day has its distinctive character. A man's life consists of his days. The day has morning, noon, and night, but each of these terms has its own specific content; what is significant is what happens, or what man does, in those periods. There are days that are so filled with content that they mean more than months of duration-time, and these days are preserved and remembered within the *nephesh* or life-soul of the person or community that experiences them. Of these special days in Israel's life the seventh is to be remembered above all others: "Remember the sabbath day to keep it holy, for in six days God made heaven and earth." It is the Sabbath that forms the culmination of the priestly story of the creation; in a sense all else is but a prologue to it. Professor Heschel has written a beautiful and profound discussion of this day in his book on the Sabbath, and I can do no better than repeat some of his words. After pointing out the meaning of "one of the most distinguished words in the Bible," the word "holy" or *qādôš*, he comments:

> It is, indeed, a unique occasion at which the distinguished word *qadosh* is used for the first time: in the Book of Genesis at the end of the story of creation. How extremely significant is the fact that it is applied to time: "And God blessed the seventh day and made it *holy.*" There is no reference in the record to any object of space that would be endowed with the quality of holiness.
> This is a radical departure from accustomed religious thinking. The mythical mind would expect that, after heaven and earth have been established, God would create a holy place—a holy mountain or a holy spring—whereupon a sanctuary is to be established. Yet it seems as if to the Bible it is a *holiness in time*, the Sabbath, which comes first.[20]

Man lives from the day of his birth to the day of his death, yet in each day he is aware that this is the day that Yahweh has made (Ps. 118:24). He knows, too, that there is a decisive, final day. Israel remembers such decisive days, such as the day of Jerusalem or of Jezreel or of Midian, and the contexts in which these expressions occur show how crucial they are. Yahweh of hosts has a day, and his day stands sovereign over the days of man (Isa. 2:6ff.). It is the day when Israel and, indeed, all the nations of the world are to be held accountable for the days that have been allotted to them. The repeated assertion that the Day is near is an expression in the category of time of the utter urgency of Yahweh's demand upon Israel's life. "My times are in thy hand," cries the psalmist in a setting that admirably expresses the relation between man's time and God's time (Ps. 31:15).

Biblical time is comprehended not by its extent but by its immediacy, not by its quantitative measurements, but by its quality, by the nature of the content with which it is filled. These characteristics are illustrated by the relationship of time to generations. Time is a succession of ongoing generations. Each generation has its specific content. It has the stamp of the progenitor upon it.[21] Thus Abraham lives on in the generations that follow him; to be the children of Abraham is to live as Abraham lived, to do the works of the father. Father and son bear a profound psychophysical relation, the son has his father within him. In the tenth chapter of Genesis the peoples of Near Eastern antiquity are comprehended in the structure of a genealogy. On Mount Sinai Yahweh declares his name to Moses: "Say to the people of Israel, 'Yahweh, the God of your fathers, the God of Abraham, the God of Isaac, and the God of Jacob, has sent me to you': this is my name for ever, and thus I am to be remembered throughout all generations" (Exod. 3:15[E]). Yahweh is Israel's God in all generations (Ps. 90:1), his faithfulness endures to all generations (Ps. 100:5), his kingdom is from generation to generation (Dan. 4:3). The Gospel of Matthew opens with the generations from Abraham to David, from David to Jeconiah, from Jeconiah to the birth of Jesus; and Luke carries his genealogy back to Adam. Thus the whole of the sacred history is understood in terms of the succession of father and son, and in this succession the time-life of Israel is comprehended. It is time lived in the ongoing movement of continuing solidarities.[22] Each generation has the stamp of the father and the son upon it.

We may now turn to another area in which the mystery of time is grasped in ancient Israel. In the dynamic, living experience of speaking and hearing the hiddenness of time is somehow, strangely, articulated and bodied forth. The concreteness of time in event is matched by the concreteness of speech in the word. What the eye was to the ancient Greek, that the ear was to the man of Israel.[23] The realm of maximum reality was that of speaking-hearing.[24] The appeal that rings throughout the Bible from beginning to end is to *hear,* to listen, to respond to words, to accept the responsibility of being addressed. Not only are the barriers of our interior isolation broken in the acceptance of this speaking-hearing relation, but all that which is implied in this encounter and engagement and participation of the "I" communicating itself in words and the "Thou" answering to the "I's" communication provides for us the final matrix in which our lives in history are lived. Yet these generalizations concerning the speaking-hearing relation are insufficient for the true understanding of the relation of speech and time. The full import of their relation is first borne in upon us when we expose ourselves existentially to the innumerable concrete moments in which concrete time is encountered with the concrete word spoken, under the immediate urgency of the demand to hear. Nature, worship, personal experience; past, present, and future; creation, revelation, eschatology; life, death, and responsibility are all of them interpreted and appropriated in the reality of words spoken and heard.

> *Hear, O heavens, and give ear, O earth;*
> *for the LORD has spoken.*　　　　　　　　(Isa. 1:2)
>
> *Give ear, O heavens, and I will speak;*
> *and let the earth hear the words of my mouth.*
> *May my teaching drop as the rain,*
> *my speech distil as the dew.*　　　　(Deut. 32:1-2b)
>
> *Hear this word,... O people of Israel.*　　(Amos 3:1)
>
> *The word of the LORD came to me.*　　　(Jer. 1:4)
>
> *I am watching over my word to perform it.*　(Jer. 1:12)

Israel, the Servant of the Lord, lives each day under the expectation of Yahweh's speech: "Morning by morning he wakens my ear" (Isa. 50:4). National and social crises are met by resort to the prophetic word (cf., e.g., Micaiah and Jeremiah). And it is the function of the prophet to respond to the specific time by speaking the word of the Lord that communicates not only the meaning of the specific time but also the context of it in the wider ranges of times past and times future, of memory and expectation. Thus prediction becomes a living reality of prophetic speech, and in Second Isaiah constitutes the reality that demonstrates not only the existence of God but also his oneness and the way by which he reveals himself. The writer of the Fourth Gospel describes a great crisis in the life of Jesus. Many of his disciples are offended by his drastic words concerning his body and blood, and many of them draw back and no longer walk with him. Jesus then says, "Will you also go away?" and Peter replies, "Lord, to whom shall we go? You have the words of eternal life, and we have believed and come to know that you are the Holy One of God." Thus throughout the Bible the mystery of time is related to the mystery of life lived in speech.

Words move ... only in time.

As in so many other aspects of biblical theology, it is Second Isaiah who sees the relation of word and event, of time and speech, in its most inclusive and spacious dimensions. His contemporaries are overborne by the meaninglessness of what is happening at the end of the neo-Babylonian and the approach of the Persian age. The incoherence of time and event plunges them into despair and doubt. To these moods the prophet replies with a triumphant declaration concerning the Word of God. God's Word rules and controls all of Nature, and the whole movement of history from beginning to end is understood by the activity of his Word. From creation to redemption His Word goes forth to accomplish his will and purpose:

> For as the rain and the snow come down from heaven,
>   and return not thither but water the earth,
> making it bring forth and sprout,
>   giving seed to the sower and bread to the eater,
> so shall my word be that goes forth from my mouth;
>   it shall not return to me empty,
> but it shall accomplish that which I purpose,
>   and prosper in the thing for which I sent it.
>   (Isa. 55:10-11)

And it is this Word—with all its tremendous cosmic and temporal perspectives— which achieves ever new and surprising depths in the prophet's eschatological drama. It is a word deep and full of mystery, a hidden word, yet its concreteness is eloquently affirmed in relation to the world-shaking events of a particular time. To this Word the Servant of the Lord listens, and in this Word he hears the meaning of his destiny, the meaning of his mission, the meaning of all his *heilsgeschichtliche* memories and *heilsgeschichtliche* hopes. Yet it is not a cryptic word which only the professionals of the cult treasure in secret. Rather, hidden word though it is, it is one that all may hear, and it is a word as long as time is long and as spacious as nature, yet dominating both by the might of its sovereign will and purpose.

Our examination of the relation of time and word introduces us to another aspect of biblical thought: the meaning of creation and its connection with time. The world is *created:* "By the word of the LORD were the heavens made, and all their host by the breath of his mouth" (Ps. 33:6). The biblical doctrine of creation is a derivative of history, the sacred history of the chosen people. The creation account in Genesis 1 is not only prologue to the history that follows it and thus to be read in relation to it, but is also a development of the election-historical life, of the redemptive history that has the Exodus as its center. It is a product of the mature reflection of Israel upon the meaning of her history within the purpose and grace of God.

But why does the priestly writer employ the Word of God as the instrument of the divine creation? If words are in time and are "timely," how are we to understand God's words in relation to creation? Augustine devotes himself to a profound discussion of this in the eleventh book of his *Confessions* (VI.8). "But how dost thou speak? In the way that the voice came out of the cloud saying, 'This is my beloved Son?' For that voice passed and the second after the first, the third after the second, and so forth in order, until the last after the rest, and silence after the last. Whence it is abundantly clear and plain that the motion of a creature expressed it, itself temporal, serving thy eternal will." The relevant passage is too long to quote here, but the upshot of it is that Augustine is unwilling to stress creation as a temporal event; such an emphasis only raises for him more questions than it answers. "This is my Word," says Augustine, "which is also the Beginning, because it also speaketh to us." "Believe me to be the Beginning because that (*sic*) you may believe, I not only am, but also speak to you." The activity of God's word in creation is the language that only faith can grasp; the appeal is not to reason, for reason would defy it, but to faith, which rejoices in the word addressed to it, and that which is said in words is the reality that only faith can discern. Thus the heavens are constantly telling the glory of God, telling it in the time-speech of the story of their creation. And in that story where words and events coalesce we apprehend the ground of our existence; we confess that we are not our own, but belong in every hour of our lives to One who has revealed himself in time, and even in the creation of the universe and ourselves addresses us in the time language of words and faith.

Nature, then, has no independent status. The conception of *physis* is alien to the Old Testament. To the ancient Israelite neither nature nor history *is,* but both are events, happenings. "The 'thing' is always the 'thing done': space is produced by event." The world of nature like the chosen people lives under covenantal bond. The world continues by God's faithfulness to his covenant, as Israel continues by his faithfulness to the Sinaitic covenant. "Thus says the LORD: If I have not established my covenant with day and night and the ordinances of heaven and earth, then I will reject the descendants of Jacob and

David my servant. . . ." "The world was not an ontological necessity" (Heschel).

Biblical faith moves in the world of time: of all kinds of times and situations, times that are never the same but shift and change kaleidoscopically. We may trace passages here and there that suggest some structure in nature or in history (cf., e.g., Jer. 31:35-37; Gen. 8:22 or the Deuteronomic framework of Judges), but the view of the Bible as a whole is that both exist under God's constant providence and care, and that both may be brought to an end at any moment. Therefore Israel lives by his promises and assurances, not by a given structure or order. The events of a particular history are Israel's Credo (cf. Deut. 26:5ff.; 6:20-24; Josh. 24:5-9; Pss. 106; 136). In the cult these events are treasured and remembered and rehearsed, transmitted from generation to generation, and celebrated on the great festival days. On these occasions the past becomes contemporary; the reality of the past event is not denied but it is experienced *now*. The present actuality of the historical event is superbly stated in Deuteronomy: "It was not your fathers with whom I made this covenant, but with you, yourselves, alive, here, today, all of you" (Deut. 5:3). The festivals had their original home in nature; in time they were all transformed into historical celebrations: the exodus from Egypt in the Passover, the giving of the Law of Sinai in the Feast of Weeks; the sojourn in the wilderness in the Feast of Booths. Israel thus remembers all that God has done for her, and the New Testament joins with the Old in its confessional recital of the mighty redemptive acts from the call of Abraham to the coming of Jesus, whom it believes to be the Messiah, and its beliefs concerning him are fashioned from memories enshrined in the Old Testament.[25]

In the practices of the cult we have seen how Israel enters into relation with the sacred and unique events of her election-covenant history.[26] The memories of the past become cultic rituals and dramatic celebrations. But they do more than merely repeat or make contemporary the gracious events that had been vouchsafed to her. They remind her of her responsibility before God. For the *kerygma* of the saving act is accompanied by the *torah* or *didache* of responsibility. Since Yahweh has of his own unmotivated goodness acted for Israel, so Israel must respond by acting and living in accordance with his holy will. Professor Eichrodt in his little monograph on *Man in the Old Testament* opens his discussion with "the unconditional obligation of the will of God as the basis of the Old Testament view of man." Yahweh's great act of deliverance at the Exodus is the ground and motive for Israel's obedience. At the head of the Elohistic decalog and Covenant Code, the *kerygma* is stated: "I am Yahweh who brought you up out of the land of Egypt," and immediately there follow all the commands and obligations that are laid upon Israel (Exod. 20:1-17). This responsibility is magnificently affirmed in the Shema:

> Hear, O Israel: the LORD our God is one LORD; and you shall
> love the LORD your God with all your heart, and with all your soul

(*nephesh*), and with all your might. And these words which I command
you this day shall be upon your heart; and you shall teach them diligently
to your children, and shall talk of them when you sit in the house, and
when you walk by the way, and when you lie down, and when you rise.
And you shall bind them upon your hand, and they shall be as frontlets
between your eyes. And you shall write them on the doorposts of your
house and on your gates.

Even today the devout Jew recites the Shema twice each day in love (*k^{e'}ittim</sup>
b^{e'}ah^abāh*). Prophet and priest are one in making known what it is that Yahweh
requires, and the apostle Paul, who appears to be most rigorous in his criticism
of the Torah, is nevertheless careful to end his letters with a series of *halakoth*.
Professor Eichrodt has stated Israel's responsibility in time and for time
succinctly:[27]

> It is evident that there is no room in this view for a self-contained and
> harmoniously rounded life, for the shaping of personality into a work of
> art in accordance with the demands of the ideal of the *kalon kagathon*.
> It has been rightly observed that the Old Testament has no heroes or
> saints. It is too vividly aware of God's constant questioning of man, and
> calling him in question, to allow any confidence to be established in an
> ideal image of human personality at rest in itself. History is a movement
> effected by God which challenges man and gives him his destiny and his
> task. In this situation time cannot become a matter of indifference, as
> merely the material form of life over which rises, as man's real home,
> the reality of the spirit with its regular and ordered world. But time
> becomes rather the unrecurring reality which is given by God and which
> urges man to a decision; the reality which inexorably calls for a decision
> here and now and permits no rest in some secure position which is valid
> once for all.

Israel's living relation with the concrete events of time is expressed in
memory and expectation. From the very beginning the sanctuaries served as
repositories of sacred memories; indeed, the sanctuaries are legitimized and
recognized as holy because it was in these places that God had made himself
known to his chosen servants in theophanic revelation. The *hieroi logoi* spoken
on these occasions are treasured and remembered, rehearsed and transmitted from
generation to generation. Thus the solidarity of Israel is maintained by a common
memory of redemptive acts. The festivals celebrate them, and in their dramatic
representations they are made contemporary. From one end of the Bible to the
other the faithful are supported by the memories of what God has done for his
people.

Yet it would be an error to suppose that biblical faith is primarily one of
recollection of past events. Rather, throughout Scripture, the movement is
generally toward the future. The promises of God to the patriarchs, to Israel,
to David, and to the prophets constitute a living and dynamic impetus toward
future realization. Yahweh has his plan, and his plan overcomes the plans of
even the most powerful (Isa. 14:24-27; 23:8-9; Jer. 29:11; Zech. 8:14b).

Yahweh has his purpose, and his purpose will be fulfilled (Isa. 44:28; 46:11). The Day of Yahweh, whether it be of light or of darkness, will come, and it is a day full of destiny. The *Heilsgeschichte* demanded fulfilment. Israel's election in the event of the Exodus was the opening event that would in God's time yield fruition. The covenant from the beginning had at its center the time when it would find realization. The land was held provisionally; it was given as a conditional inheritance, but the later prophets at least look forward to a time of Israel's return to Zion, the city of her God.

A study of the terminology of expectation shows that it emerges usually in times of social upheaval and insecurity. It is remarkable how such words as *wait* and *hope* increase in number and in depth in the period of the decline and fall of Judah. This is superbly illustrated in Jeremiah. Yahweh is Israel's Hope as he is her Savior (Jer. 14:8; 17:13). The prophet is able to overcome the despair and disappointment of exile by his faith that the future is the gracious gift of God as the events of the past had been his gifts. "For I know the plans I plan for you, says the LORD, plans for welfare and not for evil, to give you a future and a hope."[28] In many passages of the Psalter hope comes near to expressing the heart of piety (cf., e.g., 42:5, 11; 43:5; 71:14; 119:49, 81, 114; 130:5; 146:5; 147:5). This close relation of faith and hope, especially in times when the assumed continuities are severed, is expressed in Lamentations:

> *"The LORD is my portion," says my soul,*
> *"therefore I will hope in him."*
> *The LORD is good to those who wait for him,*
> *to the soul that seeks him.*
> *It is good that one should wait quietly*
> *·for the salvation of the LORD.*
>
> (Lam. 3:24-26)

Thus Israel participates in future time.

An examination of the verb "to wait" shows an equally profound identification with revealed time, i.e., time in which Yahweh is at work and in which he will fulfil his will and purpose. In a time of rejection, the prophet Isaiah waits for the LORD "who is hiding his face from the house of Jacob" (Isa. 8:17), and Habakkuk confronted with the dark mystery of theodicy receives the divine word:

> *For still the vision awaits its time;*
> *it hastens to the end—it will not lie.*
> *If it seem slow, wait for it;*
> *it will surely come, it will not delay.*
>
> (Hab. 2:3)

Similarly in Second Isaiah's eschatology the motif of waiting appears again and again. It is Job's perplexity that he cannot wait or hope. To Job's desperate grappling with the final mystery of the divine ways, the apostle Paul presents a remarkable contrast. He sees the whole creation waiting with eager longing for the revealing of the sons of God, and he has learned that "if we hope for what we do not see, we wait for it with patience"; so he rejoices in hope (Rom. 8:24f., 35-39; 15:13), and relates it to "his idea of the Spirit as an 'earnest' of full redemption hereafter." In I Peter hope is almost equivalent to faith, and it is worth noticing that this writing, too, is born in a time of darkness and despair. And for the writer of the Epistle to the Hebrews, "we have this as a sure and steadfast anchor of the soul, a hope that enters into the inner shrine behind the curtain where Jesus has gone as a forerunner on our behalf" (Heb. 6:19-20a).[29]

Finally, what is the biblical view of eternity, and how is it to be conceived? That God is transcendent to man's time is clear enough, but is this transcendence to be understood as timelessness? Does the Bible know any "infinite qualitative distinction between time and eternity"? These are questions that are not easily answered, and we must be prepared for great diversity of usage in both the Old and the New Testaments. The following comments are not only brief and inadequate but also very tentative.

1. The vocabulary of eternity is as extensive as that of time. The time consciousness of Israel is richly reflected in the many words and expressions used for both time and eternity. The most important and most common word is 'ôlām, which in late Hebrew, like the Greek aiōn, has the dual meaning of world and eternity. On the face of it, at least, this would suggest that eternity and the duration of the world are identified.[30]

2. 'ôlām is usually derived from the verb 'lm, meaning "to hide" (cf. von Orelli and others: "die verborgene unbekannte Zeit"), but more recently scholars like J. Barth, G. R. Driver, and Wheeler Robinson derive it from a cognate of Accadian ullānu, "to be remote." In a valuable monograph on the word 'ôlām (originally ālamu) Ernst Jenni demonstrates that the etymology of the word is uncertain, but that the extra-biblical usage permits the basic meaning of "farthest time."[31] This remoteness can refer either to past or future, i.e., remoteness from the present. For example, the prehistoric giants (Gen. 6:4), Israel's ancestors (Josh. 24:2), the mountains (Gen. 49:26; Deut. 33:15), and the doors of the temple (Ps. 24:7, 9) are all described as 'ôlām; similarly in reference to the future: the sun and moon (Ps. 89:26-37), the earth (Ps. 104:5; 148:6 and often), and destruction (Exod. 14:13; Isa. 25:2). It is obvious that the term in these instances and many hundreds more does not refer to endless duration although Wheeler Robinson thinks that we have here a virtual transition from that which is very remote to that which is permanent, i.e., "forever." Dan. 12:2-3 may be such an instance, but none of the texts cited by Robinson seems to me convincing.

3. The word "eternity" seldom stands alone as an independent attribute of God, but is characteristically associated with other terms, above all with life. Yahweh is a living God who does not die (cf. the true text of Hab. 1:12).

Yahweh lives forever. His eternity transcends all things. In comparison with him the heavens and the earth and the mountain fastnesses are transitory. Yet it must be remembered that precisely the same word '*ōlām* is used of God as is used of these. We are not denying God's transcendence over man's time, but we are stressing the importance of careful philological exegesis.

4. In a strict sense eternity belongs only to God. Such "eternity" as is attributed to the things of heaven and earth, the stars that shine forever and ever and the ruin of cities, is granted by God himself. Like holiness, eternity has its source only in God. In the classic expression of man's transitoriness and God's eternity we read:

> LORD, *thou hast been our dwelling place in all generations.*
> *Before the mountains were brought forth, or ever thou hadst*
>   *formed the earth and the world,*
> *from everlasting to everlasting thou art God.*
>
>   (Ps. 90:1)

But Wheeler Robinson admits that the familiar phrase *mē'ōlām wā'ed 'ōlām* here means "from the remotest past to the remotest future," and it is difficult to see how this can be denied. In Second Isaiah, however, we have for the first time an all-inclusive association of Yahweh's relation to time and space:

> *Yahweh is the eternal God,*
> *Creator of the ends of the earth.*
>   (Isa. 40:28)

Otto Eissfeldt comments on this verse: "God created all space and stands above all time."[32] Similarly Robinson: "He is set above the limitations of time as well as of space." This certainly goes without saying, for it is precisely the point toward which the whole poem is leading.

5. It is obvious, then, that in the biblical view God precedes creation and endures beyond it. Indeed, he is infinitely before man's time and infinitely after it. But there is the further question which the philosopher and theologian inevitably raises: what is the nature of God's existence antecedent and posterior to time? We repeat that God brings man's time into existence and brings it to an end. But this is not to say that he is timeless. The situation in the New Testament is much more difficult than in the Old, and many scholars find support in the former for faith in God's timelessness. Recent controversy has raged about this point, chiefly in connection with Cullmann's *Christ and Time.* Karl Barth (*Kirchliche Dogmatik,* II.1, 1940) stresses the temporal quality of eternity, and Cullmann states categorically, "Primitive Christianity knows nothing of a timeless God. The 'eternal' God is he who was in the beginning, is now, and will be in all the future, 'who is, who was, and who will be' (Rev. 5:4). Accordingly, his eternity must be expressed in this 'naïve' way, in terms of endless time."[33] Yet

there are passages in Paul and in the Fourth Gospel which seem to point beyond this. Eternal life is understood as qualitatively different from the temporality of life here and now. But can we be sure that even here the meaning of "eternal" excludes time? To say that time and eternity are qualitatively different is not to say that the contrast is between time and not-time. What God's reality is like apart from time is a mystery not only forever veiled from us, but one which does not belong to the givenness of our human situation or the givenness of revelation. To the school-boy question as to what God was doing before the creation, Luther's answer is still the best: "He went into the woods to cut rods from which to punish good-for-nothing questioners!"

6. Yet if we cannot give anything like a decisive answer as to God's existence in time or in timelessness, Scripture is eloquent from beginning to end that eternity is filled with content as time is filled with content. His name endures forever and ever, and it is blessed forever and ever. His word is everlasting (Isa. 40:3-5) and moves through all time from beginning to end. His kingdom is an everlasting kingdom, and his dominion endures to all generations (Ps. 145:13; cf. Exod. 15:18; Ps. 10:16; 29:10). He makes for David an everlasting covenant (II Sam. 23:5), and the new covenant of peace shall never be removed (Isa. 54:10; 55:3). His covenant faithfulness (RSV: "steadfast love") endures forever, and in the life of the cult his eternity is felt and known as transcending all things mundane and cosmic. Many other such passages might be cited. While the philosopher will be inclined to press the question further beyond these limits, for the ordinary man the confidence that "our times are in his hand," that all times are under his gracious dominion, that he lives eternally and slumbers not, is sufficient to withstand the gales of stormy weather, all the slings and arrows of outrageous fortune. Yet this must be added: it is conceivable and possible that at this point Greek thought had a major contribution to make to the problem. Augustine's treatment of the problem shows a profound wrestling of mind with biblical categories, but it is obvious that Greek thought has contributed to its final resolution.

7. Into the large and important question of the ages, not only this present age (ha 'ôlām hazzeh) and the coming age (ha 'ôlām habbā'), but all the ages, we cannot enter, and I am quite aware of the scandal of its omission both for New Testament and later Jewish thought. But for the New Testament Jesus is confessed to be the Coming One, introducing the New Age, the Messiah of Israel: hoti peplērōtai ho kairos kai ēngiken hē basileia tou theou. The apostle Paul describes the whole creation travailing "until now," "and not only the creation, but we ourselves, who have the first fruits of the Spirit, groan inwardly as we wait for adoption as sons, the redemption of our bodies." "For," he continues, "in this hope we are saved" and "we wait for it with patience" (Rom. 8:23-25).

NOTES TO CHAPTER TWO

1. Cf. Paul Minear, *Eyes of Faith* (Philadelphia: Westminster Press, 1946), p. 97: "The pivotal category in every philosophy of history is the *concept* of time; the pivotal reality in every perspective of life, whether or not it has been articulated in a conscious and systematic philosophy of history, is the *sense* of time."

2. H. and H. A. Frankfort, *et al.*, *The Intellectual Adventure of Ancient Man* (Chicago: University of Chicago Press, 1946), p. 23. The words are from the Frankforts' opening chapter.

3. Erich Frank, *Philosophical Understanding and Religious Truth* (London: Oxford University Press, 1945), p. 65; John Marsh, *The Fulness of Time* (London: Nisbet, 1952). Cf. his words on p. 1: "Time is perhaps the focal, as it is certainly a pressing, problem of our age. It may seem simple and harmless enough to study its nature, but the results can be revolutionary. Einstein has brought about a revolution in our understanding of the universe, and Marx has provoked a series of revolutions in history. To study time is more than to seek a definition for a word; for while time is not itself, as we believe, the ultimate reality, it cannot be properly discussed unless questions of ultimate reality are asked, and, so far as may be, answered."

4. William Wordsworth, "Ode: Intimations of Immortality from Recollections of Early Childhood."

5. Compare Ps. 39:4-6:

> Lord, let me know my end,
> and what is the measure of my days;
> let me know how fleeting my life is!
> Behold, thou hast made my days a few handbreadths,
> and my lifetime is as nothing in thy sight.
> Surely every man stands as a mere breath!
> Surely man goes about as a shadow!
> Surely for nought are they in turmoil;
> man heaps up, and knows not who will gather!

See also Ps. 144:4; Job 7:6; 13:25; 14:1-2.

6. So *RSV*. Cf. Greek, Syriac, and Targum.

7. The familiar line appears twice in Faust, first before Faust makes his pact with Mephistopheles:

> Werd' ich zum Augenblicke sagen:
> Verweile doch! du bist so schön!
> Dann magst du mich in Fesseln schlagen,
> Dann will ich gern zu Grunde gehn!

In the second part where Faust finally meets his destiny he says:

> Zum Augenblicke dürft' ich sagen:
> Verweile doch, du bist so schön!
> Es kann die Spur von meinen Erdentagen
> Nicht in Aeonen untergehen—
> Im Vorgefühl von solchen hohen Glück
> Geniess ich jetzt den höchsten Augenblick.

8. *Physics*, IV, 14, 223b21 cited by Frank, *op. cit.*, note 41, p. 82. See the detailed discussion. For a corrective to this somewhat partial and one-sided view, see Thorleif Boman, *Das hebräische Denken im Vergleich mit dem griechischen*, 2d ed. (Göttingen: Vandenhoeck & Ruprecht, 1954), pp. 111ff.; Eng. trans., *Hebrew Thought Compared with Greek* (Philadelphia: Westminster Press, 1960), pp. 125ff., and Rudolf Bultmann's review of Boman's work in *Gnomon*, 27 (1955), 55ff. For the Platonic view of time as the moving image of a static and unmovable eternity, see the remarkable passage in the Timaeus (*The Dialogues of Plato*, trans. B. Jowett, 3d ed. [New York: Macmillan, 1892], III, 456): "Wherefore he resolved to make a moving image of eternity, and when he set in order the heaven, he made this image eternal but moving according to number, while eternity itself rests in unity; and this image we call time. For there were no days and nights and months and years before the heaven was created, but when he constructed the heaven, he created them also. They are all parts of time, and the past and future are created species of time, which we unconsciously but wrongly transfer to the eternal essence; for we say that he 'was,' he 'is,' he 'will be,' but the truth is that 'is' alone is properly attributed to him, and that 'was' and 'will be' are only to be spoken of becoming in time, for they are motions, but that which is immovably the same cannot become older or younger by time...."

9. *The Idea of Nationalism* (New York: Macmillan, 1945), p. 31.

10. A. J. Heschel, "The Sabbath: Its Meaning for Modern Man," in *The Earth is the Lord's and the Sabbath* (New York: Harper & Row, Harper Torchbooks, 1966), p. 6; see also "Space, Time, and Reality," *Judaism*, 1, no. 3 (July 1952), 262-273.

11. See especially Augustine's discussion in his *Confessions*, Book XI.

12. It is significant that we owe our measurement of clock time to Mesopotamia with its sexigesimal system of reckoning: a 360° circle with degrees each of 60 minutes, and minutes each of 60 seconds. Cyrus H. Gordon, *Introduction to Old Testament Times* (Ventnor, N. J.: Ventnor Publishers, 1953), p. 1.

13. The road is understood only in relation to those who walk upon it, to those who know their starting-point and their destination, who pursue a course in life, and are called to decision at the crossroads. There are many different kinds of walking and of going; the Hebrew is careful to differentiate each.

14. H. Wheeler Robinson, *Inspiration and Revelation in the Old Testament* (Oxford: The Clarendon Press, 1946), pp. 109ff. Note especially Appendix A on "The Vocabulary of Time." The basic work on the terminology of time in the Old Testament is still von Orelli's *Die hebräischen Synonyma der Zeit und Ewigkeit genetisch und sprachvergleichend dargestellt* (Leipzig: Lorentz, 1871). While some of his linguistic observations have been superseded, his understanding of the different movements of time is perceptive and illuminating (see esp. pp. 13-40).

15. Marsh, *op. cit.*, p. 20. But this must not be taken to mean that Israel does not know chronological time. Cf. Millar Burrows, "Thy Kingdom Come," *JBL*, 74 (1955), 2ff.

16. Compare the Gezer calendar from the latter part of the tenth century B.C.:

> His two months are (olive) harvest,
> His two months are planting (grain),
> His two months are late planting;
> His month is hoeing up of flax,
> His month is harvest of barley,
> His month is harvest and feasting;
> His two months are vine-tending,
> His month is summer fruit.

17. Compare the ancient Stoic who sought to eliminate temporality from life; his *Entweltlichung* is *Entzeitlichung*. Since he sees his own being in a timeless logos and concentrated completely upon the logos-being, he extricates himself from all conditions (*Bedingungen*) and thus negates the future for himself. His present is no true present, because it knows no decision before the future. See Rudolf Bultmann, *Primitive Christianity in Its Contemporary Setting*, trans. R. H. Fuller (London-New York: Thames and Hudson, 1956), p. 144. See also pp. 149ff.

18. Johannes Pedersen, *Israel: Its Life and Culture* (London: Oxford University Press, 1926), I-II, 487.

19. *Ibid.*, p. 488.

20. Heschel, *op. cit.*, p. 9. In the Accadian creation myth, The Enuma elish, the epic culminates in the erection of the temple to Marduk at Babylon.

21. Pedersen, *op. cit.*, pp. 276-279, 475-479. Note p. 476: "When the Israelites speak of their ancestor, then it is not as a remote figure which has disappeared long ago. He constantly shares in what happens, the history of the people is his."

22. In the first nine chapters of 1 Chronicles Israel's generation history is illuminatingly comprehended in successive generations from Adam to David. "All Israel was enrolled by genealogies" (1 Chron. 9:1). Compare Wheeler Robinson, *op. cit.*, p. 106: "But history, gathering the story of many generations, can show the depth of meaning in the divine will and at the same time its dynamic force. It can show the inner and outer worlds in their ceaseless interaction (cf. Amos iv. 13), creating the very values by which history will eventually pass judgment upon itself. History can show the working out of the divine pattern of which Nature is the warp and man the woof. It is no local accident and no provincial or racial idiosyncrasy that the revelation which holds the greatest place in the world's history should itself have been made through history."

23. Kohn, *op. cit.*, pp. 32ff.

24. The relation of hearing to time is now increasingly understood. Cf. Boman, *op. cit.*, p. 142: "The sense which is plainly made for successive impressions is hearing. We *see* the spatial and *hear* the temporal." See also pp. 206f. With this judgment, compare Kohn, *op. cit.*, pp. 30ff.; Edmond Jacob, *Theology of the Old Testament*, trans. A. W. Heathcote and P. J. Allcock (New York: Harper & Row, 1958), and especially the perceptive article by Erwin W. Straus, "Aethesiology and Hallucination," in *Existence: A New Dimension in Psychiatry and Psychology*, ed. Rollo May (New York: Basic Books, 1958). His dis-

cussion of the spectrum of the senses is important for an understanding of Hebraic mentality. Note his words on p. 158: "The eye is the agent for identification and stabilization, the ear an organ for perceiving the actuality of happenings. There exists in phenomena a temporal co-existence of sound and hearing, whereas the visible is peculiarly time-less with respect to the gaze which can rest on it, turn from it, and return to it. Cochlearis and vestibularis ... are both parts of one organ, the actuality organ.... The cochlea informs us how our environment is at the moment directed toward us, the vestibularis directs us at the moment toward our environment."

25. See G. Ernest Wright, "The Faith of Israel," in *IB*, 1, 349-389 for an application of this confessional history to a statement of biblical theology.

26. For an important statement of the relationship of time to the cult, see Gerhard von Rad, *Theologie des Alten Testaments* (Munich: Chr. Kaiser Verlag, 1960), II, 115ff. "Ja, man könnte vielleicht noch einen Schritt weiter gehen und die kultische Festzeit als die einzige Zeit in vollen Sinn des Wortes bezeichnen, weil doch nur sie im höchsten Sinn des Wortes 'gefüllte Zeit' war..." (p. 115).

27. Walther Eichrodt, *Man in the Old Testament*, trans. K. and R. Gregor Smith (Chicago: H. Regnery Company, 1951), p. 27.

28. Jer. 29:11; cf. also 31:17: "There is hope for your future, says the Lord, and your children shall come back to their own country." It should be added that both of these passages are considered late by some scholars. See Walther Eichrodt, "Heilserfahrung und Zeitverständnis im Alten Testament," *TZ*, 12 (1956), 103-125. "Das enge Verhältnis von Offenbarung und Geschichte bekommt seinen unmissverständlichen Ausdruck in der Beschreibung des Handelns Gottes als Ausführung eines Heilsplanes, durch den die Offenbarung in der Geschichte zu ihrem Ziel gebracht wird. Von Gottes Heilsplan aber kann nicht anders geredet werden als durch den Hinweis auf bestimmte Punkte in der Zeit, die sich durch ihre besondere Bedeutung aus dem allgemeinen Zeitlauf herausheben und zu Marksteinen eines fortschreitenden Handelns Gottes zur Erreichung seines Zieles werden" (p. 103).

29. Millar Burrows, *An Outline of Biblical Theology* (Philadelphia: The Westminster Press, 1946), p. 247.

30. H. Wheeler Robinson, *op. cit.*, p. 118, quotes with approval Sasse's words in *Theologisches Wörterbuch zum Neuen Testament*, I, ed. G. Kittel (Stuttgart: W. Kohlhammer, 1933), 202: "This doubled meaning which *aiōn* shares with *'ōlām* points back to a conception of eternity in which eternity and the duration of the world are identified." It is very doubtful, however, whether *'ōlām* has the meaning of world in the Old Testament; rather it represents a later development.

31. Ernst Jenni, "Das Wort *'olam* im Alten Testament," *ZAW*, 65 (1953), 25.

32. "Geschichtliches und Übergeschichtliches im Alten Testament," in *Theologische Studien und Kritiken, Beiträge zur Theologie und Religionswissenschaft*, 109, no. 2 (Berlin: Evangelische Verlagsanstalt, 1947), 28: "Bewusst hat der Prophet hier die Prädikate 'Ewig' und 'Schöpfer der ganzen Erde' nebeneinander gestellt, weil beiden zusammen erst die ganze, von allem Irdischen grundverschiedene Art und Machtfülle seines Gottes zum Ausdruck bringt: die Raüme, Gott hat sie geschaffen, und die Zeit, Gott steht über ihr. Wichtig ist . . . diese Stelle auch darum, weil sie zeigt, dass Gottes Ewigkeit nicht etwas ist, was er für sich behalten will, sondern ein Wert, der seinem Volk, also Menschen, zugute kommen soll."

33. *Christ and Time*, trans. F. V. Filson (London: SCM Press, 1962), p. 63.

3

THE OATH IN THE OLD TESTAMENT:

Its Vocabulary, Idiom, and Syntax; Its Semantics and Theology in the Masoretic Text and the Septuagint

HENRY SNYDER GEHMAN

I

The taking of an oath to confirm the truth of a statement is universal, and accordingly it is not necessary to discuss instances in the Old Testament where there is recorded the mere taking of an oath without mentioning by whom or by what men swore. The anthropomorphisms of the Old Testament, however, are well known and should be considered. In this category may be cited some examples of *šāba'* (Gk.: *omnymi, omnyō*), where God is portrayed as confirming a promise by an oath. In many passages the narrative reports that God took an oath or swore to certain individuals, but it does not qualify the verb by noting by whom or by what he swore. In all these cases the LXX faithfully reproduces the sense of the MT. Thus God swears to Abraham (Gen. 26:3); to Abraham, Isaac, and Jacob (Gen. 50:24; Exod. 33:1; Num. 32:11); to the fathers, of which the examples are numerous (Exod. 13:5; Num. 14:23; Deut. 1:35; 4:31; 6:18, 23; 7:8, 12, 13; 8:1, 18; 10:11; 11:9, 21; 13:18; 19:8; 26:3, 15; 28:11; 31:7, 20; Josh. 1:6; 21:43, 44; Judg. 2:1; Jer. 11:5; 32[39]:22;[1] Mic. 7:20). In Deut. 1:35, however, the LXX omits the infinitive *tēt* of the MT. Furthermore, God swears to the fathers, Abraham, Isaac, and Jacob (Deut. 1:8; 6:10; 9:5; 29:12; 30:20; Baruch 2:34); to his people (Num. 14:16; Deut. 28:9; 31:23; Josh. 5:6; Judg. 2:15); to Jerusalem, i.e., to his people, in making the covenant (Ezek. 16:8); to the people and the fathers (Exod. 13:11); to David (2 Sam. 3:9). In a number of these passages there is a reference to the covenant or to the giving of Palestine to God's people; furthermore, election and the covenant may be implied in many of these verses.

YHWH in anger swore that Moses should not cross the Jordan (Deut. 4:21); he also swore to a whole generation of warriors (Deut. 1:34f.) and to the house of Eli (1 Sam. 3:14). The Psalmist (95[94]:11) represents God as swearing in his wrath; furthermore, the oath of God was final, and he would not change his mind (Ps. 110[109]:4). In all the foregoing cases, when God made a promise, an asseveration, or a covenant, the biblical authors in anthropomorphic fashion depict him as taking an oath, without adding by whom or by what he swore. In its interpretation the LXX consistently follows the MT and renders the *Niphal of šaba'* by *omnymi, omnyō*.

When God swears it may be supposed that his mere assertion would be sufficient without any further qualification, but there are a few references to his swearing by himself. According to Heb. 6:13, where God made a promise to Abraham, since he had no one greater by whom to swear, he swore by himself (*kath' heautou*). This goes back to Gen. 22:16-18, *kat' emautou*, but in the MT no reason for this form of the oath is given. In this category also fall Exod. 32:13, *kata seautou;* Deut. 9:27, where the LXX has an addition, *hois ōmosas kata seautou;* Amos 6:8, *kath' heautou;* Isa. 45:23, *kat' emautou;* Jer. 22:5 and 49:13 [29:14], *kat' emautou.* Furthermore, God may swear by his right hand and the arm of his strength (Isa. 62:8); in this verse is found an excellent example of the use of *'im (ei)* in a negative sense. The development of *'im (ei)* into a negative and its corollary *'im lō' (ei mē)* as an affirmative will be explained in the second section of this article. For the moment we must bear in mind that in such instances this usage developed out of an imprecation that is implied in the oath. In other citations of this division these particles will be indicated in connection with the relevant passages. In Jer. 51[28]:14, according to the MT, YHWH swears by himself, but the LXX renders, *kata tou brachionos autou;* this, however, hardly signifies that the translator had a different *Vorlage,* and may represent merely an interpretation. He may also swear *bišmī haggadōl, tōi onomati mou tōi megalōi* (Jer. 44 [51]:26, with *'im* in a negative sense). Furthermore, he may swear by his holiness (*qōdeš*): Ps. 89[88]:36, *en tōi hagiōi mou;* Amos 4:2, *kata tōn hagiōn autou;* by his *'ap (orgēi)*: Ps. 95[94]:11, with *'im (ei)* in a negative sense. God may also take an oath by his *'ĕmūnāh* (faithfulness, reliability): Ps. 89[88]:50, *en tēi alētheiai sou.* In the latter example the question may be raised, however, whether in the LXX *alētheia* is the absolute standard by which he swears or whether by an adverbial phrase it indicates the trustworthiness of his oath.

There is a difficulty in interpreting Amos 8:7 (*'im, ei*), where YHWH swears *bigeʾōn yaʿăqōb* (the pride, excellence, or majesty of Jacob). The word *gāʾōn* seems to indicate that Israel was deluding itself in depending upon a false sense of security or in the pride of having a God who had made a covenant with the nation. In other words, since God's oath must rest upon something absolute or permanent and inasmuch as he could not swear by anyone or anything inferior to himself, in the context the word appears to refer to himself. Consequently the LXX text has to be interpreted in the same sense: *omnyei Kyrios kath' hyperēphanias Iakōb.* As a matter of syntax it may be observed that generally in these cases the preposition *kata* governs the genitive of the person or object by which God swears. In the two examples from Ps. 89[88]:36, 50, however, the preposition *en* governs the dative, while in one example from Jeremiah (44[51]:26) the dative without a preposition is employed.

When men take an oath, they may swear *baYHWH, en Kyriōi*: Judg. 21:7; 1 Sam. 24:22, *'im;* 2 Sam. 19:8(7), *'im (ei);* I Kings 2:8, *'im (ei).* Or men may swear *bē'lōhīm*: 1 Sam. 30:15 (*'im . . . 'im*), where the preposition is rendered by *kata* governing the genitive, *tou theou.* In Ps. 63[62]:12, where *bō* in the parallelism refers to *bē'lōhīm* in the previous sentence, the LXX renders, *en autōi.* Sometimes Elohim is in apposition to YHWH, which is governed by the preposition *b;* 1 Kings 1:17, *en (Kōi, A) tōi theōi sou;* 1 Kings 1:30, *en Kyriōi tōi theōi Israēl.* In Gen. 31:53, Jacob swore *bēpahad 'abīw yishāq* (by the Fear of his father Isaac), which is rendered literally, *ōmosen Iakōb kata tou phobou tou patros autou Isaak.* In the examples of this paragraph the preposition *en* is employed seven times and *kata* twice.

In recording the oath of an individual, the LXX is not always bound by the syntax of the Hebrew, which employs a preposition with the name of the deity. There is a good usage as old as the time of Homer, in which *omnymi* governs the name of God in the accusative: Gen. 21:23, *hiššāb^e'āh lī bē'lōhim. hennāh* (swear unto me here by God), *omoson moi ton theon;* Josh. 2:12, *hiššāb^e-'ū-nā' lī baYHWH* (swear unto me by YHWH); the LXX with an extension of the divine name, *omosate moi Kyrion ton theon;* Josh. 9:18(24), *kī nišb^e'ū lāhem . . . baYHWH 'ēlōhē yiśrā'ēl* (because they had sworn unto them . . . by YHWH, the God of Israel) . . . v. 19(25), *'ānahnū nišba'nū lāhem baYHWH 'ēlōhē yiśrā'ēl* (we have sworn unto them by YHWH, the God of Israel), *hoti ōmosan autois . . . Kyrion ton theon Israēl . . . hēmeis ōmosamen autois Kyrion ton theon Israēl.* While dealing with this type of syntax we should also consider Isa. 65:16, *w^ehannišbā' bā'āreṣ yiššāba' bē'lōhē 'āmēn* (and he who takes an oath in the land, shall swear by the God of faithfulness [by the faithful or reliable God]). Here the LXX renders, *kai hoi omnyontes epi tēs gēs omountai ton theon ton alēthinon.* Although the examples of this classical usage are few, nevertheless it is evident from their distribution in the LXX that the translators were acquainted with this construction and did not have to be literalistic in their rendering. On the other hand, the numerous literalisms in the LXX may represent merely an attempt to be faithful to the letter of the original.

Men may also swear by the name (*b^ešēm*) of God: Lev. 19:12, *bišmī (tōi onomati mou),* where false swearing is forbidden; Deut. 6:13; 10:20, *bišmō (tōi onomati autou);* 1 Sam. 20:42, *b^ešēm YHWH (en onomati Kyriou);* Isa. 48:1, *b^ešēm YHWH (onomati Kyriou).* In Jer. 12:16, the neighbors of Judah will learn to swear by the divine name (*bišmī, tōi onomati mou*)[2]; in this verse is added the frequent formula, "as the LORD liveth," which will be subsequently discussed. In these examples the simple dative is employed five times, while *en* with the dative is used only once. In Prov. 30:9 (24:32), a pious man prays that he may not handle or use profanely, or do violence to, the name of God (*tāpaśtī šēm 'ēlōhāy*). Apparently the sense of sacrilege involved in using profanely the divine name or doing violence to it was offensive to the Greek translator, and so he toned it down, rendering, *kai omosō to onoma tou theou.* Yet in the context it seems that a pejorative sense remained in the interpreter's mind. It should further be observed that *onoma* is in the accusative, a construction discussed in the previous paragraph.

Zechariah (5:4), speaking for God, refers to a curse that shall enter the house of him who swears falsely by the name YHWH, *hannišbā' bišmī laššāqer (tou omnyontos tōi onomati mou epi pseudei).* According to Mal. 3:5, YHWH will come in judgment against false swearers, *hannišbā'īm laššāqer.* This, however, is expanded in the LXX, *epi tous omnyontas tōi onomati mou epi pseudei.* It should be observed that in both cases the Greek employs the dative without a preposition. It may furthermore be noted that some individuals took oaths by heathen gods. Men are condemned (Jer. 5:7) for swearing by no-gods (*b°lō' 'ĕlōhīm*), which the LXX renders, *ōmnyon en tois ouk ousin theois.* The same prophet (12:16) observes that the neighbors of Judah had taught the people to swear by Baal, *l°hiššābēa' babbā'al (omnyein tēi Baal).* In the first instance the translator used the preposition *en,* while in the latter the simple dative is employed. In the prophecy by Amos (8:14) against Israel for swearing by false gods, there are difficulties of interpretation. The sin of Samaria (*'ašmat šōmrōn*) probably should be understood as *'ašimat šōmrōn* (Ashima of Samaria, *RSV;* cf. 2 Kings 17:30). The LXX renders, *kata tou hilasmou Samareias.* This translation may be based on interpreting *'ašmāh* on the basis of *'āšām* (offense, guilt), whence is derived the sense of trespass, or guilt offering. At any rate, the rendering *hilasmos* (propitiation, expiation) is a free interpretation of a word of whose meaning the translator was uncertain. In the Greek text the word *theos* occurs twice through the repeated formula of an oath (*zēi ho theos sou*) occurring after this vocable, and from the context it may be inferred that the *hilasmos* expected from a deity at Samaria is employed as a surrogate for the name of a deity not known to the translator. A reference to syncretism in a religion occurs in Zeph. 1:5:

> *And them that bow down upon the housetops*
> *to the host of heaven;*
> *And them that bow down, that swear to YHWH,*
> *Yet swear by Milcom.*

In the MT the first instance of *hannišbā'īm* apparently is a dittograph for the second occurrence of the word and for metrical reasons should be deleted. Yet it seems to be old, for it occurs in the LXX, *kai tous omnyontas kata tou Kyriou kai tous omnyontas kata tou basileōs autōn.* It may be observed that in this case both the preposition *l* and *b* are rendered by *kata.*

II

The seriousness of taking an oath demands that the one making a solemn declaration is unequivocally stating the truth and that he cannot swear falsely or break an oath with impunity. In other words, retribution will be his due for perjury or for not fulfilling the promise made. Although in swearing a person asserts that he is telling the truth, he may fortify his oath by invoking an imprecation upon himself in case he swears falsely or does not fulfil his obligation. The formula *kōh ya'āseh-lī 'ĕlōhīm wᵉkōh yōsīp* (God do so to me and more also) contains the *Hiphil* of *yāsap,* which in Greek is represented by *prostithēmi.* In a conversation between Jonathan and David concerning the latter at the court (1 Sam. 20:13), from the context it is clear what Jonathan swears. After the insertion of a conditional clause, only the conjunction *w* introduces the asseveration, which is stated in the perfect consecutive.[3] The MT, with an emendation, may be rendered, "YHWH do so to Jonathan and more also; if it be pleasing to my father to bring evil upon thee, then I will declare it to thee. . . ." In this case, the LXX in a condensed interpretation renders, *tade poiēsai ho theos tōi Iōnathan kai tade prostheiē, hoti anoisō ta kaka epi se kai apokalypsō to ōtion sou.* . . . A penalty is invoked upon Jonathan in case he does not report to David the true facts of the situation. In 1 Sam. 14:44, Saul, using the above formula, says, *kī-mōt tāmūt yōnātān.* In this case *kī,* as *recitativum,* may serve only to introduce the purport of the oath, but the clause may also be rendered, "God do so (to me) and more also; verily (or, for) thou shalt surely die, Jonathan." In the LXX, *hoti thanatōi apothanēi,* the conjunction is no more than *hoti recitativum.* In 2 Sam. 3:9, Abner, in affirming his support of David, says, "God do so to Abner and more also," which continues, *kī ka'ăšer nišba' YHWH lᵉdāwīd kī-kēn 'e'ĕšeh-lō.* Unless we regard the second *kī* as resumptive of the first,[4] the passage can be rendered literally, "For, as YHWH hath sworn to David, verily so will I do to him." In this instance the LXX has in both cases rendered *kī* literally by *hoti.*

In 1 Kings 2:23, Solomon is said to have sworn by YHWH, but in the standard imprecation, probably with a *Vermilderung,* he changed to Elohim. Thus the content of the oath goes, *kī bᵉnapšō . . .* (for [or, verily] against his own life hath Adonijah spoken this word). Again the LXX translates *kī* by *hoti* (*recitativum*). When Jezebel swore to take her revenge on Elijah (1 Kings 19:2), she said, "So may the gods do (to me) and more also," *kī-kā'ēt māhār 'āśīm 'et-napšᵉkā kᵉnepeš 'ahad mēhem* (verily [or, for] at this time tomorrow I will make thy life as the life of one of them). Here the LXX once more interprets *kī* as *recitativum.* In Ruth 1:17, after the standard imprecatory cliché, the text continues, *kī hammāwet yaprīd bēnī ūbēnēk* (Verily, death [alone] shall make a separation between me and thee). In the LXX the Hebrew is rendered literalistically, *hoti thanatos diastelei ana meson emou kai sou.*

From this use of *kī* (*hoti*), when it follows the above introductory formula of an oath and introduces the substance of the asseveration, a transition may be made to study the use of *'im* (*ei, ean*) in an oath. A person may invoke retribution or damnation upon himself in case he does or will do a certain thing; this signifies that he will not do it. On the other hand, he may call retribution upon

himself if he will not perform a certain thing. In such a situation a person means
to say that he will perform or fulfil his obligation. In observing the development
of this idiom, we may start with 1 Sam. 3:17, where Eli says to Samuel, "God
do so to thee and more also, if (*'im*) thou hide anything from me," *tade poiēsai
soi ho theos kai tade prostheiē, ean krypsēis ap' emou rēma*. The implication is
that Samuel may not withhold anything. In a similar construction, David, before
meeting Abigail, says (1 Sam. 25:22), "God do so unto the enemies (*l^e'ōy^{e}bē*)
of David and more also, if (*'im*) I leave of all that pertain to him. . . ." Since
the threat was not carried out, the insertion of *'ōy^{e}bē* is probably intended to
avoid the appearance of the imprecation recoiling upon David himself.[5] In the
LXX, however, we have the reading, "God do so unto David and more also, if
(*ei*) I leave of all that pertains to Nabal." The implication of the oath is "I will
not leave anything of all that pertains to Nabal." In a similar construction,
Benhadad in a message to the king of Israel said (1 Kings 20[21]:10), "The
gods do so unto me and more also, if (*'im, ei*) the dust of Samaria shall suffice."
The signification is that the dust of Samaria shall not suffice. During the siege
of Samaria and the consequent famine the king of Israel swore, saying after this
formula (2 Kings 6:31), "if (*'im*) the head of Elisha . . . shall stand upon him."
The LXX renders literally, *ei stēsetai hē kephalē Eleisaie ep' autōi;* the sense of
the oath is that the head of Elisha shall not remain upon him.

In the incident when the people wanted David to eat (2 Sam. 3:35), the
king used the formula, "God do so to me and more also." This is followed by
kī 'im-lipnē bō'-haššemeš 'eṭ'am-leḥem 'ō kol-m^e'ūmāh (if before the sun go
down, I taste bread or aught else). In this case *kī* simply introduces the purport
of the oath, and the Greek *hoti* is to be understood in the same sense. The implication of the oath is that David will not eat anything before sundown. The LXX
freely rendered the time element, *hoti ean mē dyēi ho hēlios,* where *hoti* is
recitativum. The translator, however, having already used *ean mē* to introduce a
subordinate clause, departed from the Hebrew psychology and rendered, *ou mē
geusōmai artou ē apo pantos tinos*. At any rate, it is evident that he understood
the negative implication of the oath.

If *'im* (*ei*) in an oath gives it a negative sense, *'im lō'* logically produces
an affirmative nuance. When David appointed Amasa commander instead of
Joab, he said (2 Sam. 19:14), "God do so to me and more also, if (*'im-lō'*)
thou be not commander of the army." The obvious meanings is that Amasa will
be the commander. The Greek rendered the Hebrew literally, *tade poiēsai moi
ho theos kai tade prostheiē ei mē archōn dynameōs esēi*. In an oath, *ei mē* is the
exact equivalent of *'im lō'* in an affirmative sense.[6] In the above examples of
oaths, in which an imprecation is expressed, *'im* (*ei, ean*) and *'im lō'* (*ei mē*)
can be rendered literally with good sense. From such constructions, the conjunction *'im* (*ei*) came to express a negative, while *'im lō'* developed an affirmative
meaning, even though no imprecation is expressed. Nevertheless it should be
kept in mind that in any oath retribution is always implied.

In a narrative a reference may be made to a person's swearing by God or by YHWH, in which no formula is used. In a conference between Abraham and Abimelech the latter said (Gen. 21:23), "Now therefore swear unto me here by God (*'im*) that thou wilt not deal falsely with me." The Greek understood the sense of *'im* but avoided a literalism, *mē adikēsein me*. A similar interpretation and rendering are found in Gen. 26:29, when Abraham and Abimelech met at Gerar. In 1 Sam. 30:15, David questioned an Egyptian, who said, "Swear unto me by God that (*'im*) thou wilt neither kill me nor (*'im*) deliver. . . ." In this case also the LXX avoided the Semitism by rendering *'im* in both cases by *mē*. In 2 Sam. 19:8, Joab in rebuking David said, "for I swear by YHWH, if thou go not forth, (*'im*) not a man will stay with thee this night." In this instance the LXX renders *'im* literally with *ei*. In 1 Kings 2:8, David maintains that he swore by YHWH to Shimei, saying, "(*'im*) I will not put thee to death with the sword." This is rendered literally in Greek, *ei thanatōsō se en romphaiai*. When Nehemiah rebuked Jews who were not faithful to the traditional customs, he made them swear by God (Neh. 13:25). In the oath he dictated, *'im (ean)* is used in a negative sense. Likewise in the Song of Songs 2:7; 3:5, where the maiden adjures the daughters of Jerusalem, the appeal contains *'im* twice in a negative sense; in each verse this is reproduced by *ean (semel)*, which introduces the solemn charge. In the oath made by the elders of Gilead, they said (Judg. 11:10), "YHWH shall be witness between us; surely (*'im lō' [ei mē]*) according to thy word will we do." In all these instances the translator understood the meaning of the Hebrew and employed *ei* as a negative and *ei mē* as a positive.

As regards a witness, a cairn and a pillar could be employed for such a purpose, as in the covenant between Jacob and Laban (Gen. 31:52). By an anacoluthon[7] is found a double negative, *'im-'ānī lō'-e'ĕbōr 'ēle(y)kā . . . we'im-'attāh lō'-ta'ăbōr 'ēlay* (I will not pass over to thee . . . and thou shalt not pass over to me). In this case the LXX renders *ean . . . mē*, but in the second instance has only *mēde*. At any rate the translator understood the meaning.

The lifting of the hand[8] may be a sign of taking an oath, even though no verb of swearing is employed. In Gen. 14:22-23, Abraham said to Melchizedek, "I have lifted up my hand unto YHWH . . . (*'im*) I will not take a thread . . . nor aught that is thine"; . . . *ei apo spartiou . . . lēmpsomai*. In this case *'im (ei)* clearly has a negative meaning. In such a case the idea of imprecation may be understood, and accordingly this use of *'im (ei)* places it in the transitional category of becoming a mere negative.

This use of *'im (ei)* as a negative became standardized, and in various oaths it is not necessary to employ a formula of introduction. It could be used even in an oath sworn by God. According to Num. 32:11, YHWH's anger was kindled, and he swore (*'im*), naturally without any expression of imprecation, "These men shall not see." The LXX renders literally, *ei opsontai hoi anthrōpoi houtoi*. Again a transitional stage may be observed, and *'im (ei)* is to be understood merely as a negative. Similarly in the divine oath (Deut. 1:35) with *'im* (*ei*) a transitional stage is present. In God's displeasure with the house of Eli (1 Sam. 3:14), he swore that the iniquity (*'im, ei*) should not be expiated. In the case of David's oath or vow (Ps. 132[131]:3-4), *'im* (*ei*) occurs three times in a negative sense. As a corollary, *'im lō'* has assumed an affirmative sense also without an introductory formula. Moses swore (Josh. 14:9), saying, "Surely (*'im lō'*) the land . . . shall be an inheritance." In Isa. 5:9, on the basis of an emendation proposed from the LXX, the *RSV* renders, "The LORD of hosts has sworn in my hearing: 'Surely [*'im-lō'*] many houses shall be desolate.'"

Having now established the meaning of *'im* (*ei, ean*) and *'im lō'* (*ei mē*) in an oath, let us consider instances where no suggestion of an asseveration is expressed. In Isa. 22:14, where there is no word of swearing, God says, "This iniquity shall not (*'im*) be expiated." The LXX, however, understood the sense and rendered without the Semitism, *hoti ouk*. In Jer. 22:6, with no word of swearing, God says, "Surely (*'im lō* [*ean mē*]) I will make thee a wilderness." In Isa. 14:24, the LXX abbreviates the text by eliminating *nišba'* and rendering *tade legei Kyrios sabaōth* with the omission of *'im lō';* in consequence there is no mention of the divine oath in the translation. In fact, *'im-lō'* (*ei mē*) as a corollary assumes the meaning "surely" where there is not even a remote suggestion of an oath (Ps. 131[130]:2), "Surely (*'im-lō'*) I have calmed"; the LXX renders *'im-lō* literally, *ei mē*. Similarly in Job 22:20, "Surely (*'im-lō'*) their substance is cut off"; here again *'im-lō* is rendered *ei mē*. On the other hand, in Job 27:4 we find *'im* as a pure negative, "If (*'im*) my lips speak unrighteousness, and if (*'im*) my tongue utter deceit"; i.e., "My lips shall *not* speak unrighteousness, *neither* shall my tongue utter deceit." The translator understood the meaning and rendered *'im . . . 'im, mē . . . oude*. In Job 6:28 there is also an example of the negative use of *'im* in an asseveration, *'im-'ăkazzēb* (I will not lie). In avoiding the Semitism, the LXX rendered, *ou pseusomai*. In other words, through semantic development *'im* became a pure negative.

III

An expression occurring rather frequently in an oath is *ḥē, ḥay* with an accompanying noun or pronoun. Various theories of this formula have been proposed.[9] When the name of God or a pronoun referring to him is used with this word, the spelling is *ḥay;* otherwise it is *ḥē*. In the LXX this idiom has received a uniform rendering (*zēi Kyrios*), which became standardized from the time of the translation of the Pentateuch. Consequently the verb *zō* became accepted in the interpretation of this expression throughout the entire LXX. When God makes an asseveration, he says *ḥay 'ānī* (*zō egō*). It is apparent, however, that if this formula is placed in a divine statement, it has become a mere cliché; the absolute Deity could hardly call an imprecation upon himself.

In some cases the formula "as I live," followed by *neum* (*'ădōnāy*) *YHWH*, may introduce the divine asseveration directly, without an introductory conjunction: Ezek. 14:16; 35:11; or the oath may be introduced by *kī*. The question may be raised whether this *kī* has the sense of *hoti recitativum* or signifies "surely"; the latter interpretation makes good sense and accordingly may be accepted as a translation of the Hebrew. Among such passages may be cited Isa. 49:18; Jer. 46(26):18; Zeph. 2:9. In these cases the LXX rendered *kī* literally as *hoti*, except in the last example, which has *dioti*. In Jer. 22:24, where the formula is followed by *kī 'im (ean) . . . kī,* the LXX does not render either *kī*. Of more importance in this study, however, is the use of *'im (ei, ean)* in a negative sense after "as I live." This usage obviously implies the omission of a verb of affirmation, assertion, mere statement, or even of imprecation, after which the negative sense of the conjunction became standardized. This semantic development has been discussed in the previous section. Here[10] we may cite Ezek. 14:20 *(ean)*; 16:48 *(ei)*; 18:3 *(ean)*; 20:3, 31 *(ei)*. It is evident that the translator understood the negative sense of *'im,* for in Ezek. 33:11 he rendered *'im-'ehpōṣ* by *ou boulomai,* and thus he avoided the Semitism.

Furthermore, if *'im* has a negative sense, its corollary *'im lō' (ean mē)* has an affirmative signification. These examples of the divine oath with this idiom may be noted: Num. 14:28 *(ei mēn)*; Ezek. 5:11 *(ei mēn, ei mē, A)*; 17:16, 19 *(ean mē)*; 20:33 *(ei mēn)*; 33:27 *(ei mēn)*; 34:8 *(ei mēn, ei mē, Q)*; 35:6 *(ei mēn)*. In these cases the rendering *ei mēn* shows that the translator or the copyist understood the idiom. In this connection the question may be raised whether *ei mēn, ē mēn,* and *ei mē* are palaeographic variations, since they all bring out the Hebrew sense; the first two as a Greek idiom, and the latter as a Hebraism. In Deut. 32:40, in lifting his hand to heaven, God says, "As I live forever," which the LXX renders literally. In Num. 14:21, however, when God says, *ḥay 'ānī,* the LXX renders *zō egō,* with an addition, *kai zōn onoma mou.*

In swearing by YHWH or affirming the truth of a statement, an individual may say, *ḥay YHWH (zēi Kyrios).*[11] The contents of the oath may be stated directly without an introductory particle: Judg. 8:19; 1 Sam. 20:21. In a number of cases, however, the formula is followed by *kī (hoti)*: 1 Sam. 26:16; 29:6; cf. 2 Sam. 2:27, *ḥay hā'ĕlōhīm kī . . . kī,* where the first *kī* introduces the terms of the oath, while the second *kī* is merely resumptive of the first. Here the LXX has *zēi Kyrios* and renders the first *kī (hoti)* and also the second *kī (dioti).* For further examples of *kī (hoti),* cf. 2 Sam. 12:5; 1 Kings 22:14; 2 Chron. 18:13. In all these cases *kī (hoti)* merely introduces the contents of the oath. In 1 Kings 1:29-30, in his oath to Bathsheba, Solomon, with the formula "as YHWH liveth," extended by a relative clause, swore, saying, "Verily *(kī)* as I swore unto thee by YHWH . . . saying, 'Assuredly *(kī)* Solomon thy son shall reign after me, and he shall sit upon my throne in my stead,' verily *(kī)* so will I do this day." The LXX, however, in its literal rendering interprets the first *kī (hoti)* as *recitativum* to introduce the contents of the oath, the second as *recitativum,* and the third as resumptive. This is a possible interpretation of the passage. In 1 Kings 2:24, the same formula, with considerable extension, is followed by *kī,* "Surely today

Adonijah shall die." The LXX understood *kī* as introducing the purport of the oath and rendered literally *hoti* (*recitativum*). The LXX, however, was not always literalistic. In 1 Sam. 26:10, there is a difficulty of interpretation; the context after *kī 'im* demands the rendering, "Surely YHWH will smite him." The LXX understood it in this sense, and in its interpretation employs a Semitism (*ean mē*), which has a positive meaning. Similarly in 2 Kings 5:20, Gehazi said, "Surely (*kī-'im*) I will run after him." The translator understood this, but rendered in the LXX with a Semitism (*hoti ei mē*), which has a positive signification. Compare also Judg. 15:7, where *kī 'im* is rendered, *hoti ei mēn*. In an oath, the Hebrew *'im* in a negative sense is rendered literally in the LXX: 1 Sam. 14:45; 19:6; 28:10; 2 Sam. 14:11. The use of *'im* (*ei*) clearly implies that a verb of imprecation is understood. In Ruth 3:13, ms. B, apparently for emphasis, adds to *zēi Kyrios* the sentence, *sy ei Kyrios*. Although the formula "as the LORD liveth" is employed without the expression of an imprecation, it is a strong oath, and the person using it could hardly expect to escape divine retribution in case of perjury.

In an oath introduced by the cliché "as YHWH liveth," the name God as an appositive may be added with or without other modifiers: 1 Sam. 25:34, where the first *kī* introduces the oath and the second, a resumptive (*tote eipa*), is followed by *'im* (*ei*) in the negative sense; 1 Kings 17:1, where the LXX has an insertion, "the God of hosts" (*'im, ei*); 1 Kings 17:12; 18:10 (*'im, ei*). Moreover, the name YHWH may be qualified by "hosts" (*ṣᵉbāōt, tōn dynameōn*) together with a relative clause: 1 Kings 18:15, *kī* (surely), or the *recitativum* as *hoti;* 2 Kings 3:14, *kī . . . 'im . . . 'im;* although *kī* may mean "surely," the LXX understood it as *recitativum* (*hoti*) and continued, *ei epeblepsa*. On the other hand, in this formula the name YHWH may be qualified only by a relative clause: 2 Sam. 4:9-10, *kī* (*hoti*); 1 Kings 1:29-30, *kī* (verily, surely, or *recitativum*) . . . *kī* (assuredly, or resumptive) . . . *kī* (assuredly, or resumptive), where the LXX uniformly rendered *kī* as *hoti;* 1 Kings 2:24 (surely, or *recitativum*), the LXX, *hoti;* 2 Kings 5:16, and Jer. 38:16 (45:16), *bis, 'im* rendered *ei* in a negative sense. In all these cases the *Vorlage* of the LXX was like the MT; the same construction occurs in Judith 13:16. Moreover, in 1 Sam. 14:39, where the MT has a participle *hammōšī'a* depending on YHWH, the LXX follows literally, *ho sōsas*.

In referring conditionally to a converted Israel, Jeremiah (4:2) notes in this formula a theological principle, which leads to a knowledge of YHWH among the heathen:

> And wilt swear, "as the LORD liveth,"
> In truth, in justice, and in righteousness;
> Then shall the nations bless themselves by him,
> And in him shall they glory.

In fact, the formula "as YHWH liveth" implies a faith in YHWH, as in Jer.

16:14-15; 23:7-8; 44(51):26. This is especially evident in Jer. 12:16, where a contrast is made between swearing by YHWH or by Baal. On the other hand, this prophet (Jer. 5:2) observes that professed servants of YHWH employ this solemn expression to fortify a lie. The prophet Hosea (4:15) commands a people inclined to paganism or syncretism not to use the formula *ḥay YHWH*, which the LXX with good classical syntax renders, *mē omnyete zōnta Kyrion* (a translation which, however, supports the MT).[12] In a passage depicting a condition of syncretism or confusion of religious thought (Amos 8:14), "As liveth thy God, O Dan," the LXX could easily render by *Zēi ho theos sou, Dan,* but it encountered a difficulty in the succeeding sentence, *wᵉḥē derek bᵉʾēr-šābaʿ* (*kai zēi ho theos sou, Bērsabee*). Apparently the translator overcame the obstacle of *derek* (way) by interpreting it as the favorite or patron deity of Beersheba, which was a cultic place. The distinction, however, between YHWH and those local divinities was maintained and clearly expressed in the LXX.

The formula "as the LORD liveth" may also be extended by including the person addressed. In 2 Sam. 15:21, Ittai said to David, "As YHWH liveth and as my lord the king liveth," *kī* (*Qᵉrē*) *bimqōm . . . kī šām yihyeh ʿabdekā* (surely in what place my lord the king shall be . . . even there will thy servant be). The first *kī,* however, may be *recitativum,* and then the second one would be resumptive of the first; the LXX interprets it in this sense. When David was in disfavor with Saul, he said to Jonathan (1 Sam. 20:3), "As YHWH liveth and as thy soul liveth,"[13] *kī kᵉpesaʿ bēnī ûbēn hammāwet;* the LXX, interpreting *kī* as introducing the contents of the oath, renders it *hoti.* The Hebrew, however, could also be understood as, "Verily there is but a step between me and death." In 2 Kings 2:2, 4, 6, Elisha said, "As the LORD liveth and as thy soul liveth (*zēi Kyrios kai zēi hē psychē sou),* followed by *ʾim (ei)* in a negative sense; a similar construction occurs in 2 Kings 4:30. In fact, a person may swear merely by the life or soul of the person addressed. Abner, in asserting that he does not know David, says to Saul (1 Sam. 17:55), "As thy soul liveth, O king"; this is followed by *ʾim (ei,* Origen) in a negative sense. For a similar construction, cf. 2 Sam. 14:19. In 2 Sam. 11:11, Uriah says to David, *ḥayyekā wᵉḥē napšekā;* here the LXX has only *zēi hē psychē sou.* This form of the oath does not occur elsewhere, and the tautology implied in the MT makes it improbable. It has accordingly been proposed that *ḥayyekā* be dropped on the basis of the LXX or that it be emended to *ḥay YHWH.* An oath, moreover, may be made by the life of a monarch. In Gen. 42:15, Joseph said, *ḥē parʿōh ʾim-tēṣʾû* (as Pharaoh liveth, ye shall not go out). In this case the LXX rendered freely with a classical idiom, *nē tēn hygieian Pharaō,* but avoided the Semitism *ʾim* by translating it *ou mē.* This usage, which involves swearing by a person's life, implies a recognition of the sacredness of human personality.

In the divine oath, however, the formula *ḥay-ʾānī* does not need to precede the asseveration, but it may be imbedded in a sentence. In the illustration of individual responsibility, Noah, Daniel, and Job could save only themselves (Ezek.

14:16): ḥay-'ānī nᵉum 'ădōnāy YHWH . . . 'im-bānīm wᵉ'im-bānōt yaṣṣīlū . . .
(ei huioi ē thygateres sōthēsontai) . . . (20) . . . ḥay-'ānī nᵉum 'ădōnāy YHWH
'im-bēn 'im-bat yaṣṣīlū (ean huioi ē thygateres hypoleiphthōsin). In both verses
the negative sense of 'im is represented by ei, ean. In this connection it should
be noted that in v. 18 the Hebrew negative lō' is rendered in Greek ou mē. From
these examples it is established that with the formula of an oath involving life,
either human or divine, the conjunction 'im (ei) cannot be rendered literally
unless an implied imprecation is supplied; in other words, it has acquired a
negative meaning.

IV

From this investigation of various passages in the Old Testament, it has
been deduced from the different incidents of solemn assertions and their theological significance as reported by the biblical writers that an oath was considered
a serious matter. Of special interest here is the semantic development of 'im (if)
into a negative. Commencing with the formula, "The LORD do so to me and
more also," as a point of departure, one can observe how this conjunction came
to have a negative connotation, and how, as a corollary, 'im lō' logically assumed
an affirmative sense. In all such passages a literal rendering of the text adequately
brings out the meaning of the statement. With the establishment of the signification of 'im for the above cliché, this conjunction could be employed in any
oath in a negative sense, even though no imprecation is expressed. In the end,
'im (if) became a pure negative, even though the suggestion of an oath was
very remote. Nevertheless, in any solemn declaration there was implied the idea
of retribution upon the person who perjured himself or failed to fulfil his
inviolable promise.

Another formula employed in an asseveration is, "as the LORD liveth."
In connection with this cliché, 'im was also used in the meaning established
above. The vocabulary employed in an oath in the Old Testament reflects the
background of theological thinking, and in a solemn affirmation an individual
may manifest his belief in the one God. In the expression, "as the LORD liveth,"
there may also be found a reflection of the sacredness of the divine name, and to
swear by the soul of the person addressed suggests the concept that man is
created a little lower than God (Ps. 8:6). The LXX translators understood these
passages and generally rendered them literally. Occasionally they departed from
literalism and employed a good classical Greek idiom. In most passages, however,
their respect for the letter of the original caused them to follow the Hebrew
exactly and to incorporate a Semitic idiom, which gave the Greek of the LXX
a distinctive character in idiom and syntax. In its theological background the
validity of an oath in the Old Testament is in harmony with the commandment
(Exod. 20:7), "Thou shalt not take the name of the LORD thy God in vain
(laššāw', epi mataiōi)."

NOTES TO CHAPTER THREE

1. Where the Masoretic text and the Septuagint differ in the numbers of chapters and verses, those of the MT are given first; those of the LXX follow and are enclosed either in parentheses or brackets, as the punctuation dictates.

2. It should be noted, however, that ms. Q in this verse has the preposition *en* governing the dative, but this may be due to the influence of *omnyein*, which immediately precedes.

3. *G-K,* § 149d.

4. S. R. Driver, *Notes on the Hebrew Text of the Books of Samuel,* 2d ed. (Oxford: Clarendon Press, 1913), p. 247.

5. *Ibid.,* p. 199.

6. In cases of the divine counsel and purposes, where no form of an oath is expressed, the same idiom is employed: Jer. 49:20 (29:21); 50(27):45, *'im lō', . . . 'im lō',* which in the LXX is rendered, *ean mē . . . ean mē.*

7. *G-K,* § 167b.

8. There are instances in Ezekiel (20:6, 15, 23, 28, 42; 44:12; 47:14) where God lifts up his hand, but these passages do not involve the use of *'im.* In 36:7, however, *'im lō'* (surely) is not translated, and so the Hebrew construction is lost in the LXX.

9. Johannes Pedersen, *Der Eid bei den Semiten* (Strassburg: K. J. Trübner, 1914), p. 18; *G-K,* § 93aa, note 1; § 149a, note 1; Georg Hoffmann, "Versuche zu Amos," *ZAW,* 3 (1883), 124.

10. In Num. 14:21-23, *ḥay-'ani* is extended in the LXX: *zō egō kai zōn to onoma mou;* in v. 22 *kī* is rendered literally by *hoti,* but in v. 23 *'im* is represented by *ei mēn (ē mēn* in ms. M and a number of minuscules). The translator, however, understood the negative sense of *'im* and so added *ouk.* Thus in 14:30, "If (*'im*) you enter" signifies, "Ye shall *not* enter." The LXX reproduces literally: *ei hymeis eiseleusesthe.* In v. 35, however, *'im lō'* is rendered by *ei mēn,* which appears as *ē mēn* in ms. M and a number of minuscules, but as *ei mē* in B*.

11. In Job 27:2, *ḥay-ēl* occurs instead of *ḥay YHWH* in the first half of the line, while in the second the divine name is *šadday;* the LXX follows literally: *zēi ho theos . . . ho pantokratōr.*

12. For this use of the participle compare Dan. 12:7, *wayyiššāba' beḥē hā'ōlām,* which is rendered by the classical idiom, *kai ōmose ton zōnta eis ton aiōna theon.* Theodotion, however, rendered literalistically, *kai ōmosen en tōi zōnti ton aiōna.*

13. This formula is employed by Abigail in speaking to David (I Sam. 25:26) and wishing evil upon his enemies, but the negative use of *'im (ei)* is not involved. In 2 Sam. 15:21, where the *Qerē* has the better reading, which was in the *Vorlage* of the LXX, the formula is followed by *kī (hoti) . . . kī (hoti)* resumptive. The LXX interpreted the first *kī* as *recitativum.* In 1 Sam. 1:26, Hannah, in swearing by the soul of Eli, without the use of a connective after the cliché, simply said, "I am the woman." For the use of this formula followed by *hoti ou,* cf. Judith 12:4.

4

WOMEN AND MASCULINE THEOLOGICAL
VOCABULARY IN THE OLD TESTAMENT*

G. ERNEST WRIGHT

The Judeo-Christian heritage from the Old Testament is the matrix from which our male-dominated theological language is derived. This has come under renewed attack in our time. The central affirmations of the New Testament about God's action through Jesus of Nazareth in our behalf do not lessen the tension, but, if anything, make it more acute. With what female elements in the Bible can a woman relate? Eve, Sarah, Rachel, Miriam the sister of Moses, Hannah the mother of Samuel, etc.—these figures are all so involved in the problems of society that we may be moved to compassion for them, but not liberation. We are left with Ruth, the image of self-sacrificial love for a mother-in-law, but not all mothers-in-law whom we know are comparable to Naomi. Both Judaism and Protestantism have so sharply reacted against making a true heroine of the mother of the Messiah that the resources of Roman Catholic mariology are not available. In any event, Vatican II revealed the deep division among Catholics on the issue, for many of whom mariology is an offensive addition to tradition, so influenced by non-biblical sources as to appear a kind of unneeded and dangerous heresy appended to the biblical story. It is far too mixed with elements of polytheism's divine mother-goddess.

Small wonder, then, that Protestant theologians from time to time come out with revisionist suggestions to the biblical manner of revelation.[1] I believe, however, that a simple rehearsal of certain well-known facts about Christian theology and about the biblical creation stories need repeatedly to be brought into perspective in this connection, so that wrong ideas about the Bible's teaching on the point are not perpetuated in ignorance.

*This paper presumes the existence of a very careful study (soon to be published), entitled "The Image of Woman in the Old Testament," by Phyllis A. Bird, Professor of Old Testament at Perkins School of Theology, Southern Methodist University. The points herein stressed are a few which appear to me to supplement this otherwise excellent and full study (G.E.W.).
G. Ernest Wright died August 29, 1974. Ed.

64

I

In the first place, let us recall the strong and striking emphasis in the Old Testament against idolatry and the making of divine images. The holiness of God is viewed as so dangerous in the presence of human impurity that a human being cannot see him with the naked eye and survive. Consequently, we encounter God through mediated ways, through chosen men whom God has raised up, through the channel of the Spirit whom God sends into his elect to enable them to hear and to do, through angels/messengers, or through his "glory." The "glory of God" is a remarkably successful expression for the hiddenness, the unseeable being of God, while giving full and confident expression to his presence among us or in our world. Yet it is impossible for us (we are directly forbidden by the Second Commandment of the Decalogue) to materialize him in any manner whatever. By inference we must assume that any mental image we have of him will not be God himself but an idol we have constructed. God has withheld from us any knowledge or any way of knowing what his essence, his being, is or is like; and we are expressly forbidden to try to penetrate that mystery or to assume that anything man can make is God as he is in himself.

Such a radical viewpoint, not fully shared by other religions, has definite implications for our understanding of biblical and theological language. All descriptive statements about God must be understood as this side of his essence. The language serves solely a relational purpose: how God has chosen to relate himself to us, or how God is not simply mystery but, for example, "our/my Lord," "our/my Father," "our/my shepherd." The Bible is God's revelation of how we are to know him as our God (Paul Lehmann). Its language is God's "accommodation" of his infinity to our finite natures (Calvin), or the primary "symbols" without which our knowing could not participate in the unknowable (Tillich). And this must include our conception of the role of Jesus Christ. When Christology becomes a substitute for theology, when it ceases to be concerned primarily with God's work for our salvation, but instead attempts to push within the mystery of the ontology of God himself, then it becomes unbiblical and a primary source of Christian heresy.[2]

A structure of language that conveys particular meaning for human existence must, therefore, be drawn from a consciously chosen earthly model or models. Perhaps the most important archaeological discovery of the last twenty-five years pertaining to the Bible has been the particular model that seems to have been adapted to picture God's relation to his people. It is derived from a special international treaty form known only from Near Eastern documents of the fourteenth and thirteenth centuries B.C. That is the suzerain-vassal treaty, in which the vassal's sworn obligations are set within the context of the suzerain's gracious acts done previously and freely in the vassal's behalf.[3] Such a model suggests immediately a male image for the suzerain because female suzerains in history, though they have existed, are few and far between.

Yet at the same time that this adaptation of a particular model for Israel's understanding of God and herself is under way, there is also an open and outright rejection of one of mankind's most common religious assumptions. That is the assumption that sexuality and the fertility of the female are among the chief clues to the unlocking of the hidden meaning of the divine world. Yet the God of Israel cannot be defined; he does not partake in sexuality. He has no female consort. There is no goddess of fertility. Instead, sexuality belongs solely to the order of creation, never to the order of Divine Essence.

We have, then, two seemingly contradictory assumptions: the model of the suzerain as most adequate to portray our understanding of God and his relationship to us and our world. Yet at the same time there is the radical denial that God or the divine can in any way be defined by the sexuality of the world he created. Hence, the way God has chosen to reveal himself as our Lord, while it is dominantly a male image, is not a complete revelation but shares in the inadequacy of all human, socially conditioned language. God's essence is neither male nor female. Yet the language of suzerain-vassal says something of central importance for our religion. As people and as individuals we possess a vocational necessity. We are both free and under orders at the same time. Our obligation for social and world order becomes the center of our covenant, our treaty as God's vassal, the source of God's blessing of *shalom,* whereas failure involves our rebellion against God's past actions of love until our future becomes problematic. My life is lived in hope that by faith I may find salvation through national judgment, while a cross symbolically hanging before me always indicates the expectation of no easy or simple vocation.

II

With this background let us turn to the first two chapters of Genesis. In chapter 1, as the climax on the sixth day God creates man (*ādām*) as male and female. The Hebrew word *ādām* for man in Genesis 1-4 is not a proper name that Israelites would ever use as a boy's name. It is in Hebrew a generic term for all men, every man, mankind. *Ādām* as human being, therefore, is *created* as male and female, equally sharing in the image of God. What that means, we are not told. In context we judge that it has something to do with the assumption that mankind alone among the creatures is given capacity to converse with God, and can therefore understand the divine commands to be fruitful and fill the earth and to subdue and rule over it as would a king (Gen. 1:27-28). Man as ruler of the earthly dominion is like God as Suzerain of the universal and cosmic order. Man and woman share these commands and this capacity equally, the narrative infers, because they both compose *ādām,* humankind.

In Genesis 1, then, sexuality begins with creation and there is complete equality inferred between the sexes because both share the *imago Dei.*

When we find the question of male and female treated in the old narrative source in Genesis 2, essentially the same and additional points are made, but in a very different context where a different question is being made central to the story.

The pericope begins with chapter 2, verse 18, where the issue is more pointedly put than in chapter 1. *Ādām* as male is incomplete: "It is not good that man is always alone"—so the text begins. The rule of man over the earthly creation is implied in the verses that follow, as it is in Gen. 1:28: "So out of the ground the Lord God formed every animal of the field and every bird of the air, and brought them to man to see what he would name them; and whatever man named each living creature, that was its name . . ." (2:19). Yet here the narrative again returns to its point. Among all of these living things on earth there is for man no "companion suitable for him." The Hebrew is rather striking here and the meaning is very clear. Among the kingdom of earthly creatures, there can be found, as the passage is literally rendered, "no helper corresponding to him." Early English effort in translation created a special word to translate this phrase: there was not found "a helpmeet for him"—an excellent rendering of the Hebrew in a precisely equivalent number of words (*ēṣer kĕ-negdô*). It is unfortunate that in modern English a commentary is needed for the meaning of "helpmeet," so that the term does not survive in modern translations. In any event, the point is strongly made: male *ādām* is in an abnormal state. Something must be done. Creation must be finished.

Like the great fish in the Jonah story, the narrative element in the next two verses can be quickly passed over (2:21-22). It is simply a story-device to get on with the point. Do the deep sleep and the rib taken from the male to make woman suggest that one rib is sufficient to create a woman?! No, the sole purpose is to pin down the point that male and female *ādām* are alike, made of the same material. Thus, when God brought woman to man, the latter exclaimed: "Now this at last,"· or, "Here this time finally is (one who is) bone of my bones and flesh of my flesh." Then comes a pun on the Hebrew words: "She shall be named woman (*ishshah*) because she was taken out of man (*ish*)."

With the creation of *ādām* complete, the old epic of chapter 2 then follows with the first recorded statement in literature that the normal state for man and woman is the institution of monogamy: "Therefore a man leaves his father and his mother and cleaves to his wife, and the two of them become one flesh" (v. 24). This is a completely unexpected statement at a time when polygamy was a legally permitted arrangement, recognized as such by all contemporary law codes, including that of Israel. On the other hand, Israelite laws concerning women are chiefly those which protect her in critical situations, including polygamous marriage. Furthermore, the institution of polygamy must not be thought of solely as the product of male lust. Women and children without the protection and meaning for existence provided by a family were in a pitiable state in antiquity. No other vocation was open for them. Widows and orphans, throughout the Near East, as well as in Israel, were the first of the poor for whom special exhortations were commonly made for society's special care. Our modern era is providing an increasing number of vocational options for women besides or in addition to marriage. In antiquity, however, in the tenth century B.C. or earlier,[4] for an Israelite writer suddenly to issue a proclamation of monogamy, arising out of his reflections on the divine creation of male and female—that is a most remarkable phenomenon.

Furthermore, there is no hint in these two chapters of Genesis of any subservience of female to male. Equality and the necessity of each for the other is the normal situation. An additional observation is the remarkable insight into the nature of the marriage relation as differing from all other human relations in the statement that the two of them leave home and parents, cling to each other and become "one flesh." Again we have a profound statement, the most profound, in my view, which the Bible contains about marriage. Two individuals creating a union called "one flesh" is one of those pithy biblical statements that are never explained, but the more one considers them from a variety of viewpoints, the more remarkable they become. They possess a background quality, unelaborated and unexpressed, but which compel attention as they compel thought and freshness of expression.

If, then, monogamy and the equality of the sexes is within the order of creation, then the vision of the meaning of God in the creation becomes a judgment upon life as it is now lived, and the liberation of woman and man from anything less becomes an ideal that should direct our present and future attitudes and actions.

The Bible is very specific that while the equality of the sexes belongs to the order of God's intention in creation, the subservience of woman to man belongs to the "fallen world" and is part of the penalty placed by God upon woman along with the pain of childbirth. In Gen. 3:16 God says to the woman: "To your husband shall be your yearning; yet he will lord it over you" (*JB*).

These verses of judgment are simply descriptions of the way things are in the world as it is. They are wrong, unnatural, not according to God's original intention. Therefore, they are matters which various people through history have been concerned about. The gradual liberation of woman under the influence of the Bible has been one of the great accomplishments in Western civilization. Yet we have a long way to go. This long history of male dominance corrupts the male, just as it does the female. It is not one of the "goods" of creation. It shows our wayward and rebellious history, wherein acts of will and judgments of God combine to show us our "fallen" state.

III

Returning to where we began, we find ourselves in a most difficult position. On the one hand, sex is a most conspicuous, necessary, and significant order within God's creation. Yet it most emphatically has nothing to do with the nature or being of God or the Divine. But what are we to do when a given religious language has been carefully chosen and honed to cut through the chaos of meaninglessness in order to clear the way for a special set of images or models drawn from human experience which convey a central perception of what truth and order are for our existence? The models and the language developed on its basis are historically conditioned and do not tell us everything about the mystery of being. They reveal only what the good for us is, in what way our salvation lies.

From the earliest times and through world history, with rare exceptions, society and the models drawn from it have been male-dominated or male-centric. The Bible is strongly anti-female as far as language about God is concerned, because of the flagrant misuse of sex in religions that Israel had to fight to preserve her own monotheistic variety of fidelity to covenant. To ancient Israel God as "she" was far more dangerous than God as "he." Thus, on the one hand, we are stuck with language that has a long history behind it of both social and religious conditioning. On the other hand, we have the problem of language itself. Hebrew had no neuter. Other languages do have it, but worship and covenant cannot be built around an indefinite and impersonal "it."

Perhaps, however, the language problem is not the most important point for most women. It is rather the prejudices that society, with its long history, has placed in us. These become particularly demonic, it seems to me, when the churches prove the most intransigent of all our institutions in the acceptance of women as clergy. Even in those Protestant denominations that ordain women today, the central problems remain, especially in the pew. The equality of the sexes in church leadership is still a thing of the future, at least on the level of the local church. And those churches which still see the central content of worship as patterned after the picture of the mass, i.e., of a priest performing sacrificial rites, are in a still more difficult position, for how can a sacrificing priest be female? Priestesses are known in history, but never as altar-clergy.

NOTES TO CHAPTER FOUR

1. An example is a recent book by J. Edgar Burns, *God as Woman, Woman as God* (Paramus, N.Y.: Paulist-Newman, 1973).

2. For development of this point and for some bibliography, see the writer's *The Old Testament and Theology* (New York: Harper and Row, 1969), chapter 6.

3. George E. Mendenhall, *Law and Covenant in Israel and the Ancient Near East* (Pittsburgh: The Biblical Colloquium, 1955). For the significance of this discovery in reconstructing the history of Israel, the literature is now vast. See Wright, *op. cit.*, chapters 3-5; John Bright, *A History of Israel*, 2d ed. (Philadelphia: Westminster Press, 1972), pp. 144ff.; Delbert R. Hillers, *Covenant: The History of a Biblical Idea* (Baltimore: Johns Hopkins Press, 1961); W. Eichrodt, "Covenant and Law," *Interpretation*, 20 (1966), 302-321.

4. The oldest written form of Israel's epic is believed generally today to have been put in writing during the tenth century. Yet no basic monograph has or can at present be written to prove the date, because it is impossible with certainty to distinguish this written form's (the Yahwist's) thought patterns from the epic as known during the period of the tribal league before the monarchy.

5

JEWISH-CHRISTIAN RELATIONSHIPS:
The Two Covenants and the Dilemmas of Christology*

J. COERT RYLAARSDAM

The dilemmas of Christology today are mostly the dilemmas of history and eschatology. If Christianity is an eschatological faith, how can it be an historical faith as well? Gerhard von Rad and many who follow him uncritically to the contrary, these two are not easily reconciled. Eschatology and history stand in a paradoxical relation to each other; no synthesis is possible. So they continue as separate foci, perpetually in tension with each other. (See Excursus.[1])

However Jesus may have understood his vocation, at the outset Christians interpreted his career as an eschatological event. He had overcome the world ('ôlām), relativized history—or even abolished it. Except for some sectarian movements, Judaism thought more historically than eschatologically; it awaited the transformation and redemption of the world. So the Jews said that the Messiah had not come. But the gentiles believed. And the Christians wrote a commentary on the Hebrew Bible and called it the New Testament. Its accent is over-whelmingly eschatological. Therefore it has now become the primary occasion for the dilemmas of Christology.

Today, after nineteen centuries, the Christian ethos has almost come full circle. Christians now want to interpret the career of Jesus mainly in historical terms; given the spirit of the culture, its meaning is more communicable that way. More and more Christians of the twentieth century have recaptured the perspective of the Judaism of the first century. More and more, the commentary that was written to announce a new world is being used to define our identity and vocation in the old. The road back from eschatology to time runs through nineteen centuries. There are some interesting milestones along the way: the postponement of the Parousia, and its demythologization; the church of Constantine, and Christendom; Saint Thomas and Aristotelian realism; Calvin, and the third use of the Law; Puritanism, and the Kingdom of God in America; process theology, and Teilhard de Chardin; the Second Vatican Council, and *aggiorna-*

*Reprinted with permission from the *Journal of Ecumenical Studies*, 9, no. 2 (Spring 1972), 249-270. Copyright 1972 by Temple University.

mento. The movement is all in one direction, and so relentless that it seems to gobble up the very witness made to stay its course; consider the reaction to Karl Barth in the so-called "death of God" movement as a recent example.

Nevertheless, the tension continues. Given the paradoxical relation between history and eschatology, there is no reason to suppose that what neither Judaism nor Christianity accomplished in the first century will happen in the twentieth. Eschatology did not absorb history; and the historical did not dissolve the eschatological. Nor has a final synthesis ever been found for both. Especially in Christianity, where the temporal and historical has now reasserted itself, the prestige and status of the New Testament is alone sufficient to insure a swing of the pendulum. In the meantime, however, its overwhelmingly apocalyptic and eschatological perspective, coupled with traditional notions about its authority both within and outside the Bible, greatly complicates the contemporary dilemmas of Christology.

To what extent and how should current Christologies be controlled by the eschatological Christologies of the New Testament? Does the New Testament really frustrate the intentions of men like Pannenberg and Moltmann? And, in turn, do their formally traditional views about its authority really obscure its true function? When such questions begin to be asked a systematic theologian usually moves forward, into Christian tradition. But an Old Testament theologian moves backward, into the Bible from which the New Testament sprang. He asks about the paradox of the historical and the trans-historical in the Hebrew Bible; and he asks about the handling of it in the most influential commentary ever written, not only on the Hebrew Bible but probably also on all other sacred books.

I

In the Jewish Scriptures the paradox is given the shape of covenants. The Old Testament revolves around two covenants, not one: a covenant with Israel, and a covenant with David.[2] These two covenants probably each had a relatively separate and independent history of its own at the beginning. Each spoke in its own way about God's revelation of himself, about his relation to the world, and to Israel. So both nurtured their own distinctive and relatively independent religious, social, and cultic traditions and institutions. Each had its characteristic themes, such as "the people of God" and "the Messiah," which eventually became a part of the common legacy of Israel. But, because each covenant had its own distinct perspective, such themes often stood in some degree of tension with each other. This has continued down to the present, in both Judaism and Christianity. In Israel, the covenant with David was accommodated to the covenant with the people, but never wholly absorbed by it. In the New Testament the covenant with David was resurgent; but, again, not in such a way as to assimilate the other covenant entirely. The New Testament also revolves around the two covenants around which the Old revolves, though the proportional significance is reversed. At the bottom of the separation of Christianity from Judaism lay this tension between the two covenants.

The covenant with Israel was the older of the two. It was the *berith,* the agreement, by which Israel described its relation to Yahweh in the period before the monarchy. Thus it was the covenant of a religious confederacy of tribal groups that defined itself as a single corporate social and religious union called into being and protected by the one God to whom it vowed allegiance. It interpreted its history as the action of God in its behalf; and its continuing existence depended both on the ongoing presence of Yahweh in Israel's life and on her faithfulness to him. With minor exceptions, the whole of Israel's tradition presupposes only this confederacy covenant.

On the basis of accounts such as are found in Joshua twenty-four it seems clear that the central cultic action of pre-monarchic Israel consisted of what was probably an annual ceremony of "Covenant Renewal" at which the communal relationship to Yahweh was celebrated and reconfirmed. It is by now a matter of common knowledge that the forms for this cultic action that represented the relation between Yahweh and Israel were derived from a Hittite "suzerain ceremony" in which the great king entered into a permanent treaty relationship with a petty client he had rescued.

The beginning of the covenant lay in the initiating action of Yahweh. The account in Joshua (24:2-13) opens with a scene in which Yahweh, as the great suzerain, recalls some of the episodes in Israel's history in which, though not obligated to do so, he had come to her rescue: the preservation of the patriarchs, the deliverance from Egypt, the crossing of sea and wilderness, and the conquest of the land. The continuance of the relationship with this "saving" God depends on mutual obligations of faithfulness and responsibility: the conditions are progressively spelled out and are a matrix for Israel's laws; warnings and exhortations are issued; solemn oaths are taken; and sacrifices seal the covenant. As in the case of the suzerain treaties, the agreement is not one between equals; Israel is indebted before she enters into it, for the saving action of Yahweh that makes the covenant possible was an uncovenanted mercy. Nevertheless, the realization of the promises of the covenant—the life and security of Israel in its land as the sign and means of God's promise of blessing for all mankind—is dependent upon Israel's responsibility.

Recent form criticism and biblical theology have made much of the so-called "recital" aspect of this covenant ritual; that is, of that part which remembers the great saving acts of Yahweh that preceded the agreement and that make it possible. G. von Rad found this recital form in Deut. 26:5-10, where the great saving acts are recited not by Yahweh, as in the ceremonial of covenant renewal, but as a confession of an Israelite farmer when he comes to present the offering for his new crop. Von Rad's imagination was enthralled by the "evangelical" impulse of the recital; he called it a "Credo" and suggested that the entire Pentateuch might have developed as an expansion of the recital motif. He also noted that the giving of the Law on Sinai was not included among the list of saving acts in the recital.[3]

Von Rad thought and wrote in that way before the role of recital as one aspect of the covenant renewal ceremony had been fully grasped. The reconstruction of the covenant renewal rites as a total complex, show how divine initiative and saving action and Israel's responsibility are bound together in the confederacy covenant. For their continuing effectiveness, all parts of the agreement depend on one another; none has meaning except in the context of all the others. Hence, for example, in Exod. 20:1, the declarative "recital" to introduce the Decalogue: "I am the LORD thy God that brought thee out of the house of bondage . . ." is bound to the imperatives that follow. The covenant renewal ceremony was, indeed, a matrix for evangelical recital in Israel's traditions; but it was simultaneously, as noted already, also the matrix for the legal forms that defined Israel's responsibility. Insofar as the Pentateuch is the product of the celebration of the covenant of the confederacy in Israel it is both proclamation and instruction, for in this covenant Gospel and Law are integral aspects of a single whole. The omission of Sinai from the list of saving events recited, noted by von Rad, can perhaps best be accounted for by remembering that the rite of covenant renewal, both as Gospel and Law, represents Sinai.

This close proximity of grace and demand in a single agreement that marks the covenant of Yahweh with Israel in the confederacy contains inherently paradoxical dimensions. Therefore, what Israel had stated synthetically could, potentially, be stated antithetically as well. This is precisely what happened to this covenant in many parts of the New Testament, especially in the writings of St. Paul. For him the motif of obligation had crowded out that of recital. Yahweh's covenant with Israel was deprived of the great saving acts of God on which it rested. Its demands were treated not as a response, but as an abstract absolute. In the New Testament the saving events recited in the covenant of the confederacy tend to serve as a preface for the action of God in the career of Jesus Christ, though, actually, as we shall see, the interpretation of Jesus Christ really depended more basically on the other covenant, the covenant with David.

Before dealing with that we must take a brief look at some of the themes for biblical faith provided by the earlier of the two covenants. Virtually all of these are related to the fact that for this covenant the created world of time, space, and matter, and, most especially, the world of man and history is really the only world that matters. It bears witness to Yahweh and to his relation to men in terms of what he does in this scene. There is no concern with the transcendent in a supernatural or mythical sense; and cosmological interests are minimal. Even the accounts of creation under the inspiration of this covenant are given the form of histories. One finds scant preoccupation with God in his hiddenness and mystery; what counts most is the decisiveness of his presence in the world of human action; he makes himself known in historical events.

The locus of this historical revelation is limited. For while Yahweh presumably is God of all mankind his revelation in this world is preponderantly in

Israel's history alone. The great saving actions are events in that history. There is none of the preoccupation with "the nations" and their destiny as objects of God's interest or as actors in a divine drama, such as one meets in the books of the prophets.[4] The God of this covenant is called the God "of our fathers," and his preoccupation with other nations, whether Egyptians or Moabites, is always incidental to his concern for Israel. The accent is on particularity: the election of Israel as the people in whose history Yahweh reveals himself.

Israel told her history as a story punctuated by acts of divine rescue. Scholars have called this recital Salvation History. Yahweh always provided a "way," not only in the great historical events of the beginning of the people and its land on which the covenant rested, but also in its subsequent history when the crisis was often occasioned by its own faithlessness or disobedience. Thus, in this covenant, the direction is always towards the future. History begins with a promise, the history of Israel especially. The promise encounters a crisis from which Yahweh provides rescue, to make possible its fulfilment. Whether in the barrenness of Sarah, the oppression of the Pharaoh, or the lack of water in the wilderness, the surmounting of each crisis constitutes a salvation. Nevertheless, every "already" is superseded by a "not yet." The movement is forward; but, because both the beginning and the end lie in the temporal order, there is no visible end to the series. The Alpha and the Omega play no role in this covenant with Israel. It is open.

The term "salvation" carries very definitive and absolute connotations in Christian tradition. Therefore its application to the historical and relative events in which Israel's covenant celebrated Yahweh's revelation and redemption can be misleading. The saving act of Yahweh was completely adequate and utterly decisive to meet the crisis that was its occasion. That was its finality. But, as the very etymology of the divine name seems to show, Israel, in this covenant, did not pretend to know deity in any unchanging sense, as an absolute. The confederacy covenant makes no appeal to the hidden mystery of deity, whether as Creator or as Redeemer. Salvation in this covenant means something quite different than it does in either the covenant of David or in the Christian tradition; it is simply the reconfirmation of a promise, repeated ever anew.

Beginning in the New Testament, Christian interpreters of the Old Testament who work with Salvation History as a sort of master key by which to grasp its meaning for their own faith sometimes add the event Jesus Christ to the series of great acts of God recited in Israel's covenant renewal celebrations. But the viability of this procedure seems much more apparent than real. In the New Testament, with very limited and partial exceptions, the career of Jesus Christ constitutes an eschatological event. It discloses the Alpha and the Omega. To be sure, the event has its historical side; "born of a woman, born under the law" (Gal. 4:4); but what is distinctive about it is that it marks the end to that sort of historical contingency.[5] Here again, it was the covenant with David, rather than the covenant of the confederacy, that served the Christians who wrote the

New Testament. The latter could, presumably, contain and give meaning to the career of Jesus at a moment of fulfilment analogous to the exodus or the return from the exile. It could define it as a transforming event *in* history of a decisive sort. But it could not define it as the event that summed up history, or brought it to its destiny. And that, precisely, would seem to distinguish the Christ event in Christian tradition from the events of Salvation History. Salvation History is not *the* key to New Testament Christology.

It would be difficult to overstate the historical relativism of the confederacy covenant. The action of God begins in time and in the human scene, and it never extends beyond them. The SHALOM which marks the goal of God's plan and of Israel's mission lies within the world of man's experience. From the beginning to the end, spirit and matter are inextricably held together; the order of redemption is coterminous with the order of creation. Though the living God in his mystery may extend beyond time, his presence in it is what matters. There are no eschatological intimations in this primary covenant of the Hebrew tradition; for, properly understood, the eschatological alludes to an absolute that lies beyond the relativities of time and history, and not to any goal bound up with them. However greatly this primary covenant of the Old Testament may appeal to much in *modern* Christian experience, the Christians who produced the New Testament did not treat it as the most important biblical source for their Christology. That they found in the covenant of David, the secondary covenant of the Hebrew Bible.

II

The second pivot around which the traditions of Israel and its Scriptures revolve is the covenant of David—or with David. It attests the role given to the throne and dynasty of David and to Mount Zion and the worship there as the "signs" and means of divine revelation. We have seen that for the covenant of the confederacy, the definitive revelation of Yahweh was provided by means of a series of epochal events that together summed up the story of Israel's formation as a people and its inheritance of its land. Land and people were the signs of the LORD's presence in the world, the marks of his grace, and the basis for hope. It was a revelation that began in history and that anticipated a fulfilment in history.

David took over the sacred mountain of Zion and made it the most holy place for Israel's worship. When his own royal status and the perpetuation of his dynasty began to be treated as signs of the divine presence and the manner of it, this constituted a radical break with the past, and a radically new beginning in the religious confessions of Israel. As "events" of revelation Zion and David were truly novelties. They introduced a tension into the traditions of Israel's faith that has never been completely overcome. In Israel the covenant with David remained secondary, though eventually its characteristic motifs touched the whole tradition. The Davidic covenant precipitated the political division into two kingdoms; but eventually it accommodated itself to the older covenant of Israel. As we shall see, it was in large measure transformed by it, but never absorbed.

The primary materials relating to the confederacy covenant, before it was affected by the covenant of David, are located mostly in the Pentateuch and the book of Joshua. It is my conviction that scholarship has now located equally primary sources for our interpretation of the Davidic covenant in its original distinctiveness.[6] The fifth chapter of Second Samuel reports how David captured Jerusalem without a battle. The sixth chapter tells how he brought Israel's most venerable cultic object to Mount Zion; and in the seventh chapter we have the oath to David presented as a prophetic oracle mediated by Nathan. The story surrounding it makes clear that the dynasty of David, rather than the temple— the house that is David's family rather than the house Solomon built—provides the inner core of the Zion faith.

It is not at all improbable that David perpetuated a modified form of the worship and the priesthood that was established on Zion centuries before Israel's presence there. Here the Ugaritic materials, which give us a look into the religious scene in Canaan, and the strange account in Genesis fourteen of the priest-king Melchizedek who blessed Abram, serve to interpret each other. Melchizedek was king of Salem. His name reads "My King is Zedek (*Rightness*)." King, of course, is a title for the deity; and, significantly, it is a title that never occurs in the traditions of the older covenant, only in those of David. Melchizedek was "priest of *El elyon,*" of "God most high." El was the "high" god of the Canaanite pantheon, above Anath, his erstwhile spouse, and Aleyn Ba'al, their dying-rising son. The cult of Zion, before David captured it, seems to have featured El, the Creator of the cosmos and the ruler of nations.[7] One of his names there, in addition to his title "most high," was Zedek, which is also carried in Melchizedek's name. It alludes to the true cosmic order maintained by the creator and ruler of nature and the nations.

David did at least two things to make this ancient cult on Zion an Israelite cult: he introduced the name of Israel's God, Yahweh, and reduced all other proper names to attributes. King became a favorite title now for Yahweh; and there arose the aetiological story of how all of this had been anticipated by Melchizedek in the days of Abram.

In addition to the name of Yahweh, David brought the ark to Zion. Under the old covenant of the confederacy this sacred object had been the most conspicuous reminder and embodiment of the presence of Yahweh in the life of the whole family of Israel. It led the people through the wilderness and on pilgrimage. In battle it reminded them that Yahweh fought Israel's battles. And in some accounts of the covenant renewal ceremony it stood at the center of the solemnities, to remind the people that Yahweh heard the pledges of loyalty to which they were recommitting themselves. Now, in the covenant of David, this sacred ark, to which all Israel had deep emotional ties, announced that Yahweh reigned as King on Zion, his holy mountain, maintaining the "righteous" or cosmic order of his creation and exercising authority and rule over "the nations." Here on Zion Yahweh had established his throne; and seated on the throne at his right hand was his anointed, the ruler of the house of David.

In addition to the primary materials of the Davidic covenant noted above we must also cite the large number of psalms that belong to this classification.[8] Psalms that tell about Yahweh the Creator who establishes the mountains and walks on the deeps, or who makes the earth shake with his thundering. Psalms about his ascent to Mount Zion, accompanied by a great battle shout, to take his seat and assume his reign there. Psalms about the day of the LORD on which he comes to judge the world. Psalms about the holy mountain itself: its mystic beauty, its inviolability as the seat of the great God, its access to the mysterious waters of life, its centrality for all directions of the compass, and its temple, the house in which Yahweh is enthroned. And psalms about the king who reigns by Yahweh's decree, to whom he is related as son to father in a relationship that is antecedent to all history, and is not subject to human contingency: Yahweh's regent, his first-born son, the priest and shepherd of his people, the mediator by which the life and power of God is made available to man.

There has been much debate in the academic world about the rites on Zion, especially the rites marking the beginning of a new year. Did they correspond to the rites of the Babylonian Akitu festival? How closely? Was Yahweh annually re-enthroned as King on Zion, and what role did the ark play in this? In what ways and to what extent did the rites of sacral kingship associated with Babylon have equivalents in Jerusalem at New Year's? It is impossible to probe such questions here; nor is that necessary. For what all of the primary material of the Davidic covenant makes quite evident is that this covenant did not feature the renewal ceremonies described in our review of the older covenant. Though it remains hazardous to speak with assurance of what transpired in every respect in the cult on Zion, it is not too difficult to ascertain some of the things that did not occur there.

As reflected in its primary sources, in the cult on Zion the people did not enter into an agreement with Yahweh; they were not asked to. There is no recital of the great acts of God that made Israel a people and gave her its land; indeed, except for the personal stories of David, there is scant reference to history of any sort. There are no solemn mutual undertakings between Yahweh and man, no recital of conditions that must be observed, no warning against human aberrations by which man might forfeit the promise made to him. There is no Law in the economy of redemption. It was only later, in secondary materials in which the Davidic covenant is being qualified by the legacy of the confederacy, that the promise of the divine oath to the king is made conditional upon his moral responsibility (e.g., I Kings 3:10-15). Also, the particularity of election, represented by the focus on Israel and its land in the covenant of the confederacy, is largely lacking in this messianic covenant. It is displaced by the universality of creation and the nations. And instead of the communalism of confederacy there is individualism. The King displaces the people as son of Yahweh.

Our review of the features of the confederacy covenant that are lacking in the materials of the Zion cult sets in relief the characteristic themes of the covenant of David. In whatever rites that may have been celebrated, they stand in sharp contrast to the themes of the older covenant.

In the confederacy the historical was central, especially the history of Israel. In Genesis the creation stories serve mainly as a means of getting into the world of man. That is where the action is. But in the psalms we have cited, as well as in closely affiliated materials in both wisdom and the prophets, the testimony to creation is for its own sake. The real center of action, in the covenant of David, lies in the primordial, the cosmic, and the pre-temporal world that antedates the world of human contingency. Its psalms sing about the triumph of God as Creator by recalling his establishment of order (*zedek*), by the overcoming of chaos and anarchy in struggles that lie in that mythical past. Yahweh's Kingship, and the Davidic kingship as well, rests on a series of decrees that are eternal and unchangeable: the world is established; it will not be moved. Yahweh is King forever; mightier than the breakers of the many waters. He decrees the place of the nations in the scheme of things; and by that same immutable decree David is his first-born. He has set his right hand over the sea and the rivers, a token that coordinates his kingship and rule with that of Yahweh himself. The focus is on the Alpha of the beginning; and the psalms repeatedly appeal to this *mē az*, this primordial *illo tempore*, as the rock of assurance amid the instabilities of time and history.

Whereas the covenant celebrated at Shechem faced the future and anticipated that the ongoing sequence of promise-fulfilment would lead to the SHALOM that lay ahead, the Davidic covenant celebrated the Alpha of the primordial past, for the sake of making it available and effective in the present. It "remembered"; to reiterate or to re-effect: the primordial and the absolute for the sake of security amidst the temporal and the contingent of history. We are here clearly looking at the source of many characteristic Christian theological and liturgical motifs.

In the older covenant the revelation of God took place in history; in the Davidic covenant it took place in the primordial past of Creation. The former anticipated the future; the latter invoked the absolutes of a primordial past. Though there was great inequality in the partners, the covenant of the confederacy was bilateral. There were reciprocal pledges, mutual undertakings, and the continuing proliferation of human responsibilities. In contrast, the Davidic covenant was unilateral. It was a divine decree, an oath taken by Yahweh. God does not dwell in the midst of his people, in his land; he dwells on Zion. The chasm between man and God is bridged only by the mystical figure of the Anointed who, by the mystery of the divine decree, is both human and divine. The responsibility and freedom of human volition associated with the older covenant, and exemplified by Torah, is obscured in the covenant of David.

III

By looking at the primary materials pertinent to each of the two covenants that lie at the heart of the Old Testament we have become aware how profoundly they differ from each other. We can summarize the differences under three headings: the absolute and primordial over against the contingent and historical; the orientation to the past versus the orientation to the future; and a decreed divine determinism in tension with assumptions of human freedom and responsibility. These contrasts contain tensions of paradoxical dimensions that defy complete resolution. The story of the development of Israel's traditions, including that of the production of the Hebrew Bible, can be told best as the story of the interaction between these two covenants as both became parts of the heritage of the entire community and as both served as resources for the interpretation of its faith, century after century. In this way the paradoxical character of the tension between the two seems to have taken root in Israel's consciousness, eventually to explode in the Roman era in a variety of movements and sects. Most important among all of these was the new eschatological faith of Christianity which, in due course, again combined these same two covenants, together with their reciprocal tensions and paradoxes, as the double focus of one faith. What made this new faith distinctive from the faith of Israel, which had also combined them, was that it reversed the order of priority assigned to the covenants. Whereas in Israel the covenant of David is made subservient to the covenant of the confederacy, in Christianity the opposite is the case. We must look at the story of the development that helps us to understand that reversal.

The older covenant of Israel was futuristic and historical. Its tendency to dominate the Davidic covenant in the shaping of Israelite traditions is indicated by the fact that these themes are increasingly ascendent. The themes of the primordial actions of Yahweh as creator and king are transposed into the world of time and history. His universal assertion of his authority is relocated in the world of human events and begins to serve as the basis for anticipating events of judgment and redemption in the future. This recasting of some of the great themes of the Davidic covenant under the impact of the perspective of the covenant of the confederacy is most conspicuously discernible in the canonical books that are the special legacy of the great prophetic movement. We may recall that Martin Buber, in his book *The Prophetic Faith,* gave the title "The Turning to the Future" to his chapter dedicated to the canonical prophets. This title is a tribute to the role the prophets played in reorienting the themes of the covenant of David to the perspective of the covenant of the confederacy.

Most of the prophetic books are palpably deeply under the impact of the Zion cult and its themes. The entire book of Isaiah, for example, is permeated by Zion themes: Yahweh is enthroned on Zion; he commits his reign to his Messiah of the house of David; his rule is universal, extending to the ends of the earth, over nature and nations. One recalls the balancing of the universality of redemption with the universality of creation in chapters forty to fifty-five of the book, and also the tenacity with which the original Isaiah adhered to the theme of the inviolability of Zion. The Book of Amos opens with the announcement that "the LORD roars from Zion." And in Micah one can almost see the erstwhile securities of the Davidic covenant crumble as the prophet relocates the power of the primordial absolute of Yahweh in the historical scene in which he measures his judgments by man's moral irresponsibility.

The kingship of Yahweh and the universality of his rule over the nations become permanently embedded in the prophetic corpus. The series of "Prophecies against the Nations," found in several prophetic books, are a novelty of the prophets probably inspired by the universality of the Davidic covenant. But the static notions of eternal decrees, reconfirmed in annual cultic celebrations, by which Yahweh keeps the nations in their appointed sphere, makes way for the daring notion that the rise and fall of political powers in history is entirely at the discretion of the divine will, however obtuse it may appear. That is, the theme of the universality that comes from Zion is set in the historical perspective that is provided by the other covenant. Recall Jeremiah's interpretation of the rise of Babylonia as a new world empire (Jeremiah 27-29); and the anointed role of the conquering Cyrus in Second Isaiah. The primordial has become historical, though it has remained universal.

No change effected by the reaction of the two covenants upon each other was to be more fateful for the future than Amos's historification of the "Day of the LORD." Though Amos assumed the centrality of Zion as the divine seat, he nevertheless demythologized what was probably the central feature of its cult. Mythologically the Day of the LORD was the day of creation, the primeval day of the triumph and reign of Yahweh. Cultically it was the day on which this triumph was renewed and revitalized: the order of nature was restored, its fruitfulness insured, and nations were reassigned to their proper place. It was a day of light. But at Bethel Amos proclaimed that it would be a day of darkness. That is, mythologically speaking, creation would be undone and chaos would return in both nature and politics. Of course, Amos was no longer speaking mythologically but historically. Amos was a child of both covenants and is oppressed by the conviction that Israel has been unfaithful to its covenanted obligations. The mutuality of the older covenant, in which men can forfeit their redemption through neglect of their responsibility, had for him won out over the unilateral oath of the covenant of David. Simultaneously, he divorces the Day of the LORD from its cyclical, cultic context and projects it into an open and historical future. The day had not only become a day of judgment, but also an unpredictable future day, no longer bound to time or place. The Day of Judgment has had a long and varied career in Christian tradition. Amos only provided the first new stage of this. But his mark on it has never been undone.

In the story of the meeting of the two covenants the so-called reformation of King Josiah must count as a major reassertion of the perspective of the confederacy covenant. The king and the reformers sought to protect the status of the Davidic dynasty and of Zion and its temple by giving them a setting in the historically and communally oriented traditions of Shechem. Thus there was a final elimination of cult rites and objects that spoke to the religious mythologies that lay in the background of the royal cult: the tree and the pillar, the brazen serpent, the chariots of the sun, the *kedeshim* and the *kedeshoth,* the "vessels" used in the worship of Ba'al and Asherah, the rites of Tammuz, and Topheth. And the introduction of the ceremony of covenant renewal, with a reading of the conditions provided by the Book of the Law, reintroduces the element of volitional moral responsibility. There is communal participation, and the king is bound by the moral demands. We are told that the rites concluded with an observance of the Passover such as had not occurred since the days of the judges (2 Kings 23:21-23). The Passover, of course, carried with it the relocation of revelation in the history of Israel, in the events that made it a people with a land. Thus particularity and historical election now match universality and the absolute of the oath; and Israel, as well as its king, is the son of its God (Hos. 11:1).

For the sake of the survival of Israel, the powerful drive of the old communal covenant in the restatement of faith represented by the Reformation of King Josiah came at a very opportune time. A generation later Nebuchadnezzar destroyed the Kingdom of Judah, razed the holy hill of Zion where Yahweh had resided, and took his vicar to Babylon as a captive. In terms of the perspective of the Davidic covenant according to its original and unqualified assumptions, Marduk had triumphed over Yahweh. Israel should have ceased to exist; its name should have disappeared, along with the name of Yahweh. That was the political and social pattern in the ancient Near East where the polities were controlled by the mythology that lay in the background of the traditions of the covenant of David. The fact that Israel retained its identity in exile indicates how far the redefinition of this covenant had gone and how subsidiary it had become to the covenant of the confederacy.

The God who had ruled on Zion was able to go into captivity with his people; and, though in exile, they had no doubt that he was still the Creator and King of the nations. Review the prophetic books, and the book of Daniel. The role of place, absolutized in the Davidic cultus, had been relativized. It had not been abolished. When he prayed in Babylon Daniel turned his face to Jerusalem; and to this day in every good Jewish home there is a marker on the wall that faces Zion. Nevertheless, the process of what may be called the "etherealization" of Zion and its messiah had begun. And though, with the rise of Christianity, the themes of the covenant of David were powerfully resurgent, this process became persistent.

The mobility of Yahweh, which made it possible for him to go into exile, was rooted in the older covenant. So were the historical particularity and communalism of Israel which now reasserted themselves as the means for her survival. In Babylonia circumcision, sabbath, and diet first became systematically established as signs of the distinctiveness and vocation of Israel. There, too, the teaching and interpretation of the conditions relating to the covenant of salvation history first became the central cultic activity of the community. And, with the partial exception of the ascendency of the Aaronic priesthood and the sacrificial liturgies of the Second Temple, this preoccupation with Torah has continued until this day as the hallmark of the dominant expression of Israel's faith.

Though for a moment, on the practical level, the old covenant of Israel seemed to carry all before it, the covenant of David also persisted. The dominant focus was unable to absorb it; the relation between the two is too paradoxical for that. Even when it seemed to disappear, the Davidic covenant only went underground. Gershom Sholem's *Major Trends in Jewish Mysticism* is really a documentation of this persistent habit which has lasted over two thousand years. Apocalypticism was the first fruit of this underground vitality.

In the post-exilic world of Israel the formulae for theodicy prescribed by the ethically responsible covenant of Israel were not vindicated in the arena of historical actuality on which this covenant insisted. This gave an opening for the old primordial themes of creation and chaos, of the day of the LORD, and of a messiah who would exercise a universal reign. We have seen that these themes had already been brought into the historical scene; Amos had reinterpreted the Day of the LORD as a day of historical judgment on Israel. But in captivity Israel had acknowledged its guilt and repented. It began to hope and pray for its restoration. Its prayers were heard. Then it began to wait for the great historical assize in which the tables would be turned, so that the powers that had served so arrogantly as the instruments of her degradation might themselves be brought to judgment, and so that the reign of the messiah might begin and establish the peace of primeval paradise on earth in the shape of human society.

This anticipated historical reversal, rooted in a reading of the historicized themes of the Davidic covenant, did not occur. Empire succeeded empire, each more wicked than its predecessor; and Israel's situation in history was ever more precarious. God did not vindicate himself; history was not following the script. Now the trans-historical dimensions of the old Davidic covenant began to reassert themselves. God had left the world, for a time. He would return, in the future, soon, to execute the judgments of the Day of the LORD. We note that the futurism remains; the Alpha is beginning to point to an Omega.

Though in apocalypticism the history-transcending mystery reappears, the world of time and men remains the scene of the cosmic drama. For the moment that world has fallen prey to the forces of chaos. The nations are in the grip of wicked hierarchies of evil that have the old chaos dragon, Satan, at their head. God was not active in the world now, but he was preparing for action here. He would not act by means of historical powers, as he did in the thinking of the old historically oriented covenant, but by means of his own supernatural agents: the Son of Man, Michael, the arch-angel, the heaven-ascended Elijah, and the Messiah, who is now given the full measure of his primordial divine dignity. God is coming to destroy the forces of chaos, to destroy the nations in their grip, to cleanse the whole earth, and to inaugurate a new creation that has no end. For this coming Israel must wait, be faithful, and endure martyrdom. The analogy to the story of the Exodus is clear; but the difference is more significant. And, of course, there is the analogy with the action of God in the Christian story; what apocalypticism anticipates as imminent is there said to have happened; or, to be more precise, to be in the process of happening.

The Christians who wrote the New Testament were a Jewish sect. They were sectarian because they took such a one-sided view of the relation of the two covenants to one another. For a moment they forgot about the paradoxical character of the relationship; and they thought that the full meaning of the historical could be fitted into the perspective of the eschatological, without remainder. They quickly began to discover that they were wrong; and the story of nineteen centuries of Christian history can be told as the story of the progressive discovery, exploration, and rectification of that initial mistake. Their retention of the Hebrew Bible has served the Christians well in this matter. They have thought and said that they retained it as the sign of a *praeparatio;* but, in fact, it has served as the source of their recovery of the knowledge of foundations that are enduring because they are paradoxical.

There are, indeed, two covenants in the Christian Bible. They are not the two covenants called Testaments, placed seriatim; the former in Hebrew, the latter in Greek. They are the two covenants that run through both the Old and New Testaments, the same throughout the entire Bible.

If all of this is so, it follows that the nature of the relationship between the two faiths is radically different from all traditional Christian statements of it. If both Judaism and Christianity always continue to revolve around the same two covenants that are paradoxically related to one another, then their relationship, whatever its tensions, is forever mutually interdependent; and their separation from each other is rooted in the paradoxical character of the interrelationship of the two covenants in which both participate. If that be the case, there is a basis for dialogue, something not located hitherto. Within each, from one period to the next, and between the two faiths in every period, there is then one question that will always be in season: How are (were) we (or they) dealing with the paradox of the two covenants?

NOTES TO CHAPTER FIVE

1. *Excursus on History and Eschatology*: In this paper history refers to the whole range of contingencies bound up with the interrelated natural and human processes of the temporal world. The dominant testimony of Jewish faith and its Scriptures is that God

is accomplishing the redemption of the world, and of mankind, in, through, and by means of the processes of nature and history. That is the meaning of creation. Therefore genealogy and chronology are so important in the Hebrew Bible; and that is also why it takes the form of a history.

Eschatology is a term invented by Christian theology to make the point that, for Christian faith, man's redemption has been achieved by God in Jesus Christ in such a manner or degree that it is no longer dependent upon the contingencies of time, nature, and history. Redemption has come, partly by means of, and partly despite, this created world. It has arrived in such transcendence and finality that the world is "overcome." Creation no longer serves as the means of redemption; for redemption has come. Nor can the "rebellion" of creation undo this redemption. So genealogies are abolished, circumcision is displaced by baptism, and history is relativized. That is, Jesus Christ, the event of redemption, becomes the foundation of a new Creation that is neither historical nor temporal. He is the eschatological End of history, an absolute whose meaning cannot be synthesized with the temporal world, not even with its Salvation History, however profoundly it may be related to it. That is, the relationship between history and eschatology is paradoxical.

If, as in the dominant strand of Jewish Scripture and tradition, God is accomplishing redemption by means of creation, notably by that facet of creation called history, happenings that serve as "signs" of this anticipated redemption, and are steps on the way to it, become a sort of a framework for a "History of Salvation." They illustrate the faith that God is really using creation as the means of redemption. They do not imply that he will cease to do so, or that his manner of doing so will change. Because this is precisely what did happen when the Christian community interpreted the career of Jesus as an eschatological event, this event cannot simultaneously be added to the series of events celebrated in Jewish Salvation History. To do so is to ignore the paradoxical relation between history and eschatology. In his book, *He That Cometh*, Sigmund Mowinckel observed this distinction very carefully. But Gerhard von Rad, in his *Old Testament Theology*, blurs it; and in so doing he obscures the difference between the two faiths, Judaism and Christianity.

2. The covenant with Abraham plays no independent role in the formation of Old Testament traditions. It simply pushes back to Israel's very beginning the inception of the notion of covenant. Thus it attests the importance attached to it. Later on, both in the New Testament and in post-canonical Judaism, it did come to be treated as a source of primary significance and status. In the New Testament and in Christian interpretation it is frequently set over against the covenant with Israel. Though one may object to the intention of this, there is a way in which it makes sense: the covenant with Abraham was a retrojection into the past of a notion of covenant corresponding very closely to that represented by the covenant with David, and not to that of the covenant with the confederacy of the people of Israel. As in the case of David, it is a covenant with a single individual; and, like the Davidic covenant, it consists essentially of a divine promise, without "conditions" or laws for its validation.

3. See, especially, the first essay in *The Problem of the Hexateuch and Other Essays*, trans. E. W. Trueman Dicken (London: Oliver and Boyd, 1966).

4. See, for example, Isa. 10:5ff.; Jeremiah 27; and, in a more redemptive sense, the role of Cyrus in Second Isaiah (45:1ff.). Consider also the famous "sermon" of Amos against the nations that surround Israel and the "Prophecies Against the Nations" in several of the prophetic books.

5. Thus the genealogies of Jesus in the Gospels, together with his circumcision, perform the function of indicating that both reach their fulfilment in him and henceforth cease to have meaning outside of him.

6. Martin Noth's *Überlieferungsgeschichtliche Studien* (Tübingen: Max Niemeyer Verlag, 1967) represents the basic resource for the materials embedded in the "Deuteronomic History."

7. It is an arresting fact that in Isa. 7:14 the formula for the royal son reads *Immanuel*, not *Immanuyah*; El is with us.

8. Sigmund Mowinckel's *The Psalms in Israel's Worship*, 2 vols. (Nashville: Abingdon Press, 1962), epitomizes pioneer research in this area.

6

THE OLD TESTAMENT CONCEPT OF
THE IMAGE OF GOD

JAMES I. COOK

Instructors in biblical Hebrew usually spend more time in the opening chapters of the book of Genesis than any of their colleagues on a theological faculty. That fact may explain, at least in part, their steady interest in the concept of the image of God. My colleague, Lester J. Kuyper, revealed his interest in this subject in "The Biblical Doctrine of Man," an article published in an early issue of the *Western Seminary Bulletin*.[1] Much shared teaching and many satisfying conversations during the past decade have served not only to carry his interest forward, but also to inspire and inform my own. This essay is offered with the hope that it will be both a contribution to a continuing dialogue in biblical theology and a vehicle of appreciation and tribute.

In view of the paucity of explicit reference in the Old Testament to the image of God, this statement may be in order: the importance of a biblical teaching is not necessarily in direct proportion to its frequency of appearance; or to borrow an axiom from the text critics, biblical texts are to be *weighed,* not *counted.* The fact is that what has been termed the "outstanding feature of the conception of man in the Old Testament,"[2] the pronouncement that man is created in God's image, appears in but four verses of the Old Testament! The complete texts from the book of Genesis are these:

> Then God said, "Let us make man in our image, after our likeness; and let them have dominion over the fish of the sea, and over the birds of the air, and over the cattle, and over all the earth, and over every creeping thing that creeps upon the earth." So God created man in his own image, in the image of God he created him; male and female he created them. (1:26, 27)

> This is the book of the generations of Adam. When God created man, he made him in the likeness of God. (5:1)

> Whoever sheds the blood of man, by man shall his blood be shed; for God made man in his own image. (9:6)

Not only is explicit mention of the image of God confined to the book of Genesis, but more particularly, it appears in only one of the documents judged to underlie that book; for Gen. 1:26, 27; 5:1; and 9:6 all belong to the Priestly source. The Yahwist's narrative in Gen. 2:4b-25, which contains a second creation account, knows nothing of the concept, and, with the possible exception of Psalm 8, no other Old Testament scripture mentions it. Moreover, the references outside Genesis 1 contribute relatively little to our understanding of the image. We are left then with Gen. 1:26, 27 as the central focus of our study.

These two verses are the climax toward which the Priestly creation narrative moves. The carefully worked out literary structure of this narrative is well known to every beginning student of biblical Hebrew. The pattern that time and again delivers him from complete frustration is *wayyō'mer 'elōhîm* ("and God said"), followed by a verb in the jussive ("let there be . . ."). With majestic cadence, vv. 3, 6, 9, 11, 14, 20, and 24 repeat this formula as the various parts of the creation take substance and shape in response to the creative word. At v. 26, however, the sequence is broken with dramatic suddenness: "Then God said, 'Let us make man in our image, after our likeness. . . .' So God created man in his own image, in the image of God he created him; male and female he created them." There is here nothing of the Yahwist's vivid anthropomorphism which portrays the creator as a potter taking dust from the ground and forming and shaping a man, and then blowing into his nostrils the breath of life. The Priestly writer belongs to that period of Israel's theology which emphasized the transcendence of God. His sense of the exaltation and unapproachable holiness of God led him to separate God from such direct contact with his creation. And yet it is the unique glory of this document that God and man are linked in a remarkable manner. First the reader encounters the prelude describing a divine self-deliberation, then the threefold use of the verb *bārā'* ("to create") whose subject in the Old Testament is God alone, and finally the enigmatic creation of man in the image and likeness of God himself.

Although the beauty of the entire section is such that any attempt to investigate it approaches literary vandalism, there are questions lurking just below the surface of that beauty. What, for example, is to be made of that troublesome pair of plurals, "us" and "our"? How is the idea of man's dominant place in the creation related to the image of God? And, above all, what is this writer saying about man when he describes him as created in the image (*ṣelem*) and after the likeness (*dᵉmut*) of God? The most promising approach toward an answer to these questions lies through a consideration of the terms *ṣelem* and *dᵉmut*. Three items of particular significance may be listed at once.

1. The terms *ṣelem* and *dᵉmut* are to be understood as a joint description of a single idea. As surveys of the history of the interpretation of the image of God show,[3] Christian interpreters disregarded this fact from the time of Irenaeus to the period of the Reformation. Then it was that both Luther[4] and Calvin[5]— apparently as the result of their knowledge of Hebrew parallelism—set aside the traditional theological distinction between *ṣelem* and *dᵉmut*. Apart from the matter of parallelism, however, the legitimacy of the traditional distinction between the two terms at 1:26 is denied decisively by their use in the subsequent Genesis passages. At 1:27 *ṣelem* is repeated twice while *dᵉmut* is not mentioned.

Genesis 5:1 looks back to the creation account with these words: "This is the book of the generations of Adam. When God created man, he made him in the likeness of God." Here $d^e mut$ is used without *ṣelem* to express the very concept of 1:26. At Gen. 9:6, *ṣelem* is used without $d^e mut$.

2. The image was not lost at the time of the Fall. That is, sin did not destroy the image. Had the Priestly writer meant to convey this, he would hardly have described man after the Flood as still in possession of the image of God (9:6). E. Jacob points out that "this from the outset puts the concept into the domain of anthropology and not into that of soteriology."[6]

3. The lexical data concerning *ṣelem* and $d^e mut$ must be given due consideration. L. Koehler derives the noun *ṣelem* from the verbal root *ṣlm,* meaning "to chisel." The substantive comes to denote a carved statue such as an idol. 2 Kings 11:18, for example, records how "all the people of the land went to the house of Baal, and tore it down; his altars and his images (*ṣᵉlāmîm*) they broke in pieces." The word is also used to indicate a facsimile or copy, and in the single instance of Ezek. 23:14, a drawing or engraving, probably to be understood as a bas-relief ("she saw men portrayed upon the wall, the images (*ṣᵉlāmîm*) of the Chaldeans portrayed in vermillion"). These passages argue that *ṣelem* is a concrete term. Paul Humbert arrives at a similar conclusion after an exhaustive investigation of the language: "The semantic verdict is perfectly definite: man, according to P, has the same 'outward' appearance as the deity of whom he is the tangible effigy, and the noun *ṣelem* refers to no spiritual likeness in this case any more than in the others."[7]

The term $d^e mut$ is derived from the root *dmh,* which means "to be like, to resemble." The substantive signifies "similarity, likeness." The most illuminating example of this usage is contained in the first chapter of Ezekiel. Here $d^e mut$ is used at least nine times to underline the approximate nature of the correspondence between the writer's description of the enthroned universal Lord and the reality. The heaviest concentration of this usage is in v. 26: "And above the firmament over their heads there was the likeness ($d^e mut$) of a throne, in appearance like sapphire; and seated above the likeness ($d^e mut$) of a throne was a likeness ($d^e mut$) as it were of a human form." On the basis of his examination of this passage and other Old Testament appearances, Koehler concludes that the function of $d^e mut$ is clear: "It serves everywhere to weaken a similarity."[8] It has in his opinion the same force in Gen. 1:26. Man is created in the form (*Gestalt*) of God, but not entirely so; but only in a diminished degree. The use of $d^e mut$ by the Priestly writer in effect weakens and tempers the excessively concrete material meaning suggested by *ṣelem.*

We are now in a position to raise the essential question of how these facts are to be interpreted. Koehler, taking his stand strictly on the meaning of the word *ṣelem,* understands the image of God to consist in man's upright form (*die aufrechte Gestalt*).[9] "Only on linguistic grounds," he writes in another place, "can the explanation be offered that God creates man in such a way that he alone in contrast to the beasts has an upright form. In this respect man is clearly distinguished from the beast and with the additional words 'in our form, to look like us' is raised above the beasts and made to approach nearer to God."[10] How is the Priestly writer's use of such a concrete term for God as ṣelem to be explained? Koehler describes the concept of the image of God as the special bequest of this writer and on that basis hazards the opinion that it is then probably an innovation (Neuschöpfung) of that writer himself.[11] In the light of the fact that the Priestly writer is precisely the one whose theological concerns move away from the material, it is difficult to accept this suggestion. As W. Eichrodt says, "It is he [the author of the Priestly document] who better than any other writer knows how to convey vividly, both here and elsewhere, the absolute otherness and transcendence of the divine nature, he who eliminates all trace of anthropomorphism from his theophanies, and acknowledges no angel to mediate between God and Man because of his strict refusal to bring the divine realm down into the sphere of the creaturely."[12] It is, therefore, far more plausible to assume that ṣelem is a term that the writer inherited from an ancient source in which the image of God may well have been viewed with considerable concreteness. This hypothesis claims support both from the Old Testament stories of God appearing in human form (to Abraham in Genesis 18; to Jacob in Gen. 32:24ff.) and from such Akkadian accounts of the creation of man as the Epic of Gilgamesh.

We may further suppose that the Priestly writer did not choose to reject the term altogether because of its usefulness in helping him to express man's role in creation as the bearer of God's image. Von Rad, for example, thinks that Gen. 1:26 "speaks less of the nature of God's image than of its purpose. There is less said about the gift itself than about the task."[13] One must certainly agree with this observation to the extent that the consequence of the image is made far more explicit than its nature: "Then God said, 'Let us make man in our image, after our likeness; and let them have dominion over the fish of the sea, and over the birds of the air, and over the cattle, and over all the earth, and over every creeping thing that creeps upon the earth'" (1:26). The Hebrew verb rendered "let them have dominion" is the strong word used in Joel 3:13 (MT, 4:13) to express the treading or trampling upon grapes in the winepress. This same point is made in Psalm 8—sometimes described as Genesis 1 set to music—where man is also brought into daring proximity to God by the phrase, "Thou hast caused him to lack a little in comparison with God ('elōhîm); and Thou hast crowned him with glory (kābôd) and dignity (hādār)," terms used of the royal majesty of God himself in Ps. 145:5 and of the king in Ps. 21:5. This royal description of man is followed immediately by a description of his realm, which plainly echoes Gen. 1:26: "Thou hast given him dominion over the works of thy hands; thou hast put all things under his feet, all sheep and oxen, and also the beasts of the field, the birds of the air, and the fish of the sea, whatever passes along the paths of the sea" (vv. 6-8). This picture of man as

God's vice-regent is to be related to the concrete aspect of *ṣelem* in Genesis. "The ancient orient," says E. Jacob, "shows us with ever increasing clarity that the purpose and function of an image consists in representing someone. . . . The king had his image set up in the remote provinces of his empire which he could not visit in person. Assyrian inscriptions often repeat the ritual phrase: 'I will set up my statue in their midst.' "[14] It seems perfectly understandable, therefore, that the Priestly writer, who saw this representative function assigned not to a statue but to man, should express this teaching by the retention of the concrete term *ṣelem*.

As we have seen above, however, it was not possible for this man to speak of a physical copy of God without immediately weakening the conception by the addition of *dᵉmut*. Furthermore, we would expect a man with his theological interest not only to reduce the material content of *ṣelem*, but to deepen its theological content as well. That is to say, this writer must be read with more than lexicon in hand. If this document were simply historical in nature, pure lexicography might suffice. But since its preeminent concern is with theology, lexical data alone are not adequate. Does not the great Hebrew lexicographer himself hint at as much? Is it really on lexical grounds that Koehler concludes that man's erect posture makes him "to approach nearer to God"? In that phrase does he not—without denying the realistic meaning of *ṣelem*—open the door to a less physical, less visible and deeper interpretation of God's image? Would he not agree with Eichrodt that this writer "was bound to try to comprehend *ṣelem* in a wider sense, to advance from the idea of a tangible image to that of a parabolic similarity"?[15]

The tantalizing vagueness of such expressions as "to approach nearer to God" and "parabolic similarity" are enticements to press on to still clearer definitions. Otto Piper, with characteristic insight, discerns the following theological content of the image of God:

> First of all, this figure of speech implies that unlike its original, an image does not have life in itself. The human life lacks the creativity and absolute self-determination of God. Secondly, the degree of correspondence between the original and the image is limited by the nature of the material out of which the image is made. No divine perfection is found in man. Thirdly, all the specific features of the image correspond to features of the original. Thus man is described in the Bible as a being that is able in the mode of receptivity to respond adequately to every one of God's redemptive dealings with him.... The God of the Bible is not just perfect reality, plus personality. Rather he is a personal being who both enables man to have communion with him and whose ultimate purpose in creating a world is the accomplishment of this communion. That is to say, it is of the very essence of God to will this communion, and it is of the very essence of man to be made for this communion.[16]

Is there evidence to support an interpretation of the image of God which understands it in terms of personal relationship? F. Horst has drawn attention to a passage in the famous Mesopotamian hero legend, the Epic of Gilgamesh, in which the goddess Aruru is called upon to fashion a counterpart, a likeness, a correspondent (*Entsprechnis*) of the hero Gilgamesh. He observes that despite significant differences the Bible's language parallels the ancient Mesopotamian legend in that it defines that which makes man man as "that which corresponds to" God: "Man as the image and likeness of God is the vis-à-vis (*Gegenüber*) of God in the same manner as, in Gen. 2:20, the woman is a helpmeet 'as over against' (*im Gegenüber*) the man, corresponding to him and suitable to him. Just as man needs and should have a vis-à-vis, one corresponding to him, so God also will have a vis-à-vis, one corresponding to him, an image and a likeness."[17]

While accepting with appreciation Horst's evidence from the Gilgamesh Epic, his exegetical comments on Genesis appear vulnerable at two points. First, he in effect permits the Gen. 2:20 passage from the Yahwist's account ("a helper fit for him") to control his understanding of the image of God which, as we have seen, is a peculiar mark of the Priestly document. And second, although the linguistic parallel between Gen. 1:26 and 2:20 is perfectly clear when transposed into the German *Gegenüber* and *im Gegenüber* respectively, it is actually nonexistent in the Hebrew, which has *beṣalmēnû kideᵐûthēnû* in the one and *'ēzer keneḡdô* in the other.

It is, therefore, preferable to base the interpretation of the image of God as personal relationship on Israel's covenant faith and the theological context of the Priestly writer. Th. C. Vriezen rightly says that a "correct understanding of the doctrine of the Creation, a doctrine which figures especially in the Priestly Code, can only be attained on the basis of the Old Testament belief in Yahweh, the Saviour-God, who stands in a Covenant-relation with His people. For God, the Creator, is the same God whom Israel has come to know in its history as the Saviour."[18] The Old Testament has little concern for what we might call a general anthropology; but when man in general is mentioned, as in the creation account, he is naturally considered in the light of Israel's covenant faith as being in relation to God.

Moreover, if we ask in what form the divine nature was revealed to the Priestly writer, it becomes clear that in his account of creation everything is centered on the word. As we noted at the outset, the linguistic frame upon which his creation narrative is hung is "and God said" (*wayyō'mer 'elōhîm*). As Eichrodt points out:

> What Israel, through God's self-communication in the covenant, had experienced as the fundamental character of the divine nature, and had ever more deeply comprehended as such in her historical experience of his sovereignty, namely the personhood of the God who thus dealt with her, the Priestly writer now succeeds in bringing vividly to life as the determining force behind the process of creation. In the light of the position allotted to Man within the created order the Creator is seen as a personal Thou who discloses himself for purpose of fellowship with his noblest creature; and from this personal Thou every being that wears a human face takes its stamp. For Man to be created in the likeness of God's image can only mean that on him, too, personhood is bestowed as

the definitive characteristic of his nature. He has a share in the person-hood of God; and as a being capable of self-awareness and of self-deter-mination he is open to the divine address and capable of responsible conduct. This quality of personhood shapes the totality of his psycho-physical existence; it is this which comprises the essentially human, and distinguishes him from all other creatures.[19]

At this point we may also take note of an exegesis of Gen. 1:26, 27 that not only supports this understanding of the image of God, but also may cast light on the perplexing plurals of v. 26.[20] This approach focuses on the final phrase of v. 27, "male and female he created them," and asks, What does "male and female" mean in this context? It is natural to think immediately in terms of sex and the propagation of the race. Yet, those matters appear to be reserved for v. 28 where a special word of blessing is followed by the imperative, "Be fruitful and multiply!"[21] It is instructive to notice how closely the phrase "male and female" is joined to the concept of the image of God in v. 27: "So God created man in his own image, in the image of God he created him; male and female he created them." If male and female are not here intended to describe distinction of sex and the possibility of propagation, then it is possible that they belong to the description of the image of God. They then symbolize the basic truth about humanity: as the bearer of God's image, man is set not only in per-sonal relationship with God, but also in personal relationship with his fellowman. And if the heart of the image is differentiation and personal relationship, the plurals hint at the same thing in God.

The understanding of the image of God embraced in this study suggests not only why the Old Testament teaches that man has retained the image of God, but also why the concept is not explicitly mentioned beyond the opening chapters of Genesis. If the image means the gift of personal relationship, of an I-Thou encounter, of man's unique ability to hear and respond to the word God addresses to him, then the image has not been lost. God and man are so inex-tricably related in the Old Testament that it is impossible for the writers to say anything about man without at the same time making an affirmation about God. To think of man as creature is to affirm that God is Creator. To say man is sinner is to affirm that God is Judge. To say man is redeemed is to affirm that God is Redeemer. Thus, by teaching that man has been created in the image of God the Old Testament affirms that man is in an I-Thou relationship as creature with Creator. The Fall did not remove that basic relationship but added to it a new dimension, for man is now not only in a creature-Creator relationship, but also in a sinner-Judge relationship. Similarly, the experience of redemption adds yet another dimension, for by it man is brought into the happy relationship of redeemed and Redeemer. In the final analysis, the Old Testament is about man in these three relationships to God. There was no need for its writers to labor the concept of the image of God, then, for it is everywhere assumed.

It was most probably this common assumption combined with the new and all-embracing significance of Jesus Christ that freed the first Christian writers to develop what may be called the New Testament concept of the image of God. At its core is not the confession that man is made in the image of God, but rather the proclamation that Christ *is* the image of God. To this category belong 2 Cor. 4:4, Col. 1:15, and probably Heb. 1:3.[22] In these passages Christ is in the foreground and if there is any carry-over from the Old Testament concept it is via the assumption that, having been made man, he naturally possessed the characteristics of *'ādām* of Genesis 1, and in the fact that he demonstrated what man is when he is in an unbroken relationship with God. At the same time, once the identification between Christ and the image of God was made the concept was inevitably shifted from its original locus in the doctrine of creation to that of redemption. When man-in-sin was measured against Christ as the Second Adam, the full expression of both man and God, the image was understood in terms of restoration either to the image or likeness of God or of his Son. To this category belong Rom. 8:29, 1 Cor. 15:49, 2 Cor. 3:18, Col. 3:10, and its parallel, Eph. 4:24. In the case of the last two passages named it is important to notice that they occur, not in the doctrinal, but in the hortatory divisions of Colossians and Ephesians. That is, they are descriptive of people who have been placed in a new relationship with God in Christ and who, therefore, will also live daily in new relationships with their human partners in the new covenant.[23]

The New Testament passages that most directly restate the Old Testament concept of the image of God are 1 Cor. 11:7 and Jas. 3:9. In the former Paul writes: "For a man ought not to cover his head, since he is the image and glory of God; but woman is the glory of man." On the basis of Gen. 1:26, the Apostle declares that man is the image (*eikōn*) of God. Paul is here at one with the writer of the first creation account in appealing to the image as indicative of man's exalted status in the creation. But he diverges from that writer when, in the interest of differentiating between man and woman in the sense of husband and wife (*anēr* and *gunē*), he applies image (*eikōn*) only to the husband.[24]

It is only at Jas. 3:9, then, that we encounter what S. V. McCasland calls "an unspeculative affirmation of the Old Testament conception that man is created in the image of God."[25] The text reads: "With it [the tongue] we bless the Lord and Father, and with it we curse men, who are made in the likeness (*homoiōsis*) of God." Here is a clear reference to Gen. 1:26, 27. As in the source itself, so in the reference, there is no information provided as to the content of the image or likeness. Only the context implies that there is sufficient similarity between "the Lord and Father" and "men, who are made in the likeness of God" to render it improper to bless the one and curse the other with the same tongue. Finally, the simple repetition of the Old Testament concept (only here in the New Testament) without explanation implies that the understanding assumed in the bulk of the Old Testament was also assumed in the New. There is, then, a theological correspondence between the testaments in the sense that the New Testament begins with the Old Testament view that as bearer of the image and likeness of God, man is by creation in a creature-Creator relationship;

and by the Fall in a sinner-Judge relationship with God. To this Old Testament confession is added its own glad proclamation that the gospel of Jesus Christ is addressed precisely to this sinful creature and that those who respond to this divine address discover themselves to be in a redeemed-Redeemer relationship with God as they are progressively "conformed to the image of his Son."

NOTES TO CHAPTER SIX

1. 4, no. 3 (December 1950), 7-10.
2. Th. C. Vriezen, *An Outline of Old Testament Theology*, 2d ed., rev. and enl. (Oxford: Basil Blackwell, 1970), p. 171.
3. See, e.g., E. Brunner, *Man in Revolt* (London: Lutterworth Press, 1939), pp. 93f., and K. Barth, *CD*, III.1, pp. 192ff.
4. *Lectures on Genesis: Chapters 1-5*, in *Luther's Works*, I, ed. Jaroslav Pelikan (Saint Louis: Concordia Publishing House, 1958), 60f.
5. *Commentaries on the First Book of Moses called Genesis*, trans. J. King (Edinburgh: Calvin Translation Society, 1847), I, 93f.
6. *Theology of the Old Testament*, trans. A. W. Heathcote and P. J. Allcock (New York: Harper & Row, 1958), p. 166.
7. *Études sur le récit du Paradis et de la chute dans la Genèse* (Neuchâtel: Secrétariát de l'Université, 1940), p. 147.
8. "Die Grundstelle der Imago-Dei-Lehre, Genesis 1:26," *TZ*, 4 (1948), 21.
9. *Ibid.*, p. 20.
10. *Old Testament Theology*, trans. A. S. Dodd (London: Lutterworth Press, 1957), p. 147.
11. "Die Grundstelle," p. 20.
12. *Theology of the Old Testament*, trans. J. A. Baker (London: SCM Press, 1967), II, 123f. See also D. J. A. Clines, "The Image of God in Man," *Tyndale Bulletin*, 19 (1968), 88f.
13. *Genesis*, trans. John Marks (Philadelphia: Westminster Press, 1961), p. 57. Cf. also Clines in the article cited in footnote 12: "The image is to be understood not so much ontologically as existentially: it comes to expression not in the nature of man so much as in his activity or function. This function is to represent God's lordship to the lower orders of creation. The dominion of man over creation can hardly be excluded from the content of the image itself. Mankind, which means both the human race and individual men, do not cease to be the image of God so long as they remain men; to be human and to be the image of God are not separable" (p. 101).
14. *Op. cit.*, p. 167.
15. *Op. cit.*, II, 124.
16. "The Biblical Understanding of Man," *Theology Today*, 1 (1944), 191.
17. "Face to Face," *Interpretation*, 4 (1950), 265.
18. *Op. cit.*, p. 170. Cf. H. Berkhof, *De mens onderweg: een Christelijke mensbeschouwing* ('s-Gravenhage: Boekencentrum, 1962), pp. 26-41.
19. *Op. cit.*, II, 126.
20. K. Barth, *CD*, III.1, pp. 191-206. Especially pertinent are these comments from p. 192: "The well-known decision of early exegesis was that we have in Gen. 1:26 a reference to the divine triunity. It may be objected that this statement is rather too explicit. The saga undoubtedly speaks of a genuine plurality in the divine being, but it does not actually say that it is a Trinity. On the other hand, it may be stated that an approximation to the Christian doctrine of the Trinity—the picture of a God who is the one and only God, yet who is not for that reason solitary, but includes in Himself the differentiation and relationship of I and Thou—is both nearer to the text and does it more justice than the alternative suggested by modern exegesis in its arrogant rejection of the exegesis of the Early Church."
21. On this point see G. von Rad, *Genesis*, pp. 58f.
22. Although in Heb. 1:3 the vocabulary has shifted from *eikōn* or *homoiōsis* to *charaktēr*, the thought appears to be the same.
23. Cf., on Col. 3:10, the remarks of G. Kittel (*TDNT*, II, 397): "Here it is quite clear that restoration of the divine likeness of creation is identical with the establishment of

fellowship with Christ. The Colossian passage also shows us once more how slight is Paul's interest in mythical speculation and how strong is his concern for the supremely concrete ethical consequences of this restoration of the *eikōn*, namely, that we should put off fornication, blasphemy and lying (v. 5, 8, 9)."

24. Cf. S. V. McCasland, "The Image of God according to Paul," *JBL*, 69 (1950), 85f., who suggests that Paul's apparent restriction of the image of God to the man (as over against the woman) cannot be maintained from Genesis 1 where the Hebrew *'ādām* refers to man in the generic sense.

25. See the article cited in footnote 23, p. 93.

7

DEUTERONOMY:

Exemplar of a Non-Sacerdotal Appropriation of Sacred History*

SIMON J. DE VRIES

Joining friends and associates of Lester J. Kuyper in a venture of much-deserved felicitation, the present writer would undertake to present some distillations from his own research touching upon themes of major importance in Professor Kuyper's labors within the area of biblical theology. A life-long concern on the part of our honored colleague has been the nature of the Old Testament's authority for the Christian church, the identification of an essential principle linking the two parts of the sacred canon. Another has been Protestantism's use of Scripture, a testing of its claim and endeavor to be faithful to God's word preserved in the Bible. Lester J. Kuyper knows as well as any, and better than many, that *ecclesia reformata* must ever be *ecclesia reformanda,* "according to the word of God."

The present essay is not primarily about Deuteronomy; it is about sacred history, Deuteronomy being raised up as one unique, peculiarly influential exponent of the ongoing relevance of sacred history. We shall have observations to make about various conceptions of sacred history within the Christian church, as measured on the basis of Deuteronomy; but what we say about the church, the New Testament, and Deuteronomy itself will all be seen from the perspective of our own extensive analysis of time and history in the Old Testament, which appeared during 1975 under the title, *Yesterday, Today and Tomorrow.*[1]

What is to be said here is intended as a serious effort to stimulate churchmen of various persuasions to re-examine their respective theologies in the light of Scripture's own approach to a matter of central concern. Nothing is more central to the Bible—Old or New Testament—than sacred history, i.e., the saving/judging presence and action of God in the meaningful events of human life. The church has appropriated it in a variety of ways. For some Christians it remains alive, preserving its authority, while for others it has become a hallowed but powerless

---

*Developed from a colloquium at The Ecumenical Institute for Advanced Theological Studies, Jerusalem, April 9, 1973 (S. J. DeV.).

memory. Little wonder, in view of the Bible's own internal variety, prooftext material for every ideology! We on our part have no intent of making an apologia for any one writing or group of writings, any more than we intend to make an apologia for one form of Christianity over against other forms. The sole purpose is to clarify affinities and promote self- and mutual understanding.

I

It is no longer necessary to ask whether the Bible has its own peculiar language. There are few informed scholars who would undertake to defend the misconstructions of Thorleif Boman, John Marsh, and the Kittel Dictionary over against the penetrating criticisms of James Barr.[2] Sound linguistic methodology demolishes the notion that the Bible has its own sacred language. It is not biblical language, but the Bible's use of language that is unique. Accordingly, it is not biblical words for time, but the biblical understanding of what these words mean, i.e., the biblical perception of the factors that make time meaningful, that is different.

In the wide-ranging debate over the meaning of history for Christian theology, various polarities have been proposed, such as "God's history" versus "man's history," "superhistory" versus secular event, "linear time" versus "cyclical time"; but none of these seems to be fully satisfactory. On the basis of the present writer's very detailed examination of prominent but neglected terminology involving the Old Testament word *yôm,* "day," a more appropriate differentiation must be suggested. The only truly meaningful distinction that can be applied to the biblical data—one that is thoroughly scientific from the point of view of linguistic methodology—is that between what we would call a *quantitative* and a *qualitative* approach to the phenomenon of time. As we explain each of these, it will become apparent that it is the latter, the qualitative approach, that most centrally underlies biblical historiography, parenesis, and eschatology, where the charismatic impulse comes to expression and where the central concern is with *Heilsgeschichte,* sacred history. But it is not implied that either of these approaches appears in isolation in any given genre of biblical literature. As a matter of fact, the two depend upon and complement each other. The question is, Which of the two predominates and is more central and decisive in those documents that provide the core of biblical tradition? Which of the two characterizes most essentially God's action in human events and makes meaningful man's response in awareness of the transcendent imperative created by this action?

To avoid cumbersomeness, we shall henceforward use the terms "quantitative time" and "qualitative time" as shorthand substitutes, in full acknowledgment that these are not separate ontological entities but subjective modes of apprehension. We ask first, What is quantitative time? This is time as a quantum, something to be counted up and measured out. Days are seen as units of time that can be related numerically to one another, put into patterns of recurrence or similarity, brought into correlation with smaller or larger units. Quantitative time can be linear or cyclical, depending on whether emphasis is placed on the coincidence or the differentiation between time-units. Inevitably, quantitative time undergirds the organizational and institutional aspects of life, whether the sacral or the secular. It is the manageableness or serviceability of time that stands in the foreground. Quantitative time guarantees order and predictability. And where in the Old Testament does it predominate? In the language of wisdom and the language of the cult. This should be no surprise, for the concern of wisdom discourse is to define, and thus control, the vastly variegated but regularly recurring phenomena of human experience, while the concern of all cultic literature is to define, and thus control, all that belongs to institutional religion, wherein the otherwise irrational, threatening world of deity is brought into the service of man.

As we designate cultic language and wisdom language as prime exemplars of a quantitative approach to time, we do not lose from sight the relative place within them of qualitative time. This approach sees the uniqueness rather than the commonness of temporal event, emphasizing the special character of each separate occurrence, as once-for-all meaningful in itself. Cultic language does distinguish the special character of certain days and times, emphasizing in particular the sharp separation between holy and secular seasons; but its central concern is to regularize the sacred days, creating rituals and calendars for their appropriate observance. Wisdom language, for its part, distinguishes the various sorts or categories of temporal experience, emphasizing the distinctive quality of each *kind* of time. Here it is the species, not the individual (to use a biological analogy), that is significant. The purpose of wisdom discourse is regularization, control. The times are identified only to be classified. Wisdom's attention is on the principles of universality that relativize each event and make it part of a manageable whole.

Since it is not possible, within the limits of a short essay, to give adequate illustration of the Bible's rich stock of cultic and wisdom concepts, a single example of each must suffice. The cultic example needs no elucidation; it speaks for itself. Leviticus 23 is priestly regulation for Israel's festivals, woven in a tight pattern of time-specifications, the concern of it all being to keep each element of ritual in correct sequence. What is to be done on each separate day is important, but still more vital is *when* what is done is done.

The wisdom example is perhaps the most extreme that one can find: Ecclesiastes 3. In this familiar and much-discussed passage the distinct times are set in parallelism with each other, but in such a way that the one cancels out the other: "A time to be born, and a time to die; a time to plant, and a time to pluck up what is planted; a time to kill, and a time to heal;" etc. Inevitably comes the summation (v. 9): "What gain has the worker from his toil?" For Qoheleth the uniqueness of historical event has no purpose. Everything falls into a meaningless pattern of opposites. Man "cannot find out what God has done from the beginning to the end" (v. 11).

The essence of the *qualitative* apprehension of time is, however, an awareness that God *has* done something "from the beginning to the end." One day is not simply related, numerically or categorically, to another day. Rather, each day is seen as transcendently significant in itself; i.e., each is seen as at least potentially revelatory of God's purpose. A day may be different from all other days, not only because it may be the occasion of a decisive event in the history of men and nations, but because it may be the opportunity for crucial confrontation between God and man.

The various days in the past when Yahweh has performed his judging and saving acts are memorialized in Israel's *heilsgeschichtliche* tradition. There was a day of Israel's election (Deut. 9:24; Ezek. 16:4f.), a day of plague on Egypt (Exod. 10:13), a day of crossing the sea (Exod. 12:17), a day (or days) of the giving of quails (Num. 11:32), a day for the dedication of the tabernacle (Num. 9:15), a day of the giving of the law (Deut. 4:10), a day of victory over the Amorites (Josh. 10:12). Many passages speak of Israel's greatest day, the day when Yahweh brought them out of Egypt (Judg. 19:30; 1 Sam. 8:8; 2 Sam. 7:6; Isa. 11:16; Jer. 7:22; 11:4, 7; 31:32; 34:13; Hos. 2:17; Ps. 78:42), while other passages mention days of Israel's past judgment (Num. 32:10; Isa. 31:15; 34:12; Hos. 10:14; Obad. 11, 14; Zech. 14:3; Ps. 78:9; 95:8; 137:7; Lam. 1:12; 2:1, 21f.; 1 Chron. 28:6), also days when Israel's neighbors received God's judgment (cf. "the day of Midian," Isa. 9:4). But there were new days of salvation for Israel (Hag. 2:15, 18f.; Zech. 4:10; 8:9), even as there are recurrent days of special relief for individual believers within Israel, celebrated in the psalms of declarative praise (Ps. 18:18; 20:2; 59:17; 77:3; 138:3; 140:8; Lam. 3:57). On this model, new, unique days of divine help and divine punishment can continually be expected, and it is this that Israel's parenetic and eschatological literature has in view.

It is important to understand that prophetic eschatology is the situational counterpart of sacred historiography, projecting the future from the past, the unknown from the known. Though our argument does not depend on it, it is helpful to realize that the Hebraic terminology of time reflects this correspondence. Time for the Hebrews is more two- than three-dimensional. That is to say, to a greater degree than in Western languages several identical words are used with reference to the future and the past: *'āz* and *bā'ēt hahî'* refer to unspecified time in the past or future; *bayyôm hahû'* refers to the time of a definite past or future event; *'ôlām* refers to remote time in the past or future. The past and the future are analogically related to each other, both being measurably distant from *'attâ*, "now," *hayyôm*, "today"—the present moment from which all human experience is viewed.

This enables us to see why prophecy cannot be divorced from historiography. Today's researchers know far better than previous generations of critics the extent of prophecy's indebtedness to the historical tradition. We now see that the prophets, specially admired by historicistic criticism for their irruptive novelty, stood very much in the midst of their people and the nation's situation, drawing from the past to elicit responsible behavior in the present and in the immediate future. It is with this awareness that we must seek a solution to the day of Yahweh problem and the entire question of eschatology. The transcendent surprise of Amos' speech about the day of Yahweh (5:18-20) lay not in the fact that there would be such a day or that Israel's god would come in judgment, but that his judgment would be a threat to Israel. Israel expected a decisive coming day because they remembered many decisive days in the past.

These considerations lead us now to make a confident surmise respecting the practical purpose of historiography on the one hand and prophetic eschatology on the other. Both have this identical pastoral concern: to awaken God's people in a present moment of crisis, calling them to repentance and decision—or, if the announcement be of God's saving purpose, to awaken them to trust and hope, the proper fruits of repentance. In other words, historiography and eschatology may be taken as forms of exhortation or parenesis.

II

What we desire to say next has to do directly with Deuteronomy. This is a strange book within the Old Testament canon. It occupies a mid-place between historiography and prophecy. Although it rehearses the past (especially in chaps. 1-3, 5) and forecasts the future (in chaps. 4, 28ff.), it is massively concerned with the present. That is, apart from the lawbook contained in 12:1-26:15, Deuteronomy is a solid piece of parenesis, being shaped to move Israel to responsible decision in a recurring moment of crisis. As the historiographic literature— particularly those writings that come from the time of "pansacrality" (the time prior to Israel's emergence as a nation)—contains numerous interpretive statements with the phrase *bayyôm hahû'*, "on that day," and as the prophetic books contain numerous occurrences of *bayyôm hahû'*, epitomizing God's future, the Deuteronomic parenesis contains frequent appeals with the word *hayyôm*, "today."[3] A crucial present day occurs again and again and again, always combining a rehearsal of Yahweh's saving/judging action with an urgent appeal for Israel's definitive choice. Yahweh's demand stands prominently in view in what we have called "the promulgation formula," ". . . as I have commanded you *hayyôm*," which occurs no fewer than twenty-five times in Deuteronomy.[4] The pareneticist dramatizes Israel's choice in overwhelming urgency, most strikingly no doubt in the climactic verses, 30:15ff.: "See, I have set before you *hayyôm* life and good, death and evil. If you obey the commandments of Yahweh your God which I command you *hayyôm*, . . . you shall live and multiply. . . . But if your heart turns away, . . . I declare to you *hayyôm*, that you shall perish. . . . I call heaven and earth to witness against you *hayyôm*; . . . therefore choose life!"

It has become apparent to scholars using modern methodology that the long-fought-over book of Deuteronomy does not derive from the time of Moses but from a much later period. Following Albrecht Alt and Gerhard von Rad, we however join an emerging consensus in fixing its origin, not in Judah and in the reign of Josiah, as was held by Wellhausenian criticism, but in northern Israel shortly after the political collapse of Samaria. It is important to recognize a long and complex compositional process. Not only are there core materials—in particular, the lawbook—and late redactional elements, but one may discern distinct layers within the central parenesis,[5] reflecting a situation of renewed confrontation between God and his people.

Each "today" was crucial, though no "today" was final. This is completely in accord with the time-concept of Israel's sacred historiography and explains the meaning of prophetic eschatology. As God has had various decisive days in the past, he now renews the present day of decision. His action cannot be confined to one single time within history (a deistic, docetic notion) because every time may be his time of action. This is to say that every time is also man's moment of responsible choice since he stands constantly under the awareness that God will act savingly or judgingly according to his own—man's—response. This is history, God acting sovereignly in judgment and salvation; not in majestic aloneness but in intimate interaction with responsible man, each being bound to the other in mutual obligation.

Deuteronomy is thus a crystallization of repeated parenetical appeal, God's word ever renewed, continually calling man to choose life and blessing. The question that arises next is about its *Sitz im Leben*. In what formal setting and spiritual situation was the Deuteronomic parenesis made? Artur Weiser, Gerhard von Rad, and others have speculated that Israel observed an annual covenant-renewal festival, but this has been questioned by those who have argued that no single biblical passage points unequivocally to it. Weak as the *argumentum e silentio* may be, it is nevertheless difficult to explain the Deuteronomic parenesis on any other basis. It must be in some setting wherein the people presented themselves as morally responsible before God, and an authoritative spokesman ("Moses") presented God's demand and appeal, that it could have had any meaning. Whether or not its setting can be called liturgical may be decided, perhaps, through consideration of the very Deuteronomy-like appeal of Psalm 95. True, the covenant is not expressly mentioned here, but a covenant relationship and covenant obligation clearly are. This psalm is liturgy and a model for liturgy. In vv. 1-5 a priest/liturgist summons the worshiping congregation to praise Yahweh for his lordship over nature; then, in vv. 6-7a, renewing his summons, he shifts to a confession of the covenant bond. Suddenly, in vv. 7bff., the liturgist becomes a pareneticist, plaintively appealing to the same worshiping, covenant-bound congregation to respond otherwise on the present day of decision than a previous generation had responded in another time and place: *"Hayyôm*—if you

would obey his voice—do not harden your hearts as at Meribah, as on the day of
testing in the desert!"

III

Meagre as the evidence it offers may be, this psalm makes clear that parenesis
did have a place in Israel's formal liturgy. Thus we cannot avoid inferring that
liturgy was the proper setting for parenesis whenever and wherever it occurred.
This is true to some extent of prophetic preaching too. Though, without question,
the prophets felt free to speak outside the shrine locale, we know that there were
cult prophets and that every prophet had at least a theoretical right to speak in,
to, or even against the shrines. This is to say that, while covenant parenesis and
oracular prophecy may at times have been forcibly excluded from liturgy, even
from the cultic precincts, both had a normal, rightful role within it. How much
of a role is hard to say. We may confidently suppose that sacrificial ritual continued to occupy the dominant place so long as the temple survived. But it was
the recitation of sacred history, parenesis, and oracular prophecy that preserved
what was truly distinctive and constitutive in Israel's religion, namely, her awareness of Yahweh's past, present, and future action within her historical experience.
Sacrificial ritual, based essentially upon a cyclical, quantitative control of time,
celebrated that which is *timeless* in God. The *timely,* the unique, the historically
revelatory were rehearsed in liturgical recitation or given current relevance in
parenesis and prophecy.

In which area, then, are we to place Israel's festival cult? First, let it be
observed that strikingly little of the Old Testament's qualitative description of
time turns out to belong to the ritual of the annual festivals. Second, let us ponder
the fact that these festivals were calibrated to natural phenomena, namely, the
cycles of the sun and moon and the agricultural seasons. They had indeed been
raised up, to some extent, from pre-Yahwistic agricultural myth, and at least the
Mazzoth/Passover feast had been historicized through an explicit association with
the deliverance from Egypt. But even this festival represents a compromise as
much as a triumph, exhibiting the tendency of cultic institutionalism to reduce
the historically unique to something regularized and manageable. When the
saving act of God comes to be memorialized in a sacramental ritual, it has subjected itself to a repetitive pattern that may lead, in the hands of small-minded
defenders of the establishment, to mere repetition for its own sake.[6] The divine
may become confined within the apparatus of the sacramental cult, no longer
challenging man to historical responsibleness before the sovereign demands of an
omnipresent God, but soothing man with an assurance that God is somehow at
his own disposal, elicitable through the correct cultic manipulation that is the
secret of priests.

Some may wish to argue that biblical Israel never went so far as this. The
claim is eminently debatable. Surely in primitive times numerous Israelites were,

in fact, tempted by pagan worship, whose spiritual appeal has been carefully described in the foregoing sentences. To what degree official Yahwism succumbed may only be inferred. Relevant texts are passages from the prophets in which the cult is denounced. Amos may have wanted to abolish it completely, though the majority of prophets attempted only to reform it. Was it because of its eclecticism that they thundered against it? A clue may be found in Jeremiah's famous temple sermon (chap. 7). Whereas the people thought that the temple and its ritual guaranteed Yahweh's favoring presence, Jeremiah knew that only their moral response to the covenant demand could guarantee Yahweh's favor, and thus preserve their temple. Prophecy understands all too well how the institutional cult tends to stifle a personalistic religion. Convinced that Yahweh cannot be bound in ritual, that he can be obligated to no sacred place but works freely in every place and every time, prophecy calls the faithful to resist the temptation of resorting to "rivers of oil" in the place of what is truly good, namely, "performing *mišpāṭ*, loving *ḥesed,* and living a reverential life before God" (Mic. 6:6-8).

That this impulse represents the truly unique within biblical religion will become more clear when one recalls the history of how Yahwism came into being. Israel's etiology is found not in cultic myth but in the historically-oriented epic of Pentateuchal narrative. As we probe its form and function, we discover that cult-legend and *hieros logos,* related to sacred sites, played an infinitesimal role alongside such genres as people-related saga. We discover that Yahwism was no shrine religion at all, but a religion of the "placeless" desert. Where does Abraham experience Yahweh's theophany (Genesis 15)? No one is able to say. True, Yahweh does promise his people a place, but this is a holy land, not a city or a shrine. He promises to give Israel *this land* because *all* lands are his to give; yet no place and no land can contain him. Pre-Israel tribes provided for him a moveable shrine in the form of a tent that was transported from place to place in the desert. Moses met Yahweh *'aḥar hammidbār,* "in the remote desert"— at a nameless mountain (Exod. 3:1). Yahweh may appear anywhere because he is potentially present everywhere. He may reveal himself anytime because he is potentially present always.

This, we affirm, was Israel's constitutive insight. Never completely lost, but ever preserved in the historiographic record and given new relevance within the charismatic tradition, it provided Israel with the one thing they needed to survive the loss of land, temple, and the entire political-cultic establishment. Once under Nebuchadrezzar, a second time under Titus, Israel had to fall back on the faith of the desert. With this, Judaism learned to survive the cruelties of history.[7] Christianity, too, has often transcended deprivation of place, in spite of its susceptibility to succumb to the attractions of cultic institutionalism.

The dilemma that unremittingly imperils the ongoing awareness of sacred history and the personalistic religion that goes with it is humankind's stake in politically and culturally stable systems. Unavoidably, some adjustment will have to be made if one is to live anywhere but in a formless waste. The practical problem, then, is how to keep a charismatic and morally responsive impulse alive while functioning within the structures of institutional society and institutional religion. Israel confronted this challenge first as it settled down into an agricultural society, surrounded by urban culture; its response was in the form of accommodation and assimilation, most of it helpful but some of it harmful.[8] The Canaanite shrines were taken over, with their sacrificial apparatus intact, along with their priesthood and some of their theology.[9] Thus Yahweh moved to the *Kulturland*. Israel came to confront a still more serious challenge when it abandoned the charismatic ideal of political leadership in favor of an institutional kingship and all that went with it. Now Yahweh was moved to Zion, where he remained installed until the ultimate tragedies of Israelite history jarred him loose. Yet the postexilic prophets were not able to abandon some form of the ancient ideal for restoring Yahweh to his resting place in Zion. The Ezekiel school had a new temple (chaps. 40ff.), accompanying the new heart (36:26). According to Malachi, Yahweh would come to remedy the scandal of desultory ritual within Jerusalem's restored cultus, not by destroying but by purifying it (3:1ff.).

IV

In the few remaining paragraphs we propose to draw out some consequences that we see for ongoing theological discussion. What we shall have to say is intended to stimulate reflection, being offered out of the conviction that if our characterization of the biblical apprehension of sacred history is valid, church theology needs to be challenged by it.

First, we need to ask whether the Old Testament apprehension of sacred history finds a counterpart in the New Testament. Our observation is that the New Testament indeed stands within the same qualitative tradition. It is equally practical, situational, historically oriented, and morally concerned. Even as institutional-juridical, cultic, wisdom, and apocalyptic elements have developed as a subsidiary growth within the Old Testament canon, they can be shown to appear only on the fringes of New Testament development.

True, the New Testament is more eschatological than the Old Testament, but it has not, as a whole, fallen into the ahistorical orbit of apocalypticism, wisdom moralism, or cultic precisionism. It believes firmly that God has again acted in history, that he now involves his people and church in a shared responsibility for history's outcome. It must bring the gospel and win the world. Thus the dominant literary elements within the New Testament are historiography (Gospels, Acts) and epistolography. It makes no essential difference whether the latter emphasizes in any one place correct belief or moral behavior (e.g., in Romans versus James) because both are directed toward the church's present responsibility to respond to God's saving act in Christ. Deuteronomy-like parenesis is found in passages like 2 Cor. 6:1ff. and Hebrews 2.

Pondering the fact that the Old Testament genres bearing the *heilsgeschicht-liche* tradition involve man in moral responsibility in the very act of recalling or predicting God's saving and judging work, it is difficult to believe that the New Testament appeal to trust in Christ (justification by faith) may properly be construed in an antinomian way, as though the personal reception of the effects of God's work could ever have any consequence besides grateful and obedient moral living. If, indeed, New Testament sacred history is a genuine continuation of Old Testament sacred history, it must decisively affect the lives of those to whom the message of God's saving act is directed.

But Gospel historiography likewise has a parenetic purpose, motivating not only faith but the holy living that goes with it. When we read John 20:31, "These are written that you may believe that Jesus is the Christ, the Son of God, and that believing you may have life in his name," can the life that results from faith mean anything different from the life that is promised in Deut. 30:15, a life that is joyfully fulfilled in the acceptance of covenant responsibility?

What has Christendom made of all this? To many adherents of the gospel, of whatever persuasion, Old Testament historiography has (unfortunately) lost its authority because Israel's history is no longer received as relevant to the church's history. It is the New Testament's sacred history, then, that moves the church to pious thought and action, but in drastically different ways. The Christ event, however defined or restricted, means one thing to sacerdotal Christianity and quite another thing to non-sacerdotal Christianity. We believe the difference has very much to do with time.

Very briefly—hopefully without caricaturing—we would describe the sacerdotal apprehension of the Christ event as rooted in quantitative time. Sacerdotal ritual, participating in eternal life through sacramental manipulation and liturgical recitation, makes the sacred past present in a re-created Christ—a Christ made real not in hallowed memory but in metaphysical substance. Who can escape recognizing here the same reduction of the timely to the timeless that we have identified in the cultic tradition of ancient Israel?[10]

The non-sacerdotal approach to the Christ event, on the other hand, is essentially qualitative, allowing sacred history to remain uniquely past while emphasizing God's new action and continuing appeal primarily in the form of parenetic preaching. Protestantism, as the leading exponent of non-sacerdotal Christianity, is in fact still far too much a matter of pious thought and correct doctrine, rather than of responsible action. The active word of God needs to become more and more the dynamic of a self-aware, non-sacerdotal Christianity. If it would be true to itself, it must live up to its claim to be receptive to the approach of God in an ever-demanding, ever-renewed word of invitation and appeal.[11]

True, non-sacerdotalism also believes that Christ is genuinely present in the sacrament of the Lord's Supper; not, however, as a metaphysical substance re-created in the cult and imparted by the clergy. Christ becomes present in hallowing memory, recited in sacred historiography; then in the word of preaching, appealing to faith and moral commitment. These are aided and reinforced by the sacred elements. Whereas in pure sacerdotalism preaching may be omitted, since the sacred past is recovered only to serve as a timeless basis for the ever-recurring miracle of the Eucharist, non-sacerdotal Christendom's liturgy knows that the eating and drinking of the holy elements stand entirely in the service of God's ongoing action and man's ongoing responsible choice. This is to be done in remembrance of his timely death and timeless resurrection, thereby sanctifying all of history until his fulness comes.

NOTES TO CHAPTER SEVEN

1. *Yesterday, Today and Tomorrow: Time and History as Seen in the Old Testament* (Grand Rapids: Wm. B. Eerdmans, 1975, and London: Society for Promoting Christian Knowledge, 1975).

2. See particularly *The Semantics of Biblical Language* (Oxford: Oxford University Press, 1961) and *Biblical Words for Time* (Naperville: A. R. Allenson, 1962).

3. *Hayyôm (hazzeh)* appears in Deut. 1:10, 39; 2:18, 25; 4:4, 26, 39; 5:3, 24; 7:9 LXX, 8:19; 9:1, 3; 11:2, 26; 12:8; 15:5; 20:3; 26:3, 16-18; 27:9; 29:9, 11f., 14, 17; 30:15, 18f.; 31:2, 21, 27, and in the promulgation clauses.

4. Including a single passage in which the Septuagintal reading may be followed: 4:40; 6:2, 6; 7:11; 8:1, 11; 10:13; 11:8, 13, 22 LXX, 27f.; 13:19; 15:5; 19:9; 27:1, 4, 10; 28:1, 13-15; 30:2, 8, 11, 16. For a complete analysis of this formula, see S. J. De Vries, "The Development of the Deuteronomic Promulgation Formula," *Biblica,* 55 (1974), 301-316.

5. Cf. Norbert Lohfink, S. J., *Das Hauptgebot: Eine Untersuchung literarischer Einleitungsfragen zu Dtn 5-11* (Rome: Pontificio Instituto Biblico, 1963).

6. An illuminating example of this tendency is found in the Passover command of Exod. 13:3ff., where "Moses" begins with a command to sacramental remembrance ("Remember this day, in which you came out of Egypt....") and ends with no further obligation than "Thou shalt therefore keep this ordinance at its proper time from year to year" (v. 10).

7. A lesson that contemporary Zionism has perhaps forgotten.

8. Cf. G. von Rad, *Old Testament Theology* (New York: Harper & Row, 1962), I, 15ff.

9. Cf. H.-J. Kraus, *Gottesdienst in Israel,* 2d ed. (Munich: Chr. Kaiser, 1962), pp. 160ff.

10. We discern in current debate concerning Christ's presence in the Eucharist that much Roman Catholic theology wants to find an orientation closer to the Protestant than the Eastern Orthodox conception. It is a true mother of its daughter. The Reformation *had* to come from Catholicism; it could never have come from Orthodoxy.

11. Cf. Karl Barth, "The Need and Promise of Christian Preaching," *The Word of God and the Word of Man* (New York: Harper & Row, Harper Torchbooks, 1957), pp. 97ff.

8

THE FEAR AND LOVE OF GOD
IN DEUTERONOMY

VERNON H. KOOY

Deuteronomy is the work of a great religious innovator who brought forth a timeless message and set the religion of Israel on a basis that enabled it to endure throughout the centuries. In his endeavor to counteract the tide of idolatry and to bind the people to Yahweh with unbreakable ties, he summarized anew the covenantal obligations and set the tone of Israel's faith for all time to come. In the form of a series of three addresses by Moses,[1] patterned somewhat after the covenant[2] renewal ceremony,[3] he set forth a new interpretation of deity and called the people to undivided loyalty to Yahweh.

The attack against idolatry was more than a religious concern. Israel was a simple desert-dwelling, semi-nomadic community.

> The baals symbolized the entire agricultural commercial economy and may even be regarded as the symbol of a strongly materialistic and naturalistic world view.... They stood for a powerful culture firmly entrenched in Palestine and widely supported by powerful financial and political interests.[4]

There was a long tradition of time-tested methods for earning a living in the land. Once Israel settled in Canaan on farms and in cities there was a real temptation to take over the practices current there. Faith worked out in the discipline of the wilderness might well be exchanged for, or set alongside of, local cults to guarantee a livelihood in a land where Yahweh's power was untested. Strong measures were necessary to offset this possibility. By rehearsing Israel's history, recalling the covenant experience, and providing guidance for conduct, the writer sought to deal with the natural yearning of Israel to "be like the nations."[5]

The great concern and program of the lawgiver Moses is summed up in three texts that form the central appeal of the book and the essence of Israelite religion as the writer conceived it.

> Oh that they had such a mind as this always, to fear me and to keep all my commandments, that it might go well with them and with their children forever! (5:29)

> Hear, O Israel: The Lord our God is one Lord; and you shall love the Lord your God with all your heart, and with all your soul, and with all your might. And these words which I command you this day shall be upon your heart.... (6:4-6)[6]

> And now, Israel, what does the Lord your God require of you, but to fear the Lord your God, to walk in all his ways, to love him, to serve the Lord your God with all your heart and with all your soul, and to keep the commandments and statutes of the Lord, which I command you this day for your good? (10:12-13)[7]

Here the great themes of the fear of Yahweh and the love of Yahweh are presented. In the first two texts fear and love appear separately; in the last one they appear together.

I

The most common word for the "fear of God" in Deuteronomy is *yare'*, "to fear, to reverence."[8] Other words are *gur*, "to be afraid" (32:27); *'arats*, "to be terrified" (7:21; 31:6) *pachadh*, "to be in dread" (11:25; 28:66, 67); and *sa'ar*, "to be frightened" (32:17).

The fear of Yahweh is presented on the background of the Sinai[9] experience, which is "one great terror."[10] Yahweh is the speaker and arranges that the people should hear his voice and fear him (4:10). At the conclusion of the experience he expresses the wish that they would always do so (5:29). The awesomeness of the divine glory raises an anxiety that is akin to dread. The people are afraid; they ask Yahweh henceforth to speak to Moses and to let Moses relay his word to them (5:23-27).

Fear is prompted by theophany, "the feeling of inferiority when confronted by what is strong and incalculable,"[11] or of sinfulness when confronted by holiness (Isa. 6:5, 7). Otto terms it the *mysterium tremendum,* which is elicited by a vision of awesomeness, majesty, and energy together with a certain fascination.[12] It expresses the sense of distance between God and man, and has in it an element of anxiety that it never loses.[13] Fear, in this instance, is also set in the context of revelation. It is an emotion compatible with seeing a disclosure of the divine glory and hearing his will. It instills within the heart a deep sense of humility, brokenness, and contrition.[14]

In those passages in Deuteronomy where the object of fear is men—the enemy,[15] *yare'* also contains an element of terror. In the law code as well, the element of fearsomeness, something more than awe, is present. Extreme penalties are prescribed for serious sins so that Israel may "hear and fear."[16] Such punishments are to be administered in the presence of the congregation so that the people "may never do any such wickedness again" (13:11; cf. 17:13; 19:20).

That there is an element of anxiety in fear may be seen in the addresses. Israel is admonished to take heed lest she forget Yahweh and lest the anger of Yahweh be kindled against her and Yahweh destroy her from the face of the earth (6:12ff.). The sons are to be reminded that Yahweh delivered them from Egypt by wonders, and commanded them to do these statutes and to fear God for their good so that he might preserve them alive (6:24), implying that if they did not they would perish. In a closing passage Israel is urged to fear the glorious and awful name lest Yahweh bring upon them all the afflictions and diseases of Egypt (28:58ff.). In all these passages there is an element of threat demanding caution and preventive measures. While abject terror may not be intended, yet there is a relation to the dark side of God, his jealousy, his anger, his threat of punishment for disobedience. It would seem that more than "awe" before the divine majesty is intended. There is here a healthy respect for God as God.

Yet there is another side to the "fear of God" in Deuteronomy. In other passages fear is associated with worship—"to serve him"[17] (6:13; 10:20), and with commitment—"to cleave to him" (10:20).[18] At the sanctuary both distance and nearness are present. The people are to keep a healthy distance from the cult object, whether it is the ark, the tent of meeting, or the temple with its holy place and holy of holies. There is an aura of holiness and mystery present which demands an attitude of appropriate respect. Too close a contact with the deity would be death. This is why a fear that is more than awe is essential. Yet there is also an attraction here. Israel is to draw near to God. Here Yahweh blesses his people and makes them rejoice. Perhaps this is why Israel was to present the tithe (14:23) and celebrate the feasts (Booths, 31:10-13) at the cult site. Presence at the sanctuary assures a proper reverence and decorum at such celebrations. At the sanctuary the dominant note is worship, which comprises piety and devotion, respect and reverence, joy and dedication as the redemptive acts and gracious providence of God are remembered and celebrated.

In the Psalter, the book of worship, the blessings accompanying reverence are spelled out: "The friendship of the Lord is for those who fear him" (Ps. 25:14); his eye is upon them (33:18); there is no want to them (34:9); for the Lord pities them (103:13); his salvation is at hand for them (85:9); his mercy is upon them (103:17; cf. 103:11); he fulfills their desire (145:19); for he takes pleasure in them (147:11). These passages stress intimacy, concern, grace, and favor. The corresponding attitude of the worshiper would be dedication, obedience, and devotion. There is no anxiety here; there is rather awe which leads to gratitude, and gratitude to praise. There is a developed understanding of fear in the Psalter which goes beyond Deuteronomy.

Fear also is associated with ethical conduct: walking in his ways (8:6; 10:12f.; 13:4); obeying his voice (13:4); and keeping his commandments (6:2; 8:6; 10:12f.; 13:4; 28:58; 31:12; see also 17:19). In two of these passages (10:12 and 13:4), the elements of worship and commitment are included, cautioning against too ready a separation of worship and action. Worship implies reverence, but in the ethical activities the dark side of Yahweh is hidden, if not absent altogether. Fear of God involves morality. It includes a certain confidence and trust in Yahweh, a submission to him, obedience to him, and an acceptance of his commandments, as von Rad says.[19] The close association of fear with morality suggests that Israel is to develop a sense of obligation prompted not simply by threat of punishment, but more especially by a feeling of loyalty to and confidence in Yahweh. This aspect of fear is evidenced also in the wisdom literature, where the element of anxiety is also missing. The fear of the Lord is wisdom (Job 28:28); its beginning (Ps. 111:10); its instruction (Prov. 15:33). By it men depart from evil (Prov. 8:13); it is the way of blessing, prolonging days (Prov. 10:27). It is a strong confidence (Prov. 14:26), a fountain of life (14:27; cf. 19:23). In this literature, however, we have gone beyond Deuteronomy.

In Deuteronomy there is also an awareness that the fear of Yahweh brings blessing. Israel is to fear Yahweh for their good (6:24; 10:12), that it may be well with them and their children (3:29), that Yahweh may preserve them alive (6:24), that their days may be prolonged (6:2), for this brings good to the land (8:6ff.).

The precise meaning of the fear of Yahweh in Deuteronomy, therefore, is difficult to determine. Much will depend on the position taken as to the origin of the ideas in the book. Bamberger's concern that one must not read later religious conceptions into passages where it is foreign to the biblical writers[20] is well taken. He enjoins that the notion that "primitive fear plays an overshadowing role in the Old Testament theology must be considerably revised."[21] However, to interpret fear as "religion"[22] or simply and exclusively as "worship"[23] does not do justice to the biblical evidence and seems to practice precisely what Bamberger decries.

One finds a certain ambiguity in the concept of the fear of Yahweh in Deuteronomy. Fear hovers between the elements of dread and devotion, awe and piety, repulsion and attraction, *mysterium tremendum* and *fascinans*. Fear acknowledges distance from God and is an awareness of his transcendence. It constitutes a healthy respect for who Yahweh is and what he has done. This respect manifests itself in worship and obedience to the divine will.

What limits fear more than anything else is its association with love. Central to Deuteronomy's view of religion is not simply the fear of Yahweh, but more especially the love of Yahweh.

II

Love is set on the background of God's love and choice of Israel. It is because of God's love for Israel (7:7, 8; 23:5) that he has chosen her and is giving her a land.

The love of Yahweh comes to the fore in the Shema.[24] This passage (6:4-9) is a summary of the Torah and constitutes the primary confession of faith for Israel. It forms the counterpart to the covenantal words, "I am Yahweh your

God, who has led you out of the land of Egypt, out of the house of bondage"[25] (Deut. 5:6; cf. Exod. 20:2), and is a commentary on the initial commands of the Decalogue as well as the code that follows (chaps. 12-26).

The command of love follows a fresh understanding of Yahweh—*yahweh 'elohenu, yahweh 'echadh.*[26] However the words are to be translated, the writer emphasizes that Yahweh is the sole God[27] (4:35, 39; see also 32:17) and that he is uniquely Israel's God.[28] He has taken a special interest in her, chosen her (4:37; 7:7; 10:15), set his love upon her (7:7, 8; 23:5), and now desires to show the extent of that love by giving her a land. To assure preservation in this land, Yahweh is placing his will before her in a series of commandments which the writer has neatly summed up in one overarching demand—love (6:5).

The main word for love in Hebrew is *'ahabhah*,[29] derived from the passion of men for women and also used to describe the attachment between blood relatives, and the selfless loyalty of friends. It "always retains the passionate overtones of complete engagement of the will accompanied by strong emotions."[30] Other words are *dabhaq* (11:22; 30:20) and *chasaq* (7:7), "to cleave to someone"; *chabhah* (33:3), "to have in the bosom"; *chanan* (7:2; 28:58), "to be gracious"; and *racham* (13:18; 30:3), "to have compassion." That a strong emotional element is attached to love is seen in the fact that love is joined with "serving Yahweh" (10:12, 13; 13:3, 4),[31] "cleaving to him" (11:22; 13:3, 4), and "fearing him" (10:12, 13; 13:3, 4). These phrases are various ways of expressing that piety and devotion attendant on worship which leads to blessing.

Outside of the expansions in the Second Commandment of the Decalogue (Exod. 20:4-6; Deut. 5:9f.; cf. 7:9; Neh. 1:5; Dan. 4:9) love as the response of Israel to God is found exclusively in Deuteronomy[32] or in late passages.[33] In summarizing the will of God in terms of love the writer of Deuteronomy reveals how the laws are to be understood and applied. He replaces the negative articles of the Decalogue with a single demand that requires the dedication of the whole personality—heart,[34] soul,[35] and strength.[36] He marks out that the specific commandments, statutes, and ordinances which follow and which constitute God's will for Israel are fulfilled in one basic attitude—love. This love is prompted by the divine love (7:7; 23:5; cf. 4:37; 7:13; 10:15) and takes its patterns from it (see 10:18, 19). "By the derivation of the whole law from the command to love, the basic demand of the divine will for the surrender of the whole person to the divine Thou was brought within the comprehension of the simplest citizen."[37] By it the lawgiver sought to remove the distance between Yahweh and Israel, stressing that Yahweh had set his will before Israel in a way in which terror was removed, namely, in the law.

Love embraces more than affection and devotion. In every passage where it appears, including the Shema (see 6:5, 6), it is associated with some activity: to walk in his ways (10:12; 11:22; 19:9; 30:16), to keep his commandments (5:10; 7:9; 11:1, 13, 22; 13:2-4; 19:9; 30:16), to obey his voice (13:3, 4; 30:20; cf. 30:2, 6). Love demands an outgoing of the personality by engaging in those activities which are pleasing to God. Such activity is the means whereby the covenant partner expresses his loyalty. As Eichrodt states, "The loyalty of the treaty partner, his honest intention to live up to the new relationship is the precondition of all that follows."[38] The writer then did nothing so drastic when he spelled out the obligations of that relationship in terms of love. For what is required is not slavish obedience to a set of rules, but growing understanding and fulfilment of the divine will. One sees the perfect fulfilment of this in Jesus, whose meat and drink was to do God's will (John 4:34; cf. 5:30; 6:38; 17:4). Love, then, is "a committed participation in the service of the covenant law."[39] In thus setting the response in terms of love, the writer removes obedience from the sphere of the legal and puts it in the sphere of freedom—the free expression of the personality. It is for this reason that the suzerain treaties scarcely account for the relation between Yahweh and Israel. While the form may be similar, Deuteronomy has taken this relation out of the realm of a master-slave situation and set it in the context of love existing among friends, if not of father and son (see 1:31; 8:5). One recalls that Jesus also said, "You are my friends if you do what I command you. No longer do I call you servants . . ." (John 15:14f.).

Love is interpreted in terms of keeping commandments also in John's Gospel: "If you love me, you will keep my commandments" (14:15, 21; cf. 14:23; 15:10). There the commandment is set in terms of "love for one another" (15:12; cf. 13:34), which takes its pattern from Jesus' love for his disciples (13:34).[40] That love is marked by giving his life for his friends (15:13; cf. 10:11, 15). This is selfless giving (10:18). While the emotional element may seem to have a greater depth in John than in Deuteronomy, there is little doubt that the prototype of that love is to be found in the latter book.

Love is the way of blessing for Israel. She is to love Yahweh so that Yahweh may bless her (7:13), that her days may be prolonged (6:2), so that she may multiply (6:3; 7:13; 30:16). Israel is to love Yahweh for her good (10:13), that she may live long in the land (11:9). Then Yahweh will give the seasonal rains so that the garners will be full (11:14f.), and he will drive out the nations and enlarge the borders of her land (11:23f.; 19:8).

Quell finds a discordant undertone here. He writes, "Without intending it, this introduces into the idea of love an incongruous flavor of bargaining."[41] One might be tempted to ask, "Does Israel serve God for nothing?" But, like the response of the author of Job, the answer is No! For love is reciprocal, a response to grace that prompts additional expressions of grace. Love is always outgoing. It must express itself in activity or it is not love but admiration.

There is, in the final analysis, an awareness on the part of the writer of Deuteronomy that Yahweh through Moses is asking the impossible from his people. He has a premonition that his efforts at curbing idolatry may not succeed in spite of the demand always to keep before the individual the knowledge of the one God and his will, teaching the words diligently to his children and talking of them when sitting in the house, or when walking by the way, when lying down or rising up, or yet by binding them as a sign on the hand or as a frontlet between the eyes, or writing them on the doorposts of the house and gate (6:7-9; cf. 11:18-20). Something more is required than this zeal and constant reminder. Israel is asked to have the most intimate and distinguishing mark of Yahweh's ownership placed upon the heart (10:16), that she be no longer stubborn.[42] Yet even this seems doomed to fail. There may have to be an exile[43] and some new activity on the part of Yahweh before Israel is weaned from her waywardness. The writer recognizes that ultimately Yahweh will have to do for Israel what she would not or could not do for herself. Upon repentance, he will circumcise the heart so that the people will love him with all their heart and with all their soul (30:6). The writer thus prepares the way for the gospel and its provision for overcoming the sinfulness of man.

Where did this new concept of love originate? Was it really borrowed from the prophets, especially Hosea? When one analyzes the book of Hosea, one sees he uses two love images—that of husband and wife (chaps. 1-3)[44] and that of father and son (chap. 11). In neither case, however, is love understood as Israel's response. It is rather God's love that is emphasized and Israel's lovelessness. In Deuteronomy, God's love is not set in terms of the husband-wife relation, and there is only slight reference to God's love as a father for his son (1:31; 8:5; 14:1). There is nothing in Deuteronomy corresponding to the tender love of Yahweh for Israel expressed in Hosea 11:

> *When Israel was a child, I loved him,*
> *and out of Egypt I called my son.*
>
> . . .
>
> *Yet it was I who taught Ephraim to walk,*
> *I took them up in my arms;*
>
> . . .
>
> *I led them with cords of compassion,*
> *with the bands of love,*
>
> . . .
>
> *and I bent down to them and fed them.*
>
> . . .
>
> *How can I give you up, O Ephraim!*
> *How can I hand you over, O Israel!*
>
> . . .
>
> *My heart recoils within me,*
> *my compassion grows warm and tender.*
> *I will not execute my fierce anger,*
>
> . . .
>
> *for I am God and not man,...*
> (Hos. 11:1, 3ab, 4ace, 8abf, 9ac)

There is in Hosea a developed expression of divine grace, but no background for the appeal in Deuteronomy to love Yahweh. Israel is a faithless wife (Hos. 1-3) or a disobedient son (Hos. 11; cf. Isa. 1:2, 3). Nowhere in Hosea is the relation of Israel to Yahweh interpreted in terms of love.[45] In fact, nowhere in the Old Testament is 'ahabhah used to describe the relation of a son to his father, literally or figuratively. This should give pause to those who too easily derive Deuteronomy's thought from Hosea. In Deuteronomy, while love is kept within the context of covenant and election, the writer expresses love as the commitment of the whole person directed to pleasing God, worshiping him alone, and keeping his commandments.

It may well be that the writer felt that fear did not express the fulness of the response of the heart to God. It was bound up too much with a sense of distance from God. Some new dimension was required to express the nearness of God and the joy of his presence. Thus the writer set the response to the covenant in terms of love.

In the early period love perhaps never developed into its full potential. Formerly, covenantal words such as 'emeth, chesedh, mishpat and zedhekah were used to describe ethical and religious conduct.[46] It is to the credit of the writer that he added a new dimension to the religion of Israel. Love, for him, is the essence of true religion, injecting into covenantal obligations the elements of will and emotion. For love "continually brings men back from all externalism in religion to the most inward decision of conscience."[47] It goes beyond all legal requirements "staking man's whole being without reservation for God's cause."[48]

III

While fear and love are the desired responses to the deity, they are not identical. The fact that they are at times set side by side in the same passage and used interchangeably with the same group of responses: "to walk in his ways," "to serve him," "to obey his voice," "to cleave to him," "to keep his commandments," does not make them synonymous. While it has been suggested that what early was termed "the fear of Yahweh" later was termed "the love of Yahweh,"[49] yet there is a difference.

Fear is rooted in the Sinai experience where the divine holiness is disclosed. When used by itself it has in it an element of dread. At other times it suggests reverence, awe, or respect for God as God. In combination with other terms it loses some of its relation to the dark side of God and approaches the meaning it has in the Psalter and in the wisdom literature where it denotes that feeling of respect for God which, mindful of his gifts, causes the heart to rejoice.[50] There is a certain ambiguity in fear. It moves between dread before the deity, which is more than reverence, and a feeling of attraction and gratitude to God that expresses itself in worship and obedience.

Love, on the other hand, is set on the background of the divine love and faithfulness. It is more consistently the outgoing of the personality to God prompted by his grace and blessing. While still within the context of covenant, it brings a freedom to that relationship which delivers it from slavish obedience and makes it a matter of the heart. It thus goes beyond, or expresses in more intimate terms, the nature of religion expressed in Micah—"to do justice, to love mercy, and to walk humbly with God" (Mic. 6:8). It represents a total commitment of the total personality to the one God.

Fear and love are the desired human attitudes to counteract idolatry, even as the blessing and curse are the divine effort at its prevention. Fear responds more naturally to the warning, threat, or holy jealousy of God which prompts the curse, while love responds more naturally to the grace and love of God which prompts the blessing. In the main, fear and distance, love and nearness are related. Or, when seen from the standpoint of expression in life, fear becomes faith and love, works. So the author of Deuteronomy sets before Israel the fullness of his understanding of Yahweh—distant, yet near; jealous, yet gracious; angry, yet loving; rejecting, yet restoring; and he sets forth the fullness of man's response to deity—fear and love, reverence and dedication, faith and works.

The conflict with idolatry was not to be won by fear alone, by recalling the holy God who causes the earth to tremble and disciplines his children (8:5). It is not won even by the addition of love, recalling the gracious God who loves Israel and keeps the oath sworn to the fathers. Ultimately the problem of idolatry, as the problem of sinfulness, is resolved only by him who, out of the wonder of his love, does not destroy his people but does for them what they cannot do. Thus we catch a foregleam of the Coming One who "bore our sins in his body on the tree, that we might die to sin and live to righteousness" (1 Pet. 2:24).

NOTES TO CHAPTER EIGHT

1. 1:6-4:40; 4-44-26:19; 29:1-30:20.
2. Deuteronomy seems to combine elements of both the J (Exod. 33-34) and E (Exod. 19-24) covenant traditions. In common with J are: the concept of Yahweh as a jealous God (Exod. 34:14; Deut. 4:24; 6:15; omitting the expansions of the Second Commandment of the Decalogue, Exod. 20:5f.; Deut. 5:9); the promise of the land (Exod. 33:1; Deut. 1:8; 4:1; 6:10; 11:8f.; 28:11; 30:5; 31:20); Israel as a stiff-necked people (Exod. 33:3, 5; 34:9; Deut. 9:6, 13); a warning against making a covenant with the people of the land (Exod. 34:15; Deut. 7:2-4). Elements of E are: the concept of a holy people (Exod. 19:5, 6; Deut. 7:6; 14:2, 21; 26:19; 28:9); the choice of Moses as mediator by the people (Exod. 20:18-20; Deut. 5:22-31); theophany so Israel will fear Yahweh (Exod. 20:20; Deut. 4:10); the Decalogue (Exod. 20:1-17; Deut. 5:6-21); the altar of unhewn stone (Exod. 20:24, 25; Deut. 27:5, 6).
3. See Deut. 29:1. Cf. G. E. Wright, The Book of Deuteronomy, in IB, 2 (New York: Abingdon Press, 1953), 315; G. von Rad, Studies in Deuteronomy (London: SCM Press, 1953), pp. 14, 64, 68, who traces the tradition to Shechem; M. G. Kline, Treaty of the Great King (Grand Rapids: Wm. B. Eerdmans, 1963), pp. 27ff., who sets it in the context of dynastic covenant patterned after suzerain-vassal treaties. Such treaties have been expounded by Korošeč, Mendenhall, Wiseman, Baltzer, Beyerlin, Zimmerli, et al. One notes also certain affinities in form between Deuteronomy and the Rule of the Qumran monastics.
4. Otto Baab, The Theology of the Old Testament (New York: Abingdon-Cokesbury

Press, 1949), p. 50.

5. Deuteronomy in the form we have it may well be late. The book itself seems to pose the possibility of the Exile (see chaps. 29-30) and may be one last desperate effort to deal with the matter of idolatry. Yet it is highly probable that upon entrance into Canaan, guidance was given to assure the worship of Yahweh in what was then an alien land.

6. The passage is extended through v. 9, at which point the regular narrative begins again.

7. The passage continues through 10:22 or 11:32. One notes that von Rad divorces it completely from the previous section (G. von Rad, *Deuteronomy* [Philadelphia: Westminster Press, 1966], p. 83). Each of these texts intrudes into the context. In the first two instances the text reads smoothly should these verses be removed. In the final passage there is no continuation of 10:11. The section beginning at 10:12 introduces a series of exhortations antecedent to the code of chaps. 12-26. These passages could be conceived as later additions to the book, presenting a late interpretation of earlier traditions. Yet they seem so much at one with the whole tenor of the book that they must be considered at one with the message of the book itself.

8. 6:2, 13, 24; 10:12, 20; 14:23; 17:19; 28:58; 31:12. Cf. 4:10; 5:29; 8:6; 13:4, 11; 17:13; 19:20; 21:21; 25:18. See also 1:17, 29; 2:4; 7:18; 9:19; 18:22; 20:1; 28:10, 60.

9. Horeb according to Deuteronomy. See 4:15; cf. 1:2, 6, 19; 4:10.

10. Deut. 4:10; 5:23-27, 29; Exod. 20:20. See J. Pedersen, *Israel* (Oxford: Oxford University Press, 1959), III-IV, 625.

11. *Ibid.*, p. 624.

12. Rudolf Otto, *The Idea of the Holy* (Oxford: Oxford University Press, 1946).

13. See W. Eichrodt, *Theology of the Old Testament* (Philadelphia: Westminster Press, 1961), II, 269.

14. See S. Terrien, "Deuteronomy," in *IDB*, 2 (New York: Abingdon, 1962), 257f.

15. 3:2, 22; 20:3; cf. 1:21; 31:6. Note that the LXX consistently translates *yare'* in Deuteronomy with *phobeō*, "to be afraid" and "to reverence."

16. Death for enticement to serve other gods even by a close relative (13:6-11); for rejecting the decision of a judge or priest in difficult cases at law (17:8-13); or for rebellion and disobedience to parents (21:18-21). In the case of a malicious witness the *lex talionis* is to be applied (19:16-21).

17. See S. R. Driver, *Deuteronomy*, in *ICC* (Edinburgh: T. & T. Clark, 1951), who holds that "to serve Yahweh" implies definite and formal acts of worship.

18. *Dabhaq* means "to keep close to," implying an intimate attachment.

19. *Deuteronomy*, p. 83.

20. B. J. Bamberger, "Fear and Love of God in the Old Testament," *HUCA*, 6 (1929), 39.

21. *Ibid.*, p. 50.

22. *Ibid.*, p. 46, n. 7.

23. *Ibid.*, p. 43.

24. Deut. 6:4 in its shorter form and 6:4-9; 11:13-21; Num. 15:37-41 in its expanded form.

25. Cf. E. Koenig, *Das Deuteronomium*, in *KAT* (Leipzig: A. Deichertsche, 1917), p. 98.

26. See the discussion of this phrase by Lester J. Kuyper, "The Book of Deuteronomy," *Interpretation*, 6 (1952), 325-329.

27. "No other God can challenge the supreme and universal rule of Yahweh, the 'God of gods' (x.17); indeed there is no God beside Him" (H. W. Robinson, *Deuteronomy and Joshua*, in *NCB* [Edinburgh: T. C. & E. C. Jack, 1907], p. 33).

28. Israel's faith was not technically monotheistic in that she recognized the existence of other deities, including the baals. Yet there was a practical monotheism that excluded all other deities for Israel and extended Yahweh's concern to include nations distantly related to her (Edom, the descendants of Esau; Moab and Ammon, the descendants of Lot. See 2:9-21). The claim to be sole deity while acknowledging others is also known in Egypt. Aton is described as "sole god, like whom there is no other!" (J. B. Pritchard, *Ancient Near Eastern Texts* [Princeton: Princeton University Press, 1950], p. 370). Amon is also unique: no one knows "his true form. His image is not displayed in writings.... He is too mysterious that his majesty might be disclosed, he is too great that (men) should ask about him, too powerful that he might be known" (*ibid.*, p. 368). Certainly Israel's claim of oneness for her God requires no late date.

29. Deut. 5:10; 6:5; 7:8, 9, 13; 10:12, 15; 11:1, 13, 22; 13:3; 19:9; 23:5; 30:6, 16, 20; see also 10:18, 19; 15:16; 4:37.

30. Eichrodt, *op. cit.*, II, 250.

31. See note 17.

32. 5:10; 6:5; 7:9; 10:12; 11:1, 13, 22; 13:3; 19:9; 30:6, 16, 20; cf. Josh. 22:5; 23:11; 1 Kings 3:3, which are deuteronomic. See S. R. Driver, *Deuteronomy*, in *ICC*, p. 91, and G. A. Smith, *The Book of Deuteronomy* (Cambridge: Cambridge University Press, 1918), p. 98.

33. Pss. 31:23; 97:10; 116:1; 145:20; cf. 5:11; 69:36; Prov. 8:17, 21; Isa. 56:6; and Ps. 18:1.

34. *Lebhabh*, the inner man as to the mind and will, where a man's character is and out of which he lives.

35. *Nephesh*, the inner man as to his passion, desire, emotion; a man's human consciousness in its full extent.

36. Mᵉodh ("exceedingly"), signifying force, intensity; translated "strength" or "might."

37. Eichrodt, *op. cit.*, II, 372.

38. W. Eichrodt, "Covenant and Law," *Interpretation*, 20 (1966), 308f.

39. *Ibid.*, p. 311.

40. Love for man takes its pattern from God also in Deuteronomy. There it is expressed only in terms of love for the sojourner (10:19). Yahweh also loves the sojourner (10:18) and loved Israel when she was a sojourner in Egypt.

41. G. Quell, *Love: Bible Key Words* (London: Adam and Charles Black, 1958), p. 22.

42. See also Jer. 4:9. Paul also recognizes true circumcision as that of the heart. Cf. Rom. 2:29; Phil. 3:3; Col. 2:11.

43. Cf. 29:16-30:10. The cure in Hosea is also seen as exile (2:6-20; 3:1-5). In Jeremiah it is seen as a new covenant with the law written on the heart (31:31-34), and in Ezekiel as a new heart of flesh (11:17-20; 18:31; 36:24-28).

44. This imagery is also found in Jeremiah (chaps. 2, 3, 18) and in Ezekiel (chaps. 16, 23).

45. Because of the marriage imagery used, it may be the expected response, but it is never so stated.

46. G. Quell, *TDNT*, I, 27.

47. Eichrodt, *op. cit.*, II, 296.

48. *Ibid.*, p. 298.

49. Cf. *ibid.*, p. 299: "The requirement of love is thus nothing other than a new clarification and a deeper understanding of the old commandment to fear God."

50. Note that in the prophets fear is more closely related to that use in Deuteronomy where it appears alone. Some seventeen times it is used in the phrase "Fear not," and nine times *yare'* is used of the fear of men. When fear of God is meant, six passages contain an element of dread (Isa. 57:11; 59:19; Jer. 3:8; 5:22; Amos 3:8; Mic. 7:17); six passages reflect a sense of the *mysterium tremendum* (Jer. 44:10; Hos. 10:3; Jonah 1:16; Zeph. 3:7; Mal. 2:5; 3:5); and four passages have worship in the background (Isa. 25:3; Jer. 5:24; 32:39; Hag. 1:12).

9

THE ARK OF THE COVENANT IN JEREMIAH 3:16-18

MARTEN H. WOUDSTRA

Jeremiah's remarkable words concerning the future disappearance and loss of function of the ark of the covenant have long intrigued biblical interpreters. Depending on their understanding of the meaning of the ark for Israel's worship in general, these interpreters have differed rather widely in their assessment of Jeremiah's words. It is the object of the present study to examine Jeremiah's ark-prophecy in order to determine which of the several views propounded with respect to it would appear to do greatest justice to the intent of the biblical author.

A discussion of Jeremiah's ark-prophecy and of its divergent interpretations can best be conducted against the background of a brief resumé of the various ark-theories that have been developed in the course of the years. To give a concrete example: is the ark's "materialism," a term used by L. Koehler,[1] something about which the theologian and the student of the history of religion are bound to hold opposing views? Should the theologian be happy when Jeremiah announces the disappearance of this "material" cult-symbol? And, by contrast, should the student of the history of religion be happy when in Num. 10:35 the ark and Yahweh seem to be so closely associated that one cannot but think of a certain "primitive mentality" regarding the unity of the symbol and the thing symbolized coming to expression here? In the following lines these and similar questions will have to be considered.

A convenient starting point for the survey as proposed above may be found in the words with which Jeremiah designates the cult-object. The name of an object presumably tells us something about its function and meaning. This is also the case with the ark of the covenant. Our starting point assumes added significance in view of the fact that scholars have not been agreed as to the earliest name of the ark. Was it "ark of God," "ark of Yahweh," or "ark of the covenant"? Moreover, is the word "ark" a correct and original designation of the cult-symbol's true purpose? These are some of the questions scholars have been asking themselves.

To begin with the last question, the fact that Israel's cult-emblem was called "ark" is regarded by some to be the product of a development from a more primitive to a more rationalized concept.[2] The word "ark" is the translation of the Hebrew 'aron, which means "chest," "coffer." Throughout the entire Old Testament, whether in the Pentateuch, the book of Joshua, the Samuel stories, or elsewhere, this word is used exclusively. On the surface this would suggest that one of the functions of the ark was to serve as the container of the law-tablets.

But, so certain scholars argue, there are also ark-passages that hint at a more "direct" understanding of the cult-emblem. In that connection an appeal is made to passages such as Num. 10:35 and 2 Sam. 6:6, 7. Does not this kind of biblical material warrant the assumption that the ark has undergone a gradual transformation from a more or less numinous object, endowed with a mysterious sanctity, to that of a simple storage place for the Decalogue? And, so these same interpreters, does not Jeremiah's ark-prophecy as it were climax this process of rationalization and spiritualization? Jeremiah, so it would seem, has no use for the kind of material symbol the ark still continued to be and is happy to announce its complete loss of function.[3]

It cannot be denied that the Bible at times uses language that suggests a very close association between Yahweh and his ark. When the ark arises, Yahweh is thought to arise (Num. 10:35). When David dances before the ark, he dances before Yahweh (2 Sam. 6:17). It is no wonder, therefore, that scholars committed to the study of comparative religion have seen in these passages early stages of a gradual development of the ark concept, from material, to less material, to dispensable. Some have gone so far as to suggest that at certain points in the biblical narrative the ark is treated in a way similar to the treatment of holy objects found among ethnic religions in general. Says Hubert Schrade: "The ark . . . is Yahweh himself, just as the idol image is the god."[4]

This is not the place to make a comprehensive assessment of the role of the phenomenology of religion and of comparative religion for the better understanding of the message of God's Word. I believe that these disciplines can indeed be useful if properly pursued.[5] Extremes should be avoided. To suggest a certain "identity" between Yahweh and his cult-emblem is not necessarily contrary to biblical thought. But due care should be taken not to place this notion simply alongside similar phenomena observed outside the pale of special revelation. For the Yahweh who wants to be identified with his ark is different from all other deities. He is never just "wrapped up" with his cult-object in a naturalistic fashion but he voluntarily associates with it (Exod. 25:21; 29:42). Moreover, the same book of the Old Testament that presumably speaks of the ark in terms of its "numinous" sanctity also tells its readers that Yahweh sometimes dissociates himself from the ark (cf. 1 Sam. 6:19-21 with chap. 4). I am not prepared to call the latter emphasis part of a development away from a more "material" to a more "rational" viewpoint representing a more "advanced" theology.

One question the students of comparative religion whom Koehler has in mind may not have faced sufficiently concerns the criterion by which one must judge a certain viewpoint to be more "primitive" and less suited to a lofty conception of God than another. This may also be put as follows: neither the theologian nor the student of comparative religion should welcome one emphasis of the biblical record more than another. The fact that there are these sensory aspects to the ark should not come as an embarrassment to the theologian unless he already carries to the Bible a God-notion that is the product of abstract rationalization. And the student of comparative religion who wants to do his work well can never forget that the "materialism" of an object such as the ark was chosen as a vehicle of communication by Yahweh who is spiritual at any stage of his revelation to man.

One may therefore affirm the positive value that comparative studies have had for the elucidation of the biblical text, provided such studies be conducted on the proper basis and with due regard to the biblical claims concerning Yahweh's unique difference from the gods of the nations. Merely indiscriminate comparisons of the various cult objects found within the spectrum of religions in general will not guarantee a correct understanding of the ark of the covenant. This type of comparative study, unfortunately, often has been characteristic of the ark-studies produced in this century. Frequently, in these studies, the ark has been placed within a long series of cult-objects, ranging all the way from the fetishes of animism to the symbols of Holy Communion.[6] Naturally, all these objects have something in common which makes a comparison possible and sometimes helpful. But somewhere in our comparative studies of cult-objects we meet with an unmistakably clear divine claim that relativizes the comparison and reduces it to its proper dimension. Where this claim is not heeded, even in the area of comparative studies, there, so it seems to this observer, the biblical data are in danger of being misunderstood and misinterpreted.

The reason for our concern at this point is a very practical one. Those who consider Jer. 3:16, for example, to be more in keeping with the nature of true religion than the more "material" ark-passages such as 1 Sam. 6:19-21 and 2 Sam. 6:6, 7, proceed from a notion of religion that leaves large parts of biblical truth out of consideration. The God of the Scriptures is not so spiritual that he never can and never will make use of very material means to make his presence known and felt among men. In this respect it is interesting to note that R. H. Kennett, who regards Jer. 3:16 as setting forth the "truly spiritual conception of God," tells us that in his opinion the "prophetic" thinking of Jeremiah "has been disregarded even by those who have called themselves Christians."[7] Kennett is probably thinking here of the Christian teaching concerning such "externals" as the bread and wine of Holy Communion. These material objects are meant to be veritable pledges of Christ's presence with his people. Is this kind of teaching due to a disregard for Jeremiah's prophetic utterance concerning the ark of the covenant? Is it out of keeping with God's spiritual nature?

Questions of this kind will return later on in our study. For the time being we shall continue our review of the diverse theories concerning the ark of the covenant which have been developed over the years and which may be encountered in relevant contemporary literature on the subject.

As was noted above, the word Jeremiah uses to designate the sacred cult-object suggests its container-function. Nevertheless a widespread theory holds that the proper way of looking upon the ark is to regard it as Yahweh's throne. We are thinking here particularly of those who, like M. Dibelius,[8] have pointed to the phenomenon of the empty throne, known in ancient Near Eastern religions, as a possible prototype of the ark of the covenant. Speaking non-technically we should, of course, recognize that there is a good deal of biblical evidence for considering the ark to be in some general way comparable to Yahweh's throne. In fact the very passage under investigation would lend support to this view (cf. Jer. 3:16 with v. 17). One might also call attention to the expression *yoshebb hakkerubhim*, which has been variously translated as "who sitteth above the cheru-bim" (*ASV;* mg. "is enthroned"); "is enthroned on the cherubs" (*JB*); "he is throned upon the cherubim" (*NAB*); *NEB,* likewise; "er thront auf den Cheru-ben" (*ZB*); *"il monte les Chérubins"* [*sic*] (*BJ*).[9]

A closer look at the ark-equals-throne theory reveals some of its weaknesses. One difficulty is that the biblical references uniformly use the word *'aron,* which means "chest," "coffer." This has prompted Procksch to remark: "The ark of God must have been a coffer, since it is called that way."[10] In reply to this, those who favor the throne theory are quick to point out that the ancient Near East knew of chest-like thrones.[11] This would indeed account for some of the difficulty, but not for all of it. For why this persistence of the use of the word *'aron* if the gen-erally accepted function and symbolism of the ark was that of a throne? Why, for example, did not Jeremiah himself use the word "throne" to designate the ark if, as is apparent from what follows in Jer. 3:17, he thought of the ark in that manner?

Some scholars, therefore, consider the evidence to settle this question as to the original function of the ark too scanty to make dogmatic pronouncements. L. Koehler states: "Whether the ark of Jahweh was a throne (the later view) or a chest with a particular content (the older view) cannot be determined from the knowledge we possess."[12]

As to the expression *yoshebh hakkerubhim* cited earlier as possibly in sup-port of an ark-equals-throne theory, it should be kept in mind that attempts have also been made to construct a throne out of the *cherubim.* A distinction was thus made between an alleged cherub-throne and the ark, placed under it. It is evident that these two theories, that of a cherub-throne and that of an ark-throne, cannot very well be combined.[13]

Moreover, the question as to the precise meaning of the words *yoshebh hakkerubhim* cannot be answered easily. The Hebrew expression lacks the prep-osition. Was Yahweh conceived of as seated "between" the cherubim? This is the way the seventeenth-century Dutch translation, the *Statenvertaling,* takes it. The prepositions that have been suggested besides "on," or "above," are "beneath"[14] and "in."[15] This diversity of translations points to the degree of uncertainty as to the precise function of the cherubim-figures and makes the ark-equals-throne concept more complex than might appear at first sight. We would also call attention once again to the translation "il monte les Chérubins" (BJ). This highlights the fact (also perceived by others) that the Hebrew verb *yashabb,* often translated somewhat statically as "being enthroned," can also have the meaning, "taking one's place."

Furthermore, what should be kept in mind is that the cherubim-figures in the tabernacle were not limited to the "mercy seat" alone. They were also woven into the fabric of curtains and veil (Exod. 26:11, 31). What then, precisely, was the Old Testament saying when it referred to Yahweh as *yoshebh hakkeru-bhim?* In view of the above-mentioned uncertainties the most that can be said is that Yahweh must be understood as either "seated" or "taking place" "with respect to" the cherubim. This is not to say that Bible translators should not choose an expression that seems best to represent the thought implied. But it is to say that complete certainty as to the exact meaning is not easily obtained.

Thus far we have not spoken of the possible shape the cherubim-figures, as applied to ark and curtains, may have had. Widespread is the opinion that the physical representation of the cherubim borrowed from the composite figures discovered by archaeology showing a winged lion with a human head.[16] It is not our purpose to examine this hypothesis in detail. Whatever the case may be, the Bible's description of the cherubim figures, as, for example, in the first chapter of Ezekiel, probably contains much that is symbolic and hence should not be used to conclude what was the precise form and manifestation of the cherubim when appearing in visible form. Furthermore, on the basis of the various biblical data, we agree with M. Unger and others that the cherubim are to be considered "celestial creatures belonging to the spiritual realm and not at all to be confounded with any natural identification."[17]

A possible Egyptian connection for the ark-equals-throne theory was pointed out by W. B. Kristensen. Egyptian religion knows of thrones in the form of a box intended as a representation of the primeval hillock which, according to Egyptian thought, was the place where the fertility god Min had engaged in his first acts of generation.[18]

The above discussion clarifies the position that to consider the ark to be Yahweh's throne is possibly not as obvious as it would appear at first sight. An additional drawback to the theory of M. Dibelius is that it intends to provide a rather comprehensive explanation of how it happened that Israel was carrying about that mysterious chest on its desert journeys, and during and after the conquest. The present writer believes that while the attempt on the part of Dibelius to rescue the ark from the crassly materialistic explanations proffered by others should be appreciated, this attempt possibly goes too far in the opposite direction. For as was seen above, according to the biblical data there are certain instances in which the ark functions as more than just an empty throne of Yahweh who himself presumably is thought to be in heaven. The ark in a very real sense is one of the "representations" of Yahweh.[19] In and through the ark Yahweh very really is with his people. It is not just his empty throne.

The present writer believes, therefore, that the notion of the sacramental is probably best suited to express the biblical realism with which the relation between Yahweh and his ark is portrayed. This idea of the sacramental allows for a "real presence," while it avoids any crass identity concept akin to that of naturalistic religion.[20] This sacramental aspect of the ark has been seen by W. Lotz and others.[21] Theologians have long argued about the question in which way God is present in and with the sacrament. It is not our intention to enter into that argument here. We simply wish to point to the similarity in the problematics.[22] At the same time, by suggesting the notion of the sacramental we seek to avoid such ark interpretations as would point to Jer. 3:16 as somehow setting forth more clearly the spiritual nature of God than do other ark passages. A closer examination of Jeremiah's words will, it is hoped, make clear that his prophecy must not be understood, at least not so exclusively as is done by some, in terms of a rejecting of the material symbol, the ark.[23] If our analysis should turn out to be correct, then the lesson of God's "spirituality" is not necessarily what Jeremiah wishes to teach us here.

Thus far most of our remarks about the possible meaning of the ark of the covenant have been oriented to Jeremiah's use of the word 'aron as a designation of the cult-object. This proved to be a convenient point for offering a brief survey of some of the ark-theories that have been propounded over the years and for developing our own position along with, and sometimes in contrast to, that of others. We must now take a further look at the second part of Jeremiah's designation of the ark. To him it was "the ark of the covenant of Yahweh." Or, to say the least, his prophecy tells us that at some future time people will no longer speak of the ark in that fashion. Quite apart from the question of Jeremiah's own evaluation of the ark of the covenant at this juncture in Israel's history, it may be stated that the expression "ark of the covenant of Yahweh" was eminently suited to express some of the basic notions relative to the cult-object.

Attempts have been made by biblical scholarship to establish the earliest name of the ark. In the writer's opinion these attempts have been less than successful and have been burdened by suppositions that cannot be called biblical in the true sense of the word. At an earlier time G. Westphal,[24] for example, who held that the ark was originally dedicated to some unknown deity and only gradually transferred to the service of Yahweh, considered the name "ark of God" to be more "original" than "ark of Yahweh," for obvious reasons. Westphal based his theory on the Samuel passages dealing with the ark. These, according to certain approaches to Old Testament studies, deal more directly with the ark than do, for example, the Pentateuchal passages. On the other hand, L. Koehler, who based his remarks on the same Samuel occurrences, arrived at the conclusion that the original name was "ark of *Jahweh*"![25] This may serve as an indication of the subjective element in biblical scholarship.

In recent decades Old Testament scholarship has been more willing than used to be the case to accept a fairly early origin of the covenant idea. This has come about under the influence of certain amphictyony-theories as applied to Israel's early confederacy in Palestine. Parallels from Hittite treaty-making have also had their impact in this area of biblical research. It is not our purpose to examine this matter further at this point. This much may be inferred from the biblical data: The ark was used to house the tablets of the Decalogue (Exod. 25:21; Deut. 10:1ff.). This Decalogue was the very foundation for and expression of Yahweh's covenant with Israel. Hence the name "ark of the covenant of Yahweh," when properly understood by Israel, God's covenant people, assured Israel of Yahweh's faithfulness and challenged it to render to him due covenant-obedience. Speaking in ideal terms (i.e., in terms of the faith commitment that the covenant presupposes), this name was eminently suited to express all that the ark was to represent to Israel. Whether by the time that Jeremiah uttered his noteworthy prophecy this name had become a glib cliché in the mouth of a self-assured and disobedient covenant-people is a question that must be answered in the light of the broader context of Jeremiah's prophecies. Proceeding now to a brief analysis of Jeremiah's prophetic utterances, we first of all point to some elements in them on which scholarly opinion is divided.

The first question on which there is no unanimity among interpreters concerns the genuineness of the words here attributed to Jeremiah. B. Duhm holds that these words reflect post-exilic conditions, the same conditions, so he believes, which prompted the writers of Chronicles to comment extensively upon David's concerns for the regulation of the cultus.[26] Those who subscribe to a post-exilic origin of these words are generally inclined to hold that the thoughts expressed here are foreign to Jeremiah.[27] But others believe that the ideas contained here are "in no way inconsonant with Jeremiah's thought."[28] Eissfeldt appears to regard the materials contained in chapters 2-6 as stemming from the beginning of Jeremiah's prophetic activity,[29] whereas Aalders considers only v. 18 to be a marginal gloss reflecting later Jewish sentiment. This marginal note, so he believes, was subsequently introduced into the text.[30]

A similar lack of agreement may be discerned as to the nature of the material: is it prose, poetry, or a little bit of both? The *JB* regards the two passages, 3:6-13 and 3:14-18, to be an interruption of a larger poem that begins at v. 1 and continues with v. 19. The *JB* prints vv. 14-18 in prose format. J. Bright is not entirely sure. He calls vv. 14-15 "probably prose," and prints them as such.[31] On the other hand, the *NAB* prints vv. 14-16 as poetry, and vv. 17 and 18 as prose.

A third area of disagreement concerns the question whether, regardless of the date of these words, the ark's disappearance must be presupposed. C. von Orelli states: "That the ark no longer existed in Jeremiah's day, can no more be inferred from the way in which it is spoken of than from 2 Chron. xxxiii. 16 . . . see, on the contrary, 2 Chron. xxxv. 3."[32] Others hold that the loss of the ark has already occurred, perhaps as early as the time of Manasseh. With von Orelli and Aalders, we are of the opinion that there is no need to hold that the ark had disappeared by the time these words were spoken and written. This also has its implications for the date to which this prophecy must be assigned. If, as is admitted even by those who assign it to the post-exilic period, the thoughts expressed could well have been those of Jeremiah, there would seem to be no compelling reason to deny these words to the prophet himself.[33]

The solution of some of the earlier questions raised above is not absolutely necessary for the progress of our study. More important, in terms of the objective stated in the beginning of this essay, is the question of what prompted Jeremiah to speak and to prophesy the way he did. Was, as Kurt Galling suggests, the purpose of this prophecy to be a polemic against the easygoing attitude that Jeremiah's contemporaries assumed toward the cultus?[34] Galling believes that the ark, as well as the idea of the divine indwelling in general, had become to Judah "an unfailing earnest of salvation" (ein untrügliches Unterpfand des Heils). R. Hentschke follows a similar line of thought. Jeremiah's polemic, according to Hentschke, aims at the notion that Yahweh was somehow bound to his ark. It was this idea of a "gegenständliche Bindung Jahwes" that Jeremiah sought to oppose.[35]

Hentschke's remarks are important because they illustrate a point made earlier in this essay. To suggest that Jeremiah would aim his prophecy at "the material binding of Yahweh" raises the question of whether this kind of "binding" is to be rejected altogether in terms of the total biblical revelation concerning the ark of the covenant. Only if such "material binding" is to be considered out of keeping with the true nature of Yahweh can one expect Jeremiah to inveigh against it. But this position can only be held if the development scheme, from "primitive" to "rationalized," is applied to the biblical data. In spite of the fact that biblical scholarship has often suggested that the prophets favor a more rationalized and hence less cultic approach to the worship of Yahweh, such an antithesis does not stand up in the light of all the biblical data. To return to the notion of "material binding" once again, one might say that there are passages in the Bible in which Yahweh, voluntarily to be sure, but nonetheless really, binds himself to the material object of the ark. He still does the same today when he ordains that material objects such as bread, wine, and water are to represent him in the Christian sacraments. No amount of "prophetic" polemic can erase this kind of teaching from the pages of the Bible.

As we continue our survey of opinions regarding Jeremiah's ark-prophecy, we also encounter the view that Jeremiah was in effect making himself the mouthpiece of his contemporaries by stating that the ark would cease to be of any importance in future times.[36] Still another view, held by S. Mowinckel,[37] sees in these words of Jeremiah an expression of sadness at the loss of the ark, the greatest misfortune that could have struck the nation. Although it should be noted that Mowinckel attributes these thoughts to a post-exilic redactor, nevertheless his interpretation adds to the diversity of opinions held with respect to this prophecy.

Fortunately, the description of the divergent views concerning Jeremiah's ark-prophecy need not end at this point. There are also interpreters who have observed the connection that exists between the thoughts of v. 16 and those of v. 17. In the present writer's opinion this observation is best suited to yield the proper sense of the passage.

An examination of vv. 16 and 17 in their context produces the following result: The period in which the ark will cease to be an important cult-object is that of unparalleled prosperity and expansion. This period is, as O. Eissfeldt has correctly stated, the future "Heilszeit."[38] Felicity and fertility of paradise proportions will be experienced. One might speak of a *shalom*-situation, a situation that characterizes man's early existence at the beginning of time and which returns in the prophetic descriptions of the end-time (Ezek. 36:11; 37:26; Jer. 23:3; Joel 4:18, etc.).[39] By giving to his people shepherds after his heart (v. 15) Yahweh will restore the old theocratic ideal (cf. 1 Sam. 13:14; cf. Ezek. 34:2, 3, 13, and 23). A messianic reference need not be precluded.[40]

This, then, is the setting of the words concerning the ark's future dispensability. The restoration of the covenant people is viewed by Jeremiah as accompanied by a prosperity that recalls the blessings of paradise. Under those conditions a separate cult-symbol will no longer be necessary. The cultus among Israel had always had for its purpose to further the *shalom* of God in the most comprehensive sense of that word. The blessing the high-priest pronounced at the end of the temple service ended with the word *shalom* (Num. 6:26). This *shalom*-notion is as much cultural as it is cultic. It stands for man's comprehensive well-being and exists where the covenant comes to its fullest fruition. It is, in fact, just another way of describing the covenant-situation (cf. Ezek. 37:26).

The whole situation as described by Jeremiah points to the "eschatological end-time" (Duhm, on v. 17). This is what the expression "in that time" (v. 17) also suggests. This eschatological end-time will bring about the full fruition of all that the cultus ever stood for (cf. also Isa. 4:5, 6; Zech. 14:20, 21; Ezek. 37:26, 27). It is for that reason, and not for reasons of teaching a more "spiritualized" and less magical God-concept, that Jeremiah speaks the way he does.[41] Rather, as the people in the end-time will enjoy *shalom*-unlimited so they will also enjoy cultus-unlimited. The whole city will be called the throne of Yahweh (v. 17). As observed above, the name "throne," when not used in the technical sense of the empty-throne concept of M. Dibelius, is an apt designation of the ark of the convenant. Thus, Jeremiah means to teach us that the cult-symbol will have done its work so well that it will virtually become co-extensive with the city in its entirety.

The movement suggested by this ark-prophecy, as we see it, is not so much from the external and the visible to the internal and the spiritual.[42] What Jeremiah wants to teach his readers is that at the time of the Great Future the cultic emblem, so long hidden behind the curtains in a most holy place, will have outlasted its usefulness in view of the fact that the entire city of God will have become one giant cult-symbol, thus making it possible for all to have equal access to God.

NOTES TO CHAPTER NINE

1. *Old Testament Theology*, trans. A. S. Todd (Philadelphia: Westminster Press, 1957), p. 122.
2. For this point of view cf. K. H. Bernhardt, *Gott und Bild* (Berlin: Evangelische Verlagsanstalt, 1956), p. 151. Bernhardt speaks of a "demythologized" ark.
3. This is the view of R. H. Kennett, *Encyclopedia of Religion and Ethics*, s.v. "ark." Cf. also S. R. Hopper on Jer. 3:16 (*The Book of Jeremiah*, in IB, 5 [New York: Abingdon Press, 1956], 828), who speaks of "the localized God-idea" and of "the magical influence of the visible symbol."
4. Cf. Hubert Schrade, *Der Verborgene Gott* (Stuttgart: W. Kohlhammer, 1949), pp. 34, 36; cf. also G. Westphal, *Jahwes Wohnstätte nach den Anschauungen der alten Hebräer* (Giessen: A. Töpelmann, 1908), p. 90.
5. There is, so I believe, a way in which comparative religion can be harmful to the study of God's Word. See G. Ch. Aalders, *De Heilige Schrift en Vergelijkende Godsdienstwetenschap* (Kampen: J. H. Kok, 1919), p. 2: ". . . comparative religion seeks directly to contradict the revelation-character of the contents of Scripture."
6. This is done, e.g., by S. Mowinckel, *Religion und Kultus* (Göttingen: Vandenhoeck & Ruprecht, 1953), p. 13.
7. *Op. cit.*
8. *Die Lade Jahves* (Göttingen: Vandenhoeck & Ruprecht, 1906); cf. W. Eichrodt, *Theologie des Alten Testaments*, 5th ed. (Stuttgart: Ehrenfried Klotz, 1957), I, 44, and cf. Karl Budde, "War die Lade Jahwes ein leerer Thron?" *Theologische Studien und Kritiken*, 4 (1906), 489-507.
9. This translation, "he mounts the Cherubim," is probably based on Ps. 18:(11)10 where Yahweh is seen as "riding" upon a Cherub. The rendering "to sit down on" is possible for the Hebrew *yashabb* and should make us careful not to endorse too quickly the idea of enthronement as is done by many modern versions.
10. O. Procksch, *Theologie des Alten Testaments* (Gütersloh: Bertelsmann, 1950), p. 96.
11. Cf. W. Eichrodt, *op. cit.*, I, 45.
12. *Op. cit.*, p. 121. Koehler makes much of the "materialistic" features of the ark, calling it "the oldest, most materialistic, and therefore most quickly abandoned representation of God" (*idem*).
13. The theory of a cherub-throne was fully worked out by H. Schmidt, "Kerubenthron und Lade," in *EUCHARISTERION: Studien zur Religion und Literatur des Alten und Neuen Testaments, Hermann Gunkel zum 60. Geburtstag* (Göttingen: Vandenhoeck & Ruprecht, 1923), pp. 120-144.
14. W. Caspari translates: "Der seiner Gewohnheit nach unter Keruben Platz nehmende." See *Die Samuelbuecher* (Leipzig: Scholl, 1926), p. 59.
15. H. G. May holds that the ark may have been patterned after some of the miniature temples archaeology has discovered. These were adorned with cherub-figures on the sides. May therefore translates the phrase: "the occupant of the cherubim," which presupposes the preposition "in." See "The Ark—A Miniature Temple," *American Journal of Semitic Languages and Literature*, 52 (1936), 221.
16. Cf. G. E. Wright, "Solomon's Temple Resurrected," *BA*, 4 (1941), 27. Cf. also A. Alt, "Verbreitung und Herkunft der Syrischen Tempeltypus," in *Kleine Schriften zur Geschichte des Volkes Israel* (Munich: C. H. Beck, 1964), II, 111f. Alt speaks of the "mischgestaltigen Cherubenfiguren." This view has also been adopted by conservative scholars such as M. Unger, *Bible Dictionary* (Chicago: Moody Press, 1957), s.v. "Cherub."
17. Unger, *op. cit.* Whether the cherub-figures actually resembled the mixed beings found

in ancient sculpture should be left an open question. Moses fashioned the whole tabernacle according to the model shown to him by Yahweh (Exod. 25:9, 40). Would this allow for the kind of "borrowing" biblical scholarship has assumed?

18. Cf. W. B. Kristensen, "De Ark van Jahwe," in *Verzamelde Bijdragen* (Amsterdam: Noord-Hollandsche Uitgevers-maatschappij, 1933), p. 178.

19. Under this general heading of "representations" (Vergegenwärtigung) of Yahweh, L. Koehler treats the ark (*op. cit.*, pp. 119-126).

20. For some rather naturalistic theories about the ark's original symbolism, cf. also R. H. Pfeiffer, "Images of Yahweh," *JBL*, 45 (1926), 219ff., and A. Kuenen, *The Religion of Israel* (London: Williams & Norgate, 1874), I, 233.

21. Cf. W. Lotz, "Die Bundeslade," in *Prinzregenten Luitpold von Bayern zum 80. Geburtstag* (Leipzig: Deichert, 1901), I, 184.

22. Cf. also Calvin's discussion of the sacramental language of Holy Baptism in connection with his treatment of the Samuel passages dealing with the ark, *Opera Quae Supersunt Omnia*, 29, ed. G. Baum, E. Kunitz, E. Reuss (Brunswick: Schwetschke, 1885), 415. Commenting on Ps. 47:6, Calvin speaks of Yahweh's presence with the ark in terms of pledge (*pignus*) and earnest (*tessera*) (*op. cit.*, 31 [1887], 469).

23. F. Giesebrecht very clearly understands Jeremiah as rebuking the people's dependence upon sensory media, which he calls a lower form of piety ("eine niedere Form der Frommigkeit") (*Das Buch Jeremia* [Göttingen: Vandenhoeck & Ruprecht, 1907], *ad loc.*). Surprisingly enough Giesebrecht observes that this prophetic rebuke is not incompatible with the prophet's own expectation which views the ultimate realization of Yahweh's presence as "sinnlich fassbar." As another illustration of the way in which "spiritual" and "sensory" factors are sometimes combined, Giesebrecht invites his readers to compare Isa. 66:1ff. with 60:1ff.; 62:1ff.

24. Westphal, *op. cit.*, pp. 86ff. G. von Rad (*Gesammelte Studien zum Alten Testament* [Munich: Chr. Kaiser, 1958], p. 121) also holds "ark of God" to be the original name.

25. *Op. cit.*, p. 121. For an attempt to establish the "official" name of the ark, see a review by W. F. Albright, *JBL*, 67 (1948), 377f.

26. *Das Buch Jeremia* (Tübingen: J. C. B. Mohr, 1901), *ad loc.*

27. Cf. J. P. Hyatt, *The Book of Jeremiah*, in *IB*, 5 (New York: Abingdon Press, 1956), 827. But it is clear from this source that there is no unanimity among those who would reject some or all of the words of Jer. 3:16-18 as being from Jeremiah. Peake and Rudolph, e.g., consider v. 16 to be genuine.

28. Cf. J. Bright, *Jeremiah*, in *AB*, 21 (Garden City: Doubleday & Company, 1965), 27.

29. O. Eissfeldt, *Einleitung in das Alte Testament* (Tübingen: J. C. B. Mohr, 1964), p. 486.

30. Cf. G. Ch. Aalders, *De Profeet Jeremia*, in *Korte Verklaring der Heilige Schrift* (Kampen: J. H. Kok, 1923), I, 23.

31. *Op. cit.*, pp. 22 and 27.

32. Cf. *The Prophecies of Jeremiah* (Edinburgh: T. & T. Clark, 1889), p. 46.

33. Even S. R. Hopper (*op. cit.*, p. 828) allows for the possibility that Jeremiah may have written these words.

34. Cf. *Die Religion in Geschichte und Gegenwart*, III, 2d ed. (Tübingen: J. C. B. Mohr, 1927-31), s.v. *Lade.*

35. Cf. Richard Hentschke, *Die Stellung der vorexilischen Schriftpropheten zum Kultus*, in *BZAW* (Berlin: A. Töpelmann, 1957), pp. 71f.

36. Cf. A. Bertholet, *A History of Hebrew Civilization*, trans. A. K. Dallas (London: George C. Harrup, 1926), p. 255.

37. "A Quel Moment le Culte de Jahwe à Jerusalem est-il devenu un Culte sans images?" *Revue d'Histoire et de Philosophie Religieuses*, 9 (1929), 210.

38. Cf. "Lade und Stierbild," *ZAW*, 58 (1940-41), 215.

39. Cf. S. Mowinckel, *He That Cometh* (New York: Abingdon, 1954), p. 146, for more examples of this kind of prophetic description of the end-time.

40. This is the opinion of G. Ch. Aalders, *op. cit., ad loc.*

41. Cf. the author's "The Tabernacle in Biblical-Theological Perspective," in *New Perspectives on the Old Testament*, ed. J. Barton Payne (Waco, Texas: Word Books, 1970), pp. 88-103.

42. Cf. Aalders, "Jeremia en de Ark," *Gereformeerd Theologisch Tijdschrift*, 21 (1921-22), 273-86, which places too much stress on the idea that Jeremiah teaches us a spirit that is above the symbol. This may be part of the truth but not all of it.

10

HOW TO UNDERSTAND MALACHI 1:11

Th. C. Vriezen

It was with great pleasure that I received the invitation to contribute to the *Festschrift* honoring Professor Lester J. Kuyper. The memory of time spent with him in the Netherlands, and most of all in Holland, Michigan, is still present to my mind. The stay at Western Theological Seminary, the opportunity to become acquainted with its staff and students, with its solid training, and with the whole entourage of Dutch-American life in Michigan, have made a lasting impression on Mrs. Vriezen and me. We felt immediately at home in this old-new world that the Dutch immigrants created during the last century and a half in the American Middle West. A small period of Dutch church history, which in general the Netherlanders know only from one or two pages in books, became a living reality for us.

I am sorry not to have been able to find a theme in the Old Testament related to this sense of enduring community between stay-at-homes and distant immigrants. Therefore I have simply chosen a subject that held my attention at the time that I received the invitation: the interpretation of Mal. 1:11. Penetrating more deeply into this text, I became more and more fascinated by its unexpectedly broad-minded theological message and by the many scholarly controversies it has evoked. As it brought to mind New Testament words, I became conscious of the fact that in the last century B.C., Israel grew steadily into the new religious understanding that the New Testament voices. At the same time Mal. 1:11 is so controversial that it represents an irresistible challenge to academic workers. I have, therefore, attempted to give my own independent answer to the problems it raises. Although I dare not expect that my scholarly colleague will find every aspect of my discussion convincing, I do hope that he will be pleased to read the exegetical remarks I offer in order to elucidate Mal. 1:11.

The exegesis of this passage is most complicated and has resulted in quite different interpretations. The text itself not only contains problems of textual criticism, but also raises questions concerning its place in the context, and the connection between Mal. 1:6-10 and 11-14. In the first part of the passage (vv. 6-10), the prophet is clearly protesting against the inferior sacrifices the priests accept and then offer in the temple, for by this practice they desecrate Yahweh who is called Father, Lord, and God. He concludes his oracle by remarking that it would be better if the temple were closed, since Yahweh takes pleasure neither in such sacrifices nor in the priests who offer them. In the second part (vv. 12-14) there is a denunciation of those who dare to offer these sacrifices. In between is v. 11, a verse that is very difficult to relate to its context. As a result, v. 11 is often either explained separately, or considered to be a later addition that has in turn given rise to further enlargement by the addition of vv. 12 and 13, or 12-14. In literal translation the text of v. 11 reads as follows:

(a) For from the rising of the sun to its setting my name is great among the nations;

(b) in every kind of place (or, everywhere?) is kindled, is offered to my name and a pure sacrifice (or, and pure sacrifice),

(c) for great is my name among the nations, says Yahweh Sabaoth.

Because this reading of 11b obviously does not make sense, there is abundant occasion to make slight changes in the text.[1] The "and" in front of "pure sacrifice" does not fit into the text and the two masculine participles (*muqtar*, "kindled," and *muggash*, "offered"), consecutive but unconnected, are rather strange. One also wonders whether the rendering "offered to my name" is correct (nowhere else is this said of sacrifices) and if "offered to me" would not be better (cf. 2:12).

Even more important than the precise reading of the text is the relation of v. 11 to the preceding and following verses, that is, the question of whether or not 1:6-14 is a unity. The connection with v. 12 seems certain from a grammatical and literary point of view; the connection with v. 10 is more problematic. Actually, v. 10 might very well serve as a conclusion to the preceding, and vv. 12-14 be understood to be raising a somewhat different matter. These last verses, especially vv. 13 and 14, are no longer concerned with reprimanding the priests for bringing inferior sacrifices but rather with the judgment upon the offerers themselves who bring these animals to the temple. On the other hand, the possibility that both matters have been linked together (whether secondary or not) by the prophet himself is not to be denied. Because of this the place of v. 11 in the context is difficult. The question arises whether it would be meant by him to be the conclusion of the preceding or the transition to the next subject. In both cases v. 11 could have been an originally independent liturgical text, a kind of doxology put into Yahweh's mouth as self-glorification (as is also found in Amos 4:13, 5:8f., and 9:6). Or it is possible to consider it as neither conclusion nor transition, but rather with, for example, Friedrich Horst[2] and Karl Elliger,[3] as an alien element which because of its content cannot be reconciled with the beginning of Malachi 1 (vv. 2-5), and to which yet later additions have been made. Thus vv. 11-14 would be a conglomerate of texts added by different commentators.

The connection between both parts is too close for this, however, and v. 11 is too well in place here. I consider vv. 11-14 to be at the least an additional commentary on vv. 6-10. This commentary could have originated with the prophet himself because of the similarity in style, especially since v. 11 can be understood to fit in with both the following and the preceding passages. It adds another grave aspect to the prophet's criticism of the actions of the priests in Jerusalem: Their misdemeanor is judged to be extremely serious because even among the nations of the world such things do not occur. There, beyond the boundaries of Israel, are offered pure sacrifices to Him whose name is great among the nations.

Apart from literary objections to the unity of 1:6-14, two more essential ones have been made: (a) the universalism expressed in v. 11 is completely opposed to the particularism of vv. 2-5; (b) v. 11 presupposes a recognition—not to be found in Malachi's day—of Yahweh as God also among the nations, for the text states that the nations magnify his name (Yahweh) in their cult. This statement is considered to be improbable because it is conceivable only at a much later date.

As far as the authenticity of v. 11 is concerned, the question is this: May one attribute to Malachi such an "optimistic" view of the recognition of Yahweh by the nations? Of interest is the remark of Julius Wellhausen,[4] in which he attributes this verse to Malachi, but because of that, stresses the tension between this universalistic text and the particularistic remarks in vv. 2-5. Somewhat disapprovingly he adds: "Aber so widerspruchsvoll war das Judentum, infolge seiner geschichtliche Belastung." The Old Testament scholars who deny that this verse is Malachi's do so on the grounds that it is irreconcilable with vv. 2-5. Wellhausen accepted the possibility of its authenticity because according to him, as a result of its history, later traditional Judaism is full of contradictions.

For the sake of a balanced judgment, I advance here certain points that are either absent from or inadequately expressed in the commentaries.

First of all, there is the question of the usage of the divine name. In Malachi this usage is remarkable for its great variety. On the one hand, the specifically Jewish names Yahweh and Yahweh Sabaoth are used; on the other hand, the general names El, Adonai, and Elohim occur, together with such very general designations as Father and King (cf., e.g., 1:6, 9, 14; 2:10; 3:8, 14f.). In a text as short as the book of Malachi, this variety is rather conspicuous. The use of the names Father, El, Adonai, King, as well as the conception of creation (2:10), give an especially broad aspect to Malachi's conception of God.

Remarkable in 2:10 is the occurrence of 'el 'echād, which calls to mind Yahweh 'echād in Deut. 6:4. As far as I know, this is the only time 'echād is used in connection with 'ēl. Here 'ēl is just as much 'echād as Yahweh. This profession reminds one of the thought of Second Isaiah:[5] Yahweh is God, he alone, and the nations will acknowledge him as God (45:14). Although Malachi does not mention the "God of heaven" as is done in Ezekiel, Nehemiah, and Daniel—possibly because he does not use the official terminology of the Persian state—his conception of God is essentially closely related to it. Apparently he uses these expressions interchangeably: Yahweh or El, Ab or Adonai, all mean the same to him. This already indicates that Malachi's concept of God is of wide scope and not just particularistically oriented. Here Malachi is not far removed from the author of Jonah who has the sailors calling upon Yahweh (1:14), and Jonah mentioning Yahweh, the God of heaven (1:9).

In Malachi, nevertheless, the typically Jewish names Yahweh and Yahweh Sabaoth do indeed remain dominant, but in many of these passages the expression "says Yahweh Sabaoth" was probably introduced by later editors. Most important is the relation between vv. 6ff. and vv. 2-5. It is a misunderstanding to contrast the universalistic view of the former with the alleged purely particularistic character of the latter. To interpret Mal. 1:2-5 in this way is to neglect the most important element in the text, namely, that the prophet is involved in a dispute with his compatriots and addresses persons among his people who were denying the love of God for Israel and the reality of any manifestation of his grace. Many Jews who had repatriated after the exile must have been deeply disappointed by the situation they encountered in their old-new fatherland, which had been penetrated by the Edomites. These experiences led those Israelites to reject the message, "I love you," proclaimed by the prophet to be the word of God. By responding to that word with the question, "How hast thou shown love to us?" (NEB), the people indicated that they disputed the truth of the prophet's message. He therefore earnestly entreated them to be steadfast in their faith, because the God of Jacob was still their God. They would not be harmed by the Edomites; on the contrary, the Edomites had already experienced the anger of the Lord, and upon endangering Israel once more, would be ruined once and for all. By his message of election the prophet calmed the fears of his people. Although he does not mention the word election, the idea is the hidden foundation of his words. By virtue of this faith he proclaimed the faithfulness "of the Lord, who is great beyond the border of Israel."

We must explain the words of Malachi from the *historical* situation in which they originated. If we do so, then the conclusion that Malachi is a nationalistic, particularistic prophet is not justified. He does not consider the election of Israel at all as an eternally established fact, in the sense that the Israelites could be sure of prosperity and safety evermore. On the contrary, he criticizes very sharply many groups among his people; and for him the day of the coming of the LORD is—as for Amos and Zephaniah—a day of awe and judgment. He makes a rigid distinction between the arrogant and the evildoers, and those who fear God. We therefore conclude that Malachi is anything but a purely particularistic preacher; the comforting words at the beginning of the book do not contrast with the later message.

Of particular significance in Mal. 1:1-5 is the last sentence: "great is the LORD, beyond the border of Israel," because it reminds us immediately of the theme of v. 11, though of course with this difference: in v. 5, the greatness of Yahweh is proclaimed by the prophet; in v. 11, his greatness is supposed to be acknowledged by the peoples of the world. So we may return to our main subject, the universalism of v. 11.

The breadth of Malachi's conception of God calls to mind Second and Third Isaiah, and Zechariah (2:10f.). The idea of the election of Israel as a sign of God's love reminds one of Second Isaiah (see below for the relation between Mal. 3:1a and Isa. 40:3, *et al.*). The strong emphasis Malachi places on the purity of the cult in Jerusalem puts us in mind of the prophecy of Haggai, who links the salvation of the new Israel to the restoration of the temple and the temple cult. Malachi may therefore be considered as a prophet who faithfully continues the tradition of his predecessors, the prophetic creators of a reborn Israel. Verse 11 surpasses these insofar as that which they foretold concerning the nations and that to which they called them—namely, to serve Yahweh—is here portrayed as already in the process of realization.

This view may be closely bound up with the fact that the prophet realizes that he is being called upon to prepare his people for the imminent coming of Yahweh, as is evident from 3:1a (which, with Elliger,[6] must be attributed to the prophet himself); he is the messenger sent by Yahweh to prepare his way. This preparatory mission immediately reminds one of Second and Third Isaiah (cf. 40:3; 57:14; and 62:10), even though in Malachi it is used in a different context—not as promise of salvation, but as announcement of the coming judgment. The earnestness with which Malachi reprimands the levity of many among his people indicates that he is aware of living *zwischen den Zeiten,* at the beginning of the fulfilment of the promise. It is apparently because of his awareness that he also has expectations of something new happening among the nations. They are considered to be participating already in the worship of the God of Israel who may be called Yahweh Sabaoth, El, Adonai, or Ab. Mal. 3:12 also mentions the nations who will call Israel blessed at the coming of God's kingdom. Those who deny v. 11 to Malachi have continually stumbled at this view of the nations, since they start from the conviction that this does not agree with the historical situation in the days of Malachi. Some, therefore, have tried to explain the message as a prophecy along the lines of Third Isaiah (chaps. 60ff.) and to assign a future meaning to the verbs, which are clearly in the present tense. Then v. 11 would have to be considered eschatologically as a prefiguration (so, for example, A. von Hoonacker in *Les Douzes Petits Prophètes*[7] and, in similar manner, most Roman Catholic exegetes). This, however, cannot be maintained on grammatical grounds. This and the following passage are written in the present tense and intend to confront the people with their present situation, while Malachi, in v. 11, holds up the nations as an example to the Jews.

Finally, we must go into the matter of the possibility or impossibility of the words of v. 11 having their origin in Malachi's day. According to some, it was possible during the time of the prophet since Jews in the Persian world and in Elephantine in Egypt (here they apply this remark to the Jewish Diaspora which extended from Persia to southern Egypt) did in their cult serve Yahweh, albeit in far from orthodox ways. The objection correctly made to this view is that the passage gives the impression that it concerns the worship of Israel's God by the nations of the world themselves, even though the subject in v. 11b is stated in the passive and therefore is impersonal. This passive form indicates a subject otherwise not mentioned, but which in this context can hardly indicate anything other than the nations. A further objection is that one could hardly expect Malachi to have accepted Jewish sacrifices offered outside Jerusalem, while at the same time stressing the requirement for purity in sacrifice. Others consider this remark historically justifiable since the God of heaven is worshiped among the nations as well as in Israel, and they suggest that Malachi equated this cult of the Gentiles with the worship of Yahweh, or that he recognized in this, as Wellhausen and others suppose, the monotheism known in Israel. It is difficult to suppose, however, that Malachi would so easily have equated the religions of the nations who spoke of a God of heaven with Israel's monotheism. Actually, this passage is not concerned with an appraisal of the faith of the non-Jewish world, but with the fact that the cult was celebrated in a pure manner among other nations. Morton Smith suggests that the syncretistic cults of the nations in which, before and after the exile, Yahweh must have frequently been involved were accepted as Yahweh worship.[8] Here he refers to Naaman, to 1 Kings 8:41f., to Isa. 56:7, and to Jonah 1:16, and takes into consideration the thrice-used expression "my name" in Mal. 1:11. Because this would imply that syncretism was here consciously accepted by the prophet, Smith accordingly numbers him among the syncretistic group of Jews from the period after the exile. To class Malachi with the syncretistic Jews does seem a rather bold supposition; one would sooner be inclined to see here the prophet's recognition of the worship of the one great God of heaven which many peoples had in common.

One final consideration remains to be discussed in this connection. First of all, there is the question of whether or not one can acknowledge the prophetic oracle as "authentic" (in this case as spoken by Malachi himself), only if one can prove that historically it is in agreement with the relevant period. Would it be impossible for a prophetic oracle applied to one's own age to anticipate the future, just as other prophetic oracles applied to the future do? From several prophecies it is apparent that prophetic oracles are not always actually fulfilled in the manner they suggest. Isaiah 16:13f. clearly rectifies an earlier prophecy[9] and the expectation concerning *Koresh* (Cyrus) expressed in Second Isaiah was not fulfilled in the way expected by the prophet, so that an "irrender Glaube" has been spoken of.[10] This could also be the case with an oracle that is intended to give a description of one's own age.

The oracle in Mal. 1:11 delineates the glorification of Israel's God among the nations as already a reality in "every kind of place" (a rendering that is probably better than "everywhere"). The precise situation in this regard in the time of Malachi (*ca.* 475 B.C.) is unknown to us and probably will remain so. The prophet who more obviously than his predecessors lived in the expectation of the nearness of the revelation of God's kingdom, also, as appears from this oracle, lived in the certainty of the visible spread of the acknowledgment of Israel's

Lord by the nations. Certainly there must have been reasons for this. Smith rightly refers to passages such as Isaiah 56 and 1 Kings 8:41f.,[11] which may have been written at about this same post-exilic time, and which show that there were among the nations people who associated themselves with the faith of Israel. In addition, expectations such as those expressed in Isa. 45:14, spoken by Second (or Third) Isaiah, are to be considered (some would also include here Isa. 44:1-5).

A beginning of Yahweh worship among the nations may, with Smith, be assumed, and not only in syncretistic form. Malachi in particular, whose faith was so wide-ranging that he was able to speak of Yahweh as El, Lord, and Father, was apparently open to what he heard and expected of non-Israelite forms of worshiping God and acknowledged the earnestness with which the nations worshiped Yahweh through incense and offerings. In any case, what he knew about the accessibility of Yahweh to people from among the nations, and about what was spent in his service in the world, gave him the right to hold up the cult of the nations as an example to the priests in Jerusalem. The Gentiles who had been converted only recently would certainly have performed the rites of the cult of Yahweh in all earnestness, although they were not necessarily all Naamans, as Smith supposes. Taking this into consideration, one cannot definitely deny Malachi's authorship of 1:11. This passage could very well form part of the first half (6-10) of the text, and be read in connection with v. 9 in which the priests in Jerusalem are stimulated by mockery to try to entreat the favor of God (El) with their inferior sacrifices. Verse 11 explicitly states once more why God takes no pleasure in these offerings: Yahweh is the God whose name is great among the nations from the rising of the sun to its setting, and his name receives pure sacrifices from many unexpected directions. He is not dependent upon the offerings of Jerusalem!

The style of this text is reminiscent of the liturgical hymns of praise with which the glory of Yahweh is sung in the Psalms (e.g., Pss. 113 and 50), but at the same time of songs of praise used in the eastern world (Egypt and Mesopotamia) to extol the majesty of the nations' rulers. Similarly, the Amarna letters have preserved a statement by the king of Jerusalem, who describes the power of the Egyptian king "who has established his name from the rising of the sun and its setting." What is expressed in this way is the universality of his power. Although in this instance such universality cannot be fully realized, the speaker does not utter these words as mere flattery. They are spoken with serious intent at that particular moment. For him the king is the dominant power on whom he has set his hopes.

The primary difference between the style of the Psalms and of the political praise outside Israel, and that of Mal. 1:11, is that in the latter case this expression is advanced as Yahweh's own oracle. By this divine declaration of his glory, underlined by the remark that his name is shown due respect cultically among the nations (the remark in the Amarna letters that the Pharaoh has es-

tablished his name means, *mutatis mutandis,* the same thing), the incredibly care-
less behavior of the priests in Jerusalem, whom one might certainly expect to
acknowledge the greatness of his name, is harshly exposed. This text, passed on
from Yahweh, gives great emphasis to the denunciation of the priestly negligence.
Seen from this point of view, one has to admit that the text is essentially meant
to denounce sharply the attitude of the priests.[12] The cultic rituals in their
charge, which to them ought to have been sacred above all else, were in sad contrast to what was happening among the nations of the world.

The humiliation experienced by Israel and the priesthood in Jerusalem as
a result of this prophetic word must have been very painful. That it was not
unique, however, is evident from expressions such as those of Ezekiel (16:45ff.)
in which Judah is portrayed as being worse than Sodom and Samaria, or the introductory verses of Isaiah (1:2f.) in which the behavior of Israel is held to be
more foolish and unreliable than that of an ox or ass. In fact, these accusations
are possible because the prophets realize that they can demand more of Israel than
of others, since they are convinced of Israel's special relation to God. The same
may be said of Mal. 1:11. This passage, therefore, does not deny Israel's election
any more than do Ezek. 16:48ff. or Isa. 1:2f., but actually reaffirms it. It calls
attention to the decay of religious life in Israel in the second and third generation after the exile and summons the nation to repentance and conversion. Seen
in this way, Mal. 1:11 is not in conflict with the first pericope of Malachi 1. Even
"tension" may not be the right word here. It does, however, point out marked
contrasts in the early post-exilic Jewish world. That these contrasts continued to
sharpen is evident from later history.[13]

There is much in Malachi that reminds one of the contrasts that the Qumran sect expressed at a later time. The Qumran community, like Malachi, lived in
expectation of the nearness of God's kingdom and realized the cultic consequences
of this situation for life and faith. It also strongly emphasized the ideas of election and community, the unity of faithful Israel. Like Malachi, the sect came
into conflict primarily with the priesthood in Jerusalem. There are also important
differences, however, since the Qumran sect was a completely introverted community, whereas Malachi—in spite of his explicit affirmation of the special position Israel occupies over against other nations (at least Edom)—evidently remained open to the world outside Israel, where also, he said, "Great is the Lord."

In this respect the preaching of Malachi surpasses that of the Qumran sect
and anticipates the universalistic elements of the New Testament. Dr. Verhoef
(see his article cited in footnote 13) is justified in referring in this connection
to John 4:20ff. The same point may also recall, to mention only some passages,
Matt. 8:5-13, Acts, chapters 10f., and Romans, chapters 1f. Thus, from a *Christian
theological* point of view, there is some reason to place the collection of prophetic books at the end of the Old Testament canon (even though this order is
no older than the Reformation),[14] so that the prophets—and especially the last
prophet, Malachi—are linked with the Gospels of the New Testament.

NOTES TO CHAPTER TEN

1. Elsewhere in the text of Malachi 1, several changes are also desirable (cf. *BH*[3] and *BHS*). In some cases the phrase "says Yahweh Sabaoth" is redundant and to be seen as an editorial addition. Sellin, to name one example, suggests reading—with the inversion of one word and one letter—*muqtar lishmi umuggash mincha*, i.e., "to my name is kindled, and offered (a) pure sacrifice(s)." Through editorial reissuing or copying, several irregularities must have entered the text; some manuscripts offer different versions in more than one text. A later conscious improvement of the text (*tiqqun sopherim*) has even been introduced by the scribes. In 1:13 the Hebrew text reads "him," i.e., "my name," instead of the original "me." This textual problem and its possible solutions will not detain us any longer. They should be discussed in connection with the whole problem of the textual transmission of Malachi. Unfortunately, no text has yet been found in Qumran.

2. *Die zwölf kleinen Propheten: Nahum bis Malachi*, in *HAT* (Tübingen: J. C. B. Mohr, 1938).

3. *Das Buch der zwölf kleinen Propheten II*, in *ATD* (Göttingen: Vandenhoeck & Ruprecht, 1951).

4. *Die kleinen Propheten* (Berlin: Walter De Gruyter & Co., 1963), p. 205.

5. Or Third Isaiah; cf. C. Westermann, *Das Buch Jesaja: Kap. 40-66*, in *ATD* (Göttingen: Vandenhoeck & Ruprecht, 1966).

6. *Op. cit.*

7. (Paris: J. Gabalda, 1908).

8. *Palestinian Parties and Politics that Shaped the Old Testament* (New York: Columbia University Press, 1971), pp. 93f.

9. Cf. O. Procksch, *Jesaia I*, in *KAT* (Leipzig: A. Deichert, 1930).

10. Cf. J. Hempel, *Vom irrenden Glauben* (1929), later included in *Apoxysmata* (Berlin: A. Topelmann, 1961).

11. Isa. 56:3 and 6 speak of *ben hannekar* and 1 Kings 8 of the *nokri* (foreigner) who join themselves to the Lord!

12. As Dr. J. Blommendaal rightly observes in his thesis, *El als fundament en als exponent van het Oud Testamentische universalisme* (Utrecht: Elinckwijk, 1972), pp. 79f.

13. For further literature, we refer the reader to the detailed treatment in the commentaries of F. Horst, K. Elliger, and A. van Hoonacker cited above, as well as those of J. M. P. Smith, *A Critical and Exegetical Commentary on the Book of Malachi*, in *ICC* (New York: Charles Scribner's Sons, 1912), E. Sellin, *Das zwölfprophetenbuch II*, 2-3, in *KAT* (Gütersloh: Gerd Mohn, 1930), G. Smit, *Kleine Profeten III*, in *Tekst en Uitleg* (Gronigen: J. B. Wolters, 1926), and to P. A. Verhoef, "Some Notes on Mal. 1:11," *Biblical Essays* (Proceedings of the Ninth Meeting of *Die Ou-Testamentlische Werkgemeenskap in Suid-Afrika* held at the University of Stellenbosch, July, 1966).

14. Cf. A. C. Sundberg, *The Old Testament of the Early Church* (Cambridge: Harvard University Press, 1964), pp. 58f.

11

EXEGETICAL PATTERNS
IN I CORINTHIANS AND ROMANS

E. EARLE ELLIS

Within 1 Cor. 1:18-3:21a two passages, 1:18-31 and 2:6-16, display similar exegetical patterns. The first opens with a citation (19f.) of Isa. 29:14, supplemented by Isa. 19:11f., and is followed by a christological exposition making use of two concepts in the opening texts, *sophia/mōria* (*mōrainein*). This leads to a final quotation (31) of Jer. 9:22, whose motif-word, *kauchasthai*, also has been caught up in the exposition (29). Similarly, 1 Cor. 2:6-16 gives a composite and highly interpreted citation (9, ?10a) followed by an eschatological exposition containing a repetition of words from the cited text (*eiden*, 9, cf. 12), including at least one word that has been interpolated, *pesher*-like, into the citation (*anthrōpos*, 9, cf. 11; ? *pneuma*, 10a, cf. 10b-14). This leads to a final quotation (16), Isa. 40:13, whose term *ginōskein* also has been caught up in the exposition (14).

There are some grounds for supposing that 1 Cor. 1:18-31 and 2 Cor. 2:6-16 are independent expositions, i.e., midrashim in their origin. That is, Paul is probably not himself creating the two pieces in the process of writing the letter but is adapting to his own purposes a midrash (or midrashim) already in hand. The several non-Pauline expressions in each passage[1] as well as an examination of the larger context support this conclusion.

1 Cor. 1:18-3:21a consists of five sections: 1:18-31, 2:1-5, 2-6-16, 3:1-17, and 3:18-21a. The first and third, i.e., the midrashic sections, appear to be used as foundation "texts," which are then applied to the Corinthian situation in the second and fourth sections. The "application" sections are distinguished by a shift to the past tense and to the first person singular, by personal and Corinthian allusions, by an absence of Old Testament references, and by similar introductory phraseology:

> *kagō elthōn pros humas, adelphoi* ... (2:1)
> *kagō, adelphoi, ouk ēdunēthēn lalēsai humin* ... (3:1)

At the same time they are verbally tied to the expository or midrashic sections. The fifth section concludes the piece with a final quotation-commentary (3:18-21) and application (3:22f.) into which are incorporated the words and motifs of the earlier midrash: *sophia, mōria, kauchasthai, anthrōpos.* The passage thus discloses the following form:

1:18-31	Midrash
2:1-5	Application
2:6-16	Midrash
3:1-17	Application
3:18-23	Concluding Text and Application

The midrashic sections appear to form authoritative foundation "texts" from which the application to the Corinthian situation proceeds. As such, key-words of the first "text" (1:18-31), e.g., *sophia/mōria, anthrōpos,* are repeated not only in the second "text" (2:6f., 9, 11, 13f.) and the concluding text (3:19, 20), but also in the application sections (2:1, 4f.; 3:3f., cf. 10). 1 Cor. 3:21b-4:21 appears to continue (the application of) the midrash beyond the concluding text. Thus, the Apostle's dismissal of the Corinthians' judging (4:3) of his work is based on his earlier exclusion of them from the pneumatics, whose role is to judge all things (2:15; cf. 3:1).[2] And his warning not to go beyond what is written (4:6) likewise refers to the texts that he has just expounded to them. From these observations one may conclude that the first division of 1 Corinthians not only contains midrashim but also reflects in its own literary formation a midrashic pattern.

Professor Wuellner has shown[3] that the pattern in 1 Cor. 1:18-3:21a is not unlike that found in some rabbinic discourses on Scripture. The literary form of the two pericopes, 1 Cor. 1:18-31 and 1 Cor. 2:6-16, also is similar to a rabbinic pattern in which the appointed text of Scripture is supplemented by a second text and followed by commentary (repeating certain words in the texts) and by a concluding citation, usually but not always a repetition of the initial text. An example may be drawn from Pesikta Rabbati 17:1:[4]

> "And it came to pass at *midnight,* that the Lord smote all the first-born in the land of Egypt" (Exod. 12:29). R. Tanhum of Jaffa, in the name of R. Mana of Caesarea, began his discourse by citing the verse, "When I pondered how I might *apprehend* this, it proved too *difficult* for me" (Ps. 73:16). By these words David meant that no creature could be so knowing as to *apprehend* the instant of *midnight*—only the Holy One, blessed be He, could. For the likes of me, said David, it is too *difficult.* And so because no creature can be so knowing as to *apprehend* the instant of *midnight*—only the Holy One, blessed be He, can—therefore Scripture says, "And it came to pass at *midnight,* that the Lord smote."

Often, of course, the piskas are more elaborate, containing additional supporting texts, parables, and longer commentary. But the above example is sufficient to show the basic pattern of a considerable number of these expositions. S. Maybaum[5] found a pattern like this to be typical in Palestinian midrashim, i.e., an initial (Pentateuchal) text plus a second (proemial) text from the Prophets or Writings, followed by exposition, and concluded by a further reference to the initial text.

A commentary-pattern in Philo, which Dr. Borgen[6] has shown to be comparable to that in Rom. 4:1-22 and Gal. 3:6-29, also is somewhat similar to the pattern in 1 Cor. 1:18-31 and 2:6-16. An example is provided by *leg. alleg.* III, 169-173, in which an initial citation (Exod. 16:13-15) is followed by commentary utilizing words from the text, supplemented by a subordinate text (Exod. 15:8), and concluded by an allusion back to the initial text.

The rabbinic and Pauline exegetical patterns are too similar to be independent developments, and yet they scarcely show a direct dependence. Therefore, even though the rabbinic pattern is extant only in (later compilations of) third- or fourth-century homilies, it may be presumed to reflect a type of exegesis used in first-century Judaism. The similar literary form in Philo confirms this.

As might be expected, the Pauline pattern in 1 Cor. 1:18-31; 2:6-16 varies somewhat from both Philo and the rabbinic midrash. Like some rabbinical patterns, but unlike Philo, it uses a second opening text (1:20) and concludes with a citation different from the initial text.[7] Also unlike Philo, it lacks subordinate texts and moves from the initial text(s) and commentary directly to a concluding text. Unlike the rabbis, the "second text" is little more than an allusion at 1:20 and only part of a composite citation at 2:9. However, these variations cannot conceal the basic affinity of these literary forms. 1 Cor. 1:18-31; 2:6-16 are midrashim, i.e., pieces of exposition with characteristics similar to the commentary-patterns used elsewhere in first-century Judaism. Furthermore, they appear to constitute the "texts" on which the larger midrash, 1 Cor. 1:18-3:21a, is constructed. This observation is important for the analysis of the commentary-pattern in Romans 1-4.

In Romans, two sections, which on other grounds have been recognized to be distinctive literary units,[8] also display a midrashic structure. The first, Rom. 1:17-4:25, is like 1 Corinthians 1-4 in its commentary pattern and in employing a (?pre-formed)[9] expository piece as the concluding "text" of the midrash (4:1-25). Furthermore, it uses as a supporting text (3:10-18) a combination of Old Testament passages or, if Professor Otto Michel is right,[10] a Christian hymn or a part of a hymn created out of such passages. In either case, this thematic and interpretive summary of Old Testament verses, essentially an implicit midrash that interpolates the key-word *dikaios* into the summary, is used as an authoritative "text" for the larger exposition. The concluding "text" (4:1-25) is an explicit, proem-like midrash that, as Dr. Peder Borgen has shown,[11] is in some ways more similar to Philo's exegetical practice. The section as a whole, and the verbal connectives among the various elements, reveals the following sequence:

Proem text:[12]	1:17	(Hab. 2:4, *dikaios, pistis*)
Exposition:	1:18-2:5	(2:1, 3, *krinein*)
?Supporting text:	2:6	(Prov. 24:12, *ergon*)
Exposition	2:7-23	(7, *ergon;* 13, *dikaios, dikaioun;* 12, 16, *krinein*)
?Supporting text:	2:24	(Isa. 52:5, *blasphēmein*)
Exposition:	2:25-3:3	(2:26, cf. *dikaiōma, logizesthai;* 3:3, *pistis*)
Supporting text:	3:4	(Ps. 51:6, *dikaioun, krinein*)

Exposition: 3:5-9 (5, *dikaiosunē, krinein;* ?8 *blasphēmein*)
Supporting text: 3:10-18 (10, *dikaios*)
Exposition: 3:19-31 (20, 27, *ergon, dikaioun;* 21f., 25f., *dikaio-sunē;* 22, *pisteuein;* 22, 25f., 27f., 30f., *pistis;* 24, 26, 28, 30, *dikaioun;* 26, *dikaios*)
Concluding
"text":   4:1-25 (2, *dikaioun;* 3, *pisteuein;* 3, 8f., *logizesthai, dikaiosunē;* 9, *pistis; etc.*)

In sum, the first part of Romans, like that of 1 Corinthians, is a commentary, a teaching piece built upon an elaborate midrashic pattern. It is true that the linguistic tallies in the exposition are not so specifically related to the elucidation of the cited texts as they are in the more compact forms of midrashim. But the commentary-pattern and the general exegetical intention are unmistakable.

The second section, Romans 9-11, has affinities with the *yelammedenu*-type discourse in which a question or problem is posed and then answered by a biblical exposition. The basic questions in Romans 9-11 are not difficult to identify:

9:6-29:   Do all those from Israel belong to Israel?
9:30-10:21: Why have the Gentiles achieved righteousness and the Jews stumbled?
11:1-36:   Has God abandoned his people?

However, unlike the rabbinic homilies,[13] the questions proceed more from a current event—Israel's rejection of the Messiah—than from a problem in the biblical text. They also lack the stylized form of the rabbinical pattern and are more interwoven, the second question arising out of the answer to the first, the third out of the second. Also, they are supplemented by subordinate questions (e.g., 9:14; 10:18f.) that add to the complexity of the whole passage. In spite of the differences the pattern and techniques in Romans 9-11 reflect sufficient similarities with the rabbinic discourses to suggest that they arose in a common milieu. In the following excerpts the procedures in Rom. 9:13, 14-23 may be compared with those in Pesikta Rabbati 50:1:[14]

... (Hos. 14:2). This verse is to be considered in the light of what Isaiah was inspired by the Holy Spirit to say, "For Sheol cannot praise thee..." (Isa. 38:18). Can this verse in Isaiah really mean what it seems to be asserting of the Holy One, blessed be he,... that a man who has merit... will go down into Sheol? Of course, this is not what the verse means.... As it is written, "Everyone that calls... upon my glory, [for this] I created him..." (Isa. 43:7), any man who calls upon my name... will be safe from the punishment of Sheol. Isaiah asked further..., Is it not thy delight to forgive so that the man lives... [for] as David said, "The dead praise not the Lord" (Ps. 115:17)? The Holy One ...replied to Isaiah, "My son, what David said applies to the wicked...."

As it is written, "Jacob have I loved..." (Mal. 1:2f.).

What shall we say then? Is there un-righteousness with God?

God forbid. For he says to Moses, "I will have mercy...." So it is not of him who wills... but of God who shows mercy. For the Scripture says to Pharaoh, "Even for this purpose...." Then you will say to me, "Why does he still find fault? For who can resist his will?"

But who are you, a man, to answer back...? Will the pot say... (Isa. 29:16; 45:9)?

A further comparison may be drawn between the pattern in Piska 44:1 and that in Rom. 9:29, 30-33:

"Return, O Israel . . ." (Hos. 14:2). Let our master teach us. If one who keeps committing sin keeps saying that through repentance he will be forgiven, what answer shall be made to him? Our masters taught thus, "He who keeps saying, 'I will sin and then repent . . .', will never have strength enough to repent" (Yoma 8:8).

Why not? Because if a man repents and then goes back to his transgressions his repentance was not true repentance . . . [parable]. Scripture says, "Let the wicked forsake his way . . ." (Isa. 55:7).

"Except the Lord Sabaoth had left us a seed . . ." (Isa. 1:9).

What shall we say then? That the Gentiles who followed not after righteousness, even the righteousness that is from faith. But Israel who followed after the law of righteousness did not attain to the law of righteousness. Why? Because they sought it not from faith but as though it were from works. They stumbled over the stumbling stone. As it is written, "Behold, I lay in Zion . . ." (Isa. 28:16).

The pattern in the larger pericope, Rom. 9:6-29, also is somewhat similar to that found in the rabbis. The opening text, Gen. 21:12, is supplemented by Gen. 18:10. The key-words, *kalein, sperma,* and *huios* are repeated in the exposition (8, 12, 24) and in the supporting quotations (25-27). The word *sperma* (29) in the concluding citation (Isa. 1:9, LXX) refers back to the opening text.[15]

In conclusion, the exegetical patterns in 1 Corinthians and Romans are suggestive both for the formation of the Pauline letter and for the structure and interpretation of a number of individual passages. They probably point not only to the creative mind of the Apostle but also to that of some of his co-workers, the circle of prophets and teachers whose exegetical labors Paul participated in and used.

NOTES TO CHAPTER ELEVEN

1. E.g., in 1 Cor. 2:6-16: "rulers of this age" (6), "before the ages" (7), "the spirit of the cosmos" (12), "the spirit that is from God" (12); there is one Pauline hapax *didaktos*. 1 Cor. 1:18-31 is somewhat more Pauline in word and idiom and is, perhaps, more likely to have been created by the Apostle; Pauline hapaxes are *suzētētēs* (20), *eugenēs* (26), *agenēs* (28); in the quotation: *sunetos, grammateus* (19f.). Expressions occurring only in the pericope, 1 Cor. 1:18-3:21a, are *mōria* (18, 19); "wisdom of the cosmos" (19, cf. 3:19), "wisdom from God" (30).
2. Later (1 Cor. 9:3; cf. 14:37) it is on the basis of apostolic privilege that Paul dismisses their judging him. In 1 Cor. 14:24, 29 judging is similarly used of the prophets' role in discerning (24, *anakrinein*) a person's true state before God or discerning (29, *diakrinein*) the measure of divine truth in another prophet's message (cf. Rom. 12:6). The Corinthian pneumatics apparently wish to test Paul's word and work in this way.
3. W. Wuellner ("Haggadic Homily Genre in 1 Corinthians 1-3," *JBL*, 89 [1970], 199-204) limits the midrash to 1 Cor. 1:19-3:20. He regards this traditional theme, divine sovereignty and God's judgment on all wisdom, to have its *Sitz im Leben* in school or synagogue "discussion with disciples" (pp. 202f.; cf. Pirke Aboth 6:6; D. Daube, *The New Testament and Rabbinic Judaism* [London: Athlone Press, 1956], pp. 158-169).

Midrashic procedures appear elsewhere in Corinthians, e.g., 1 Cor. 10; 15; 2 Cor. 3; 6:14-7:1. In some instances they may reflect Paul's use of a pre-existing piece of exposition; in some they may provide the literary frame for the Apostle's argument. But, if so, the pattern is neither as clear nor as comprehensive as that which one observes in 1 Cor. 1-4. On 1 Cor. 2:1-5 as exposition cf. L. Hartman in *SEA*, 39 (1974), 11ff., 118ff.

4. Cf. W. G. Braude, *Pesikta Rabbati*, 2 vols. (New Haven: Yale University Press, 1968), I, 361, cf. 300f. Piskas 15-18, 32 represent "fairly unified expositions of single themes" (p. 4). Braude regards the *Pesikta* as a seventh-century compilation of the teachings of third- and fourth-century Palestinian Amoraim (p. 26). For a midrash whose concluding text is not a repetition of the initial text cf. I, 363-365 (Piska 17:3); II, 591-597.

5. S. Maybaum, *Die ältesten Phasen in der Entwicklung der jüdischen Predigt* (Berlin: Dummer, 1901), pp. 15ff., as cited in Borgen, p. 51 (see note 6).

6. P. Borgen, *Bread from Heaven* (Leiden: E. J. Brill, 1965), pp. 47-50, cf. 51-58.

7. W. Bacher, *Die Proömien der alten jüdischen Homilie* (Farnborough: Gregg International [Eng.], 1970 [1913]), p. 19, believes that the second opening text, the proem, developed from the earlier practice of supplementing an initial text with subordinate, non-Pentateuchal quotations. However, 1 Cor. 1:19, 20 (cf. Gal. 3:6, 8) suggests that a second opening text may have been an acceptable pattern from a very early time, even if it did not have the formal character of a rabbinic proem.

8. P. Minear (*The Obedience of Faith* [London: SCM Press, 1971], pp. 46-56) sees a close connection between Rom. 1:18-4:25 and 14:1-15:13, a section that also exhibits some characteristics of a commentary-pattern.

9. This would account for the awkward transition at Rom. 4:1.

10. O. Michel, *Der Brief an die Römer* (Göttingen: Vandenhoeck & Ruprecht, 1955), p. 85.

11. Borgen, *op. cit.*, pp. 29-33, 48n. Like Paul (e.g., Rom. 4:23-25; 1 Cor. 3:20f.; Gal. 4:31-5:1), Philo (e.g., *leg. alleg.* III, 162-168: *de mut.* 253-263) adds to the concluding text of the exposition a further comment or application. It should be observed that, unlike the midrash on Gen. 15:6 in Galatians (3:6-?29, cf. 11), Romans 4 contains no explicit reference to Hab. 2:4, the text that opened the exposition (Rom. 1:17), although the catch-words provide an allusion to it.

12. Rom. 1:17 not only concludes the preceding section but also serves as an "opening" for the following one. This is evident from the literary connection with 1:18 and from the verbal tallies with 1:18-4:25.

13. But the sequence, current event ⟶ scripture, is occasionally present in Qumran midrash. Cf. E. E. Ellis, "Midrashic Features in Acts," *Melanges bibliques en hommage au R. P. Béda Rigaux*, ed. A. Descamps (Gembloux: Duculot, 1970), pp. 308f.

14. Braude, *op. cit.*, II, 770, 843.

15. A number of commentators mark Rom. 9:29 as the conclusion of a section, e.g., Michel, *op. cit.*, pp. 205f.

12

EXODUS IN THE LETTER TO THE HEBREWS

RICHARD C. OUDERSLUYS

Speaking of the theology of Deuteronomy, Lester Kuyper says that "the deliverance of Israel, a weak people, from mighty Egypt, the wonder of God speaking to them, and the driving out of the powerful Canaanite nations to give their land for an inheritance to Israel (Deut. 4:33-38) can but produce one conclusion, that 'Jahweh he is God, there is none else beside him.' This is not a conclusion reached by speculations of philosophy, but by a common sense interpretation of history."[1] No doubt, the most determinative event in Israel's history was the Exodus from Egypt, because it gave Israel a distinctive history, a revelation and faith, even a new way of remembering and speaking. Scholars are bound to continue their discussion and probing of the date and nature of the event or events that constitute the whole complex of data known as the Exodus, but there can be little questioning of its centrality both for the Old and the New Testaments. Since the relationship of the two testaments has been one of the lively concerns of the thought and work of my colleague, perhaps this brief examination of the Exodus theme in the New Testament and especially the Letter to the Hebrews may serve as a tribute to his distinguished teaching career.

I

At the Exodus, Israel came to know God in his essential nature as Lord and Savior (Exod. 12:12; 15:1-2), and to experience his sovereign grace and judgment. Much of the nation's identity and self-understanding was a direct outcome of that event. The Exodus itself was unique (Deut. 4:32-35), and was understood to be God's act of election whereby he chose Israel to be his people, for reasons lodged solely in his own love (Deut. 7:6-8). It was to the Exodus that Israel traced its deliverance from Egypt, the constituting of the nation (Exod. 19:3-7), its unique covenant-bond with God (Deut. 7:7; 9:6; 8:3, 12-18); and it was from the Exodus that Israel learned to look for a continuing relation between God and its own history. It is not surprising that this event came to stand at the heart of Israel's most ancient confession of faith (Deut. 26:5-10), and at the heart of its most characteristic liturgy (Exod. 12:17-18, 26ff.; Deut. 16:1ff.).

Even the casual reader of the Old Testament is impressed by the recurring frequency of the familiar refrain: "I am the Lord your God, who brought you out of the land of Egypt, out of the house of bondage" (Exod. 20:2; Deut. 5:6). Other festivals—Unleavened Bread, Weeks, and Tabernacles—became occasions for remembering the Exodus events in a manner that contemporized them for the celebrators (Josh. 24:6-7). The memory of Egypt became registered in much of Israel's covenant code, its rituals (Exod. 19:3-8; 24:1-18), the proper attitude to strangers (Exod. 22:21; Deut. 10:18-19), the merciful treatment of slaves (Deut. 15:15).[2] And the Exodus remembered appears to be that whole series of word-and-deed disclosures of God, encompassing the Passover and the deliverance from Egypt, the crossing of the Red Sea and the victory over the Egyptians, the giving of the Law at Sinai (Exod. 20:1-17), the instruction of the people before entering the land of promise (Exod. 13:11ff.), and their discipline in the wilderness (Deut. 8:2-3).[3]

Both the revelational meaning of the Exodus and Israel's existential response and decision continued to furnish a kind of pattern or structure for the subsequent revelational and redemptive events of Old Testament history. On numerous occasions, the Psalms celebrate the Exodus-faith (114:1-4; 135:8-12; 136: 10-22; etc.), and in some of the more historical psalms (78, 105, 106) the deliverance from Egypt and the experiences of the desert period are described with considerable detail. It is in the period of the Exile, however, that the hopes of the people turned again to Yahweh with whom their previous history had been bound up. In the firm conviction that history belongs to God and that God had given Israel its history at the Exodus, the prophets did not hesitate to establish a typological relationship between the earlier event and subsequent redemptive acts. When they speak to a beleaguered people, it is to assure them that God, who had acted once before on their behalf, would again act in a new and more glorious Exodus. Points of correspondence are brought forward between God's primal deed of salvation in the creation conflict, his act of redemption at the Exodus, and the expected deliverance from the Babylonian exile.

As once before (Exod. 14:19-20), God will again go before his people in the day and follow them through the night (Isa. 48:21-22), leading them in the wilderness (Deut. 8:2ff.; cf. Isa. 43:19-20) and through the sea (Exod. 14:21ff.; cf. Isa. 43:16; 51:9-11). He will again provide water in the desert as of old (Exod. 17:6f.; cf. Isa. 41:18; 43:20; 49:8-10). As Miriam once sang a victory song (Exod. 15:1ff.), so this new deed of deliverance will be celebrated in exultant hymns (Isa. 42:10ff.; 44:23). As God's powerful word was once heard at Sinai (Exod. 20:1ff.), once more it will be heard as an irresistible power and reality (Isa. 55:10-11). The typology of the prophets, however, is more than a list of correspondences between earlier and later events. God's actions in history, while always consistent and conspicuous in their continuity, nevertheless are ever new and unrepeatable. Elements of contrast are as important as those of correspondence. The new Exodus will outdo the wonders of the old. As James Muilenburg says, "the uniqueness of events and 'times' is such that they cannot be cata-logued and classified; at least, what is important in them is new and unrepeat-able."[4] The first Exodus was made in haste (Exod. 12:39), but the second will be deliberate (Isa. 52:12). The second will make Israel forget the first one (Jer. 23:7-8; Ezek. 20:33f.; Isa. 43:18). The first was followed by a notable covenant (Exod. 20:1ff.); the second will be followed by a new and greater covenant (Jer. 31:31-33; 32:40; Ezek. 16:60ff.; Isa. 54:8). The first brought Israel out of the land of Egypt at which time the Lord pleaded with the fathers "in the wilderness of the land of Egypt," but now in a new act of deliverance the Lord declares he will bring them from the "wilderness of the nations" into his holy mountain (Ezek. 20:35, 36, 40-44).[5]

Indeed, the second Exodus introduces an age so new and transforming that its prophetic dimensions exceed the particular exile-event, and point to a new eschatological time. As Bernhard W. Anderson points out, this prophetic use of typology uses historical memory to feed and formulate eschatological faith.[6] Yahweh is about to do a new thing, and what will emerge is a new creation.

> From this time forth I will make you hear new things,
>   hidden things which you have not known.
> They are created now, not long ago;
>   before today you have never heard of them,
>   lest you should say, "Behold, I knew them."
>   (Isa. 48:6-7)

It is characteristic of God's redemptive acts that they are likewise creative acts (40:21-31; 44:24-28; 45:12-13), but it is especially true when the prophets speak of the coming of a new eschatological time that they employ the traditions both of creation and the Exodus. There will be not only a new Exodus and a new covenant, but a new gift of the Spirit to the new messianic king (Isa. 11:2), and a new messianic people (Joel 2:28-30; Ezek. 43:2, 4-7). More importantly, there will be a return of the Lord's presence in the midst of his people (Exod. 19:18; Isa. 40:3, 5, 9; Ezek. 43:2, 4-7). And perhaps most significant of all, the hope of God's salvation for Israel now becomes a hope for all nations (Isa. 45:22-23; 2:2-4), inaugurated by a messianic king who will rule with justice and righteous-ness (2 Sam. 23:4; Isa. 9:2-7; 11:1-9), and who will bring his salvation to the ends of the earth (Isa. 42:6-7; 49:6). Commenting on this time of Exile-de-liverance and delayed hope, A. G. Hebert observes:

> Certainly it is to these prophets of the Exile that our Lord and His apostles regularly go back to explain what it was that was happening in the events of the Gospel; and if the Messianic hope was not fulfilled in Him, then it has never been fulfilled, but remains as "a hope which failed."[7]

The Old Testament, however, stops here. Using the Exodus theme, the proph-ets could interpret and anticipate the meaning of history. They could remember the past, interpret the present, and hope for the future, but nowhere do they assert that the hope that they proclaimed was ever fulfilled.

II

Before proceeding directly to the use of the Exodus in the Letter to the Hebrews, it may be helpful to pause, if only briefly, with its utilization by other New Testament writers. Taking their cue from the typological interpreting of events by the prophets, the New Testament writers see the Exodus repeated but in a new and more glorious way both in the personal experience of Jesus and in the experience and history of the church. The writers of the Synoptic Gospels make it a part of their witness that Jesus interpreted his person, word, and work in terms of Old Testament prophecy and typology.[8] Mark's Gospel, for example, begins significantly enough with Jesus in the wilderness with the wild beasts (Mark 1:12-14).[9] Matthew furnishes us with a portrait of Jesus as the second Moses (Deut. 18:15, 18), who gives his people a new law and leads them into the new and final salvation.[10] Luke mentions the word Exodus with the specific intent of declaring that it was something Jesus would accomplish by his death (Luke 9:30). Commenting on this Lukan statement, S. H. Hooke has said,

> We have seen Abraham's Exodus from Ur, the Exodus of Israel under Moses from Egypt, the Exodus of the remnant out of Babylon, and the Exodus of the Servant of Jahweh by way of rejection and death from Israel's dream of national restoration. Now, from the Transfiguration onwards the final Exodus begins. We see Jesus with his face set towards Jerusalem, leading an uncomprehending and reluctant company of followers who were to be the new Israel, carried with him through the waters of death, baptized with his baptism.[11]

In the Gospel of John, the promised future dwelling of God with his people and the return of his glory (*kabod*) are fulfilled in the Word made flesh (John 1:14). Again the wilderness imagery reappears (3:14, 15), and numerous parallels connect Moses and his signs with Christ and his signs; i.e., the Manna and the Bread of Life (Exod. 16:4-9, 15; John 6), the Living Water and the Rock (Exod. 17:6; Num. 20:11; John 7:37ff.), the Pillar of Fire and the Light of the World (Exod. 13:21-22; 14:19f.; John 8:12f.).[12] This kind of close typological correspondence between the Exodus and the Messiah appears frequently in rabbinic literature, and even prompted false Messiahs to begin their work, as Moses had done, in the desert.[13]

Paul's use of the Exodus also needs to be sketched only briefly.[14] His sermon at Antioch of Pisidia probably serves as a sample of his customary synagogue-preaching (Acts 13:16ff.), and the hearers could not have missed the significance of the recitation of God's mighty acts at the Exodus at the beginning of the sermon. And if W. J. Phythian-Adams is granted his point, then even in his Gentile preaching Paul was never far away from Exodus parallels, because at Colossians 1:13-14 he speaks of a deliverance from bondage, a journey into a new kingdom, and finally an inheritance through a mighty redeemer.[15] Harald Sahlin believes there are some forty references or allusions in Paul to the history of the Exodus, and even if all the passages cited are not equally convincing, one must still grant the importance of the theme for the thought of Paul. As do other New

Testament writers, Paul sees the Exodus fulfilled in the death of Christ: "Christ, our paschal lamb, has been sacrificed" (1 Cor. 5:7). He extends the typology, however, to the new people of God, when he enjoins them to remember that the Christian life is a continuing festival, the ideal Passover celebration (1 Cor 5:8). At 1 Corinthians 10:1f., Paul speaks of the deliverance at the Red Sea as being a type of the redemption of the new Israel, and of the Exodus manna and water as forerunners of Christian Baptism and the Lord's Supper. In these sacraments, as John Marsh says, "the Christian lives all the great 'moments' of his redemption, the Exodus at the Red Sea, the fulfilled Exodus at Jerusalem, the last 'Exodus' at the end of the world."[16] And it should not escape our notice that the most striking instance of Exodus typology in Paul and, for that matter, in the entire New Testament, is his taking over of the designation *ekklēsia* for the New Testament people of God, the word once used for the Old Testament "congregation/people in the wilderness" (Acts 7:38). The church as the people of the new Exodus is a familiar theme of 1 Peter, where the author describes Christian baptism using many of the motifs of the old event: the girding of the loins (Exod. 12:11; 1 Pet. 1:13), the need to be holy (Lev. 11:44f.; 1 Pet. 1:16), and their redemption (Exod. 6:6; 15: 13; 1 Pet. 1:18) by the blood of the lamb (Exod. 12:5; 1 Pet. 1:19). The new people of God now have all the honored titles once given to the first Israel (1 Pet. 2:9-10). There is also in the letter to Jude that striking reference to "he who saved a people out of the land of Egypt," where the textual evidence suggests that the original reading might well have been "Jesus who saved a people out of the land of Egypt."[17] Other allusions or references could be examined, but those mentioned above will suffice to introduce the usage of the theme in Hebrews and to warrant the declaration of F. F. Bruce when he says that "the events of the Exodus and the wilderness wandering . . . are treated in the apostolic age as parables of Christian experience."[18]

III

The author of Hebrews uses the typological reading of the Exodus previously noted in the Old and New Testament writings, but he extends this reading to the entire Old Testament cultus. Jesus as a high priest is so much superior to the Levitical priests (7:1-10) that the best available model or analogy is Melchizedek (4:14-5:10; 7:11-28). Jesus offers the perfect sacrifice of the new and better covenant (8:1-13), in a new and better sanctuary (9:1-10), with a new and better ministry (9:11-14), which provides an eternal inheritance (9:15-22) of final, ultimate efficacy (10:1-18). While these impressive contrasts exalt the new above the old in the hope that the new will enable the people to forget the old, this is not their only or most important function. These contrasts must be seen in the perspective of the journey that Jesus, as a greater than Moses (3:1-6), made for and before his people as the pioneer and perfecter of their faith; a journey that culminated with his session at the right hand of the throne of God (10:12; 12:2). His journey accomplished for his people that which the covenant and journey of the old Exodus never provided, immediate access to God, the freedom to draw near to God (4:16; 7:19, 25; 9:8-12, 24; 10:1, 22). The author of Hebrews speaks of this as the inability of the old cultus "to make perfect" (7:11, 19; 9:9; 10:1, 14; 11:40). Christ's "perfection" is nothing other than his saving work (2:10, 14-15, 17), by which he secures the "perfection" or salvation of his people (2:11-14; 7:25-28). The relationship here is clearly causal, and nowhere better indicated than in the statement at 11:39-40: "And all these, though well attested by their faith, did not receive what was promised, since God had foreseen something better for us, that apart from us they should not be made perfect." As Du Plessis has said, "What they were denied was the historical experiencing of the Messianic *teleiōsis*. God in His providence deferred the bestowal of the full reward till the advent of Christ."[19] As the pioneer and perfecter of his people, Christ introduced a better hope (7:19), under a better covenant (7:22; 8:6), which is enacted on better promises (8:6), by one who offered a better sacrifice (9:23, 26) in a better sanctuary (9:24).

As a consequence of this journey undertaken by Christ for his people (1:1-10:18), they are in the new eschatological situation of inaugurated fulfilment, and yet nonetheless are a pilgrim people who journey on to the promised future of God (11:1-13:24). On the one hand, the Exodus deliverance of their forerunner is already an experienced possession, and the church has already entered upon the "rest" of the gospel (4:1) with unimpeded access to God. It has come to Mount Zion and to the city of the living God, the heavenly Jerusalem (12:22f.). Therefore, there can be no returning to Egypt, no turning back for those "who have once been enlightened, who have tasted the heavenly gift, and have become partakers of the Holy Spirit, and have tasted the goodness of the word of God and the powers of the age to come" (6:4f.). On the other hand, the church, as the wandering people of God,[20] is still en route to its appointed destiny (13:14), confessing that on earth it appears as a stranger and an exile (11:13f.). There is a Sabbath-rest that still remains for the people of God (4:9), and the author warns that considerable exertion and faithfulness will be needed to avoid the wilderness disaster that overtook the people of the old Exodus (3:7-19; 4:6-8). While the Exodus deliverance is past, the Exodus journey of the people is still in progress, and to negotiate their perilous wilderness, they will need the grace of continuance (6:9-12) and the faith that perseveres (11:39-12:3). In his own characteristic fashion, the author takes the three themes of the journey that Jesus made as his people's high priest, the present journeying of his people, and their final rest, and makes them serve his eschatological faith.[21]

There is no doubt that the author takes time and history seriously, and that he employs the two-ages pattern of salvation history found elsewhere in the New Testament. One-sided derivations of the author's conceptuality and vocabulary from Gnostic themes,[22] from Philo,[23] or from Qumran circles[24] are bound to be something less than persuasive in the light of the prominence given to the doctrines of the two ages, the two covenants, and the categories of promise and fulfilment. It is true that the author's use of such terms as *hypodeigma*, "copy" (8:5; 9:23), *skia*, "shadow" (8:5; 10:1), and *parabolē*, "parable" (9:9; 11:19) refer to heavenly realities. And when he uses the term *antitypa*, "antitype" (9:24), he means that the Old Testament cultus is the antitype of heavenly reality. The movement of thought is downward (from heaven to earth), and not forward (from Old Testament to New Testament).[25] On the surface, this seemingly represents an Alexandrian outlook and mode of thought, and apparently many scholars are persuaded that it is so, and present their exegesis in this framework.[26] This exegetical approach, however, becomes exceedingly dubious in the light of the author's consistent eschatological faith, and his spatial imagery and downward movement of thought may be no more than his way of speaking of the Old Testament as divine revelation. The bulk of the typology of Hebrews points forward and the tabernacle ordinances of chapters 9 to 13 foreshadow Christ. The once-for-all high-priestly work of Christ (9:12, 26; 10:10) not only fulfils the Old Testament priesthood, but also perfects it, that is, brings to completion in the new covenant that which was but anticipated in the old. The Exodus typology represents no interior journey of the mind as in Alexandrian thought, but the journey Jesus took that led to the right hand of the throne of God by way of the cross, and the journey his people now make to their eternal rest. In the theology of the writer of Hebrews, the Old Testament cultus was a faithful reproduction of heavenly reality, the antitype of the true tabernacle revealed to Moses on Sinai, but, as such, it forecast or foreshadowed the genuine and new cultus that came with the new age and the new covenant. The new is not a reproduction but the reality itself, *tēn eikona tōn pragmatōn* (10:1); therefore the Old Testament is a foreshadowing of the New Testament realities. The thought of Hebrews, then, stands in close relationship with the eschatological outlook of the early church.

It would be an exaggeration to claim that the eschatology and Exodus typology of Hebrews shed light on such problems as date, destination, and readers. The author's preoccupation with the Old Testament and his typological exegesis seem to argue for an audience of Jewish readers,[27] but it is of no great moment if they are disaffected Hellenists [28] or ritually strict Jewish Christians. [29] It may be quite otherwise, however, when it comes to the purpose of the letter and our construction of the peril in which the readers of the letter stand. The contention that the readers were in peril of apostasy and relapse into Judaism surely outruns the evidence, but there is no mistaking their perilous situation. Apostasy is the impossible possibility inherent in their situation (6:1-8; 10:26-31), and it turns on the impossibility of repenting (6:6); but it is a boundary line still distant to the readers as far as the author is concerned. Following every admonition, there are words of warm, pastoral confidence and encouragement (2:1-4; 3:12ff.; 4:1, 11; 6:9-12; 10:19-39; and chapters 12-13). The nature of the pastoral admonitions in chapter 13 is interesting in this respect. The ten key themes of the chapter discussed by F. V. Filson[30] relate directly to the failure of the readers to sense their eschatological situation between the "now" and "not yet." The once-only, redemptive work of Christ took place "yesterday" (13:8), and this "yesterday" inaugurates God's gracious dealing with human sin, a work of such enduring worth that Christ can now be described as "yesterday and today the same and into the ages."[31] Failure to understand and act upon their present eschatological situation is one facet of the peril of these people. The other facet is their failure to understand and act upon the "not yet" of their situation: running the race still before them (12:1-2), remembering that "here we have no lasting city" (13:14), and going with Jesus "outside the camp" (13:12). The distinction between the Exodus deliverance and the Exodus journey apparently can shed some light on the situation of the readers.

It should also be noticed that when the author speaks plainly about the danger that threatens the faith of the Hebrews, he turns to the wilderness theme of the Exodus, read and interpreted through Psalm 95. For him, the wilderness is chiefly the place and symbol of Israel's disobedience and wandering, the place where God's past deliverance was forgotten and where God's promise for the future no longer moved the people to response. It is difficult to see how the relevance of all this could be lost upon the readers of this letter, living as they were between the "now" and the "not yet." And when the author turns his "exhortation"[32] to what he would like his readers to be doing, it is to urge upon them the grace of continuance and the faith that perseveres. Obviously, he wants them to be an Exodus church, knowing that here they are only strangers and exiles on the earth (11:13), and that here they have no lasting city (11:14; 13:14). The journey commended to them is no symbolic one. His eschatology involves everything that the word really means, an end for history that is bound up with the nearness of the parousia (10:25). The *telos* of the journey is precisely where our forerunner has already entered (6:19-20). The future in view is not the reflex of faith, as in some recent theologies of hope, but is rather a future that shapes faith (11:1-40), and has observable proleptic impacts upon the present (13:1-22). The immobility of the church over against its mission and task constitutes part of the motivation for the letter to the Hebrews and does help to clarify part of its message.

The readers have stood firm under persecution and suffering (10:32-34), and now should not hesitate to move on and out in witness while they wait for the coming of the Lord (10:36-39). In their journey outward and onward, the heroes of faith in ages past, like a "cloud of witnesses" (12:1), will serve to encourage them, but their chief encouragement will be our forerunner, who ran the race and made the journey before and for them.

To be an Exodus-church was not easy then, nor is it now. Abandonment of the faith is not the foremost or only way in which the church courts peril. When the church falters in its mission to the world (13:13), when it neglects witness and worship (10:25), when it can no longer exercise the power of negative thinking and strongly disapproves what exists in the present (13:1-5), when it no longer celebrates the journey Jesus made for his people, when the presence of the future is no longer proleptically realized, then it is time to read again the letter to the Hebrews.

NOTES TO CHAPTER TWELVE

1. Lester J. Kuyper, "Deuteronomy, A Source Book for Theology," *Hervormde Theologiese Studien,* 7 (1951), 184.
2. James Muilenburg, *The Way of Israel: Biblical Faith and Ethics* (New York: Harper & Brothers, 1961), pp. 48-54.
3. For a discussion of whether "disobedience and punishment" or "revelation and love" dominates in subsequent formulations of the desert motif, see Shemaryahu Talmon, "The 'Desert Motif' in the Bible and in Qumran Literature," *Biblical Motifs: Origins and Transformations,* ed. Alexander Altmann (Cambridge: Harvard University Press, 1966), pp. 31-63.
4. *Op. cit.,* p. 135. For further discussion of typology as a biblical way of looking at historical events, see A. C. Charity, *Events and Their Afterlife: The Dialectics of Christian Typology in the Bible and Dante* (Cambridge: Cambridge University Press, 1966); G. W. H. Lampe and K. J. Woollcombe, *Essays on Typology,* Studies in Biblical Theology, no. 22 (Naperville: A. R. Allenson, 1957); G. E. Wright, *God Who Acts,* Studies in Biblical Theology, no. 8 (Chicago: Henry Regnery Company, 1952), pp. 59-66; and the well-known essays of Gerhard von Rad, Martin Noth, and Walther Eichrodt in *Essays on Old Testament Hermeneutics,* ed. Claus Westermann (Richmond: John Knox Press, 1963).
5. See Walther Zimmerli, "Le nouvel 'exode' dans le message des deux grands prophetes de l'exil," *Maqqel Shaqedh. Hommage a Wilhelm Vischer* (Montpelier: Causse-Graille-Castelnau, 1960), pp. 216-227.
6. B. W. Anderson, "Exodus Typology in Second Isaiah," *Israel's Prophetic Heritage,* ed. Bernhard W. Anderson and Walter Harrelson (New York: Harper & Brothers, 1962), pp. 177-195; U. E. Simon, *A Theology of Salvation* (London: S.P.C.K., 1953), pp. 97-109.
7. A. G. Hebert, *The Bible From Within* (London: Oxford University Press, 1950), p. 108.
8. R. E. Nixon, *The Exodus in the New Testament* (London: The Tyndale Press, 1963); Jean Daniélou, *From Shadows to Reality* (London: Burns & Oates, 1960), pp. 153-174; Leonhard Goppelt, *Typos: Die typologische Deutung des Alten Testaments im Neuen* (Gütersloh: C. Bertelsmann, 1939).
9. Ulrich W. Mauser, *Christ in the Wilderness,* Studies in Biblical Theology, no. 39 (Naperville: A. R. Allenson, 1965).
10. W. D. Davies, *The Setting of the Sermon on the Mount* (Cambridge: Cambridge University Press, 1964), pp. 61ff.
11. S. H. Hooke, *Alpha and Omega* (London: James Nisbet, 1961), p. 181. For an extended discussion of Lukan usage of the theme, see J. Manek, "The New Exodus in the Books of Luke," *Novum Testamentum,* 2 (1958), 8ff.
12. T. F. Glasson, *Moses in the Fourth Gospel,* Studies in Biblical Theology, no. 40 (Naperville: A. R. Allenson, 1963); and L. Goppelt, *op. cit.,* pp. 215ff.
13. T. F. Glasson, *op. cit.,* pp. 15-19. See also the article on Moses by J. Jeremias in *TDNT,* IV, 859ff. The typological connection between Moses-desert-messiah may be reflected in such other New Testament passages as Matt. 24:26; Acts 21:38.
14. Paul's use of the theme has been explored by Harald Sahlin, "The New Exodus of Salvation according to St. Paul," *The Root of the Vine: Essays in Biblical Theology,* ed. Anton Fridrichsen (London: Dacre Press, 1953), pp. 81-95; and by L. Goppelt, *op. cit.,* pp. 169ff.
15. W. J. Phythian-Adams, *The Way of At-one-ment* (London: S.C.M. Press, 1944), p. 23.
16. John Marsh, *The Fulness of Time* (New York: Harper & Brothers, 1952), pp. 137f.
17. F. F. Bruce, *The Epistle to the Hebrews,* in *NICNT* (Grand Rapids: Wm. B. Eerdmans, 1964), p. 63, note 46.
18. *Ibid.,* p. 372.
19. P. J. Du Plessis, *Teleios: The Idea of Perfection in the New Testament* (Kampen: J. H. Kok, 1959), pp. 224f.

20. E. Käsemann, *Das wandernde Gottesvolk* (Göttingen: Vandenhoeck & Ruprecht, 1957), sets out in detail the role played by the theme of the journeying people of God in Hebrews.

21. C. K. Barrett, "The Eschatology of the Epistle to the Hebrews," *The Background of the New Testament and its Eschatology*, ed. W. D. Davies and D. Daube (Cambridge: Cambridge University Press, 1956), pp. 363-393; A. Feuillet, "L'eschatologie de l'Epitre aux Hebreux," *Studia Evangelica*, ed. F. L. Cross (Berlin: Akademie Verlag, 1964), II, 369-387.

22. The dependence of Hebrews upon Gnostic themes is the main contention of Ernst Käsemann, *op. cit.*

23. Once the contention of older scholars such as James Moffatt, *The Epistle to the Hebrews*, in *ICC* (Edinburgh: T. & T. Clark, 1924), and E. F. Scott, *The Epistle to the Hebrews: Its Doctrine and Significance* (Edinburgh: T. & T. Clark, 1923), Alexandrian background via Philo has become characteristic of Roman Catholic commentators, largely through the massive work of C. Spicq, *L'epitre aux Hebreux* (Paris: J. Gabalda, 1952), I-II. Sidney G. Sowers, *The Hermeneutics of Philo and Hebrews*, Basel Studies of Theology, no. 1 (Richmond: John Knox Press, 1965), grants considerable Alexandrian influence in Hebrews, but subjects it to the two-age pattern of salvation history. Such advocates will need in the future to grapple with the careful research of Ronald Williamson and his conclusion that possibly "the Writer of Hebrews had never been a Philonist, had never read Philo's works, had never come under the influence of Philo directly or indirectly" (*Philo and the Epistle to the Hebrews* [Leiden: E. J. Brill, 1970], p. 579).

24. H. Kosmala, *Hebräer-Essener-Christen, Studien zur Vorgeschichte der frühchristlichen Verkündigung* (Leiden: E. J. Brill, 1959); M. De Jonge and A. S. Vander Woude, "11Q Melchizedek and the New Testament," *New Testament Studies*, 12 (1965-66), 301-326.

25. See Geerhardus Vos, *The Teaching of the Epistle to the Hebrews* (Grand Rapids: Wm. B. Eerdmans, 1956), p. 58.

26. While expressing reservations at many points, both Jean Héring, *The Epistle to the Hebrews* (London: Epworth Press, 1970), and Hugh Montefiore, *A Commentary on the Epistle to the Hebrews* (London: A. & C. Black, 1964), are representative of recent interpreters who posit some borrowing by the writer of Hebrews from Alexandrian thought.

27. The only specific clue in the letter to the readers is that of 13:24 where *hoi apo tēs Italias* probably means "those who come from Italy" (so the RSV, NEB, TEV, etc.), and therefore a small congregation of Jewish-Christians in Rome.

28. So William Manson, *The Epistle to the Hebrews* (London: Hodder and Stoughton, 1951).

29. E. Earle Ellis, " 'Those of the Circumcision' and the Early Christian Mission," *Studia Evangelica*, ed. F. L. Cross (Berlin: Akademie Verlag, 1968), IV, 390-399.

30. F. V. Filson, *'Yesterday'; A Study of Hebrews in the Light of Chapter 13*, Studies in Biblical Theology, 2d series, no. 4 (Naperville: A. R. Allenson, 1967), pp. 27-81.

31. *Ibid.*, pp. 31f.

32. *Ibid.*, pp. 27f.

A BIBLIOGRAPHY OF THE WRITINGS OF LESTER J. KUYPER

Articles published in the *Western Seminary Bulletin*:
"Our Church and Other Churches," 1, no. 4 (March 1948), 11-14.
"The Servant of Jahweh," 2, no. 4 (March 1949), 10-13.
"Theology in Deuteronomy," 4, no. 1 (June 1950), 1-4.
"The Biblical Doctrine of Man," 4, no. 3 (December 1950), 7-10.
"The Message of Apocalyptic," 5, no. 3 (December 1951), 1-4.
"The Revised Standard Version," 6, no. 3 (December 1952), 4-7.
"The Church Reformed According to the Word of God," 7, no. 4 (March 1954), 1-6.

Articles published in the *Reformed Review*:
"Our New Look," 9, no. 1 (October 1955), 1-4.
"The Repentance of Job," 9, no. 4 (June 1956), 30-44.
"Israel and Her Neighbors," 10, no. 3 (April 1957), 11-20.
"The Holy One and The Holy Spirit," 11, no. 3 (April 1958), 1-10.
"Report from Palestine," 12, no. 3 (March 1959), 1-23.
"Interpretation of Genesis Two-Three," 13, no. 2 (December 1959), 4-14; no. 3 (March 1960), 17-29.
"The Netherlands Reformed Church," 13, no. 4 (May 1960), 18-31.
"Grace and Truth," 16, no. 1 (September 1962), 1-16.
"Endurance or Enjoyment?" 16, no. 2 (December 1962), 44-46.
"How Long, O Lord, How Long?" 17, no. 4 (June 1964), 3-12.
"The Repentance of God," 18, no. 4 (May 1965), 3-16.
"The Bible for the Church and the School," 20, no. 1 (September 1966), 11-22.
"The Old Testament Used by New Testament Writers," 21, no. 1 (September 1957), 2-13.
"The Old Testament in the Church," 21, no. 3 (March 1968), 9-25.
"The Biblical View of Nature," 22, no. 3 (March 1969), 12-19.
"Are We at an Impasse?" 23, no. 2 (Winter 1970), 102-105.

Articles published in various journals:
"To Know Good and Evil," *Interpretation*, 1 (1947), 490-492.
"Deuteronomy, a Source Book for Theology," *Hervormde Theologiese Studien*, 7 (1951), 181-190.
"The Book of Deuteronomy," *Interpretation*, 6 (1952), 321-340.
"The Church Reformed According to the Word of God," *Interpretation*, 12 (1958), 157-173.
"Grace and Truth: An Old Testament Description of God, and Its Use in the Johannine Gospel," *Interpretation*, 18 (1964), 3-19.

"The Repentance of Job: A Study of *MA'AS*," *Vetus Testamentum*, 9 (1959), 91-95.

"The Meaning of *CHASDO*, ISA. XL 6," *Vetus Testamentum*, 13 (1963), 489-492.

"The Suffering and the Repentance of God," *Scottish Journal of Theology*, 22 (1969), 257-277.

"The Hardness of Heart According to Biblical Perspective," *Scottish Journal of Theology*, 27 (1974), 459-474.

Unpublished doctoral dissertation: "The Doctrine of Sin in the Old Testament with Special Consideration Given to the Position of Reformed Theologians of the Netherlands." Union Theological Seminary, New York, 1939.

Printed Address: *The Righteousness of God in the Old Testament*, Holland, Michigan, 1943. Convocation Inaugural Address.